ULYSSES S. GRANT

THE AMERICAN NATION: A HISTORY

VOLUME 21

OUTCOME OF THE CIVIL WAR

1863–1865

BY

JAMES KENDALL HOSMER, LL.D.

RECENT LIBRARIAN OF THE MINNEAPOLIS PUBLIC LIBRARY

NEW YORK AND LONDON
HARPER & BROTHERS PUBLISHERS

CONTENTS

EDITOR'S INTRODUCTION

ALTHOUGH independent in field and arrangement, this volume is a continuation of the same author's *Appeal to Arms* (*American Nation*, XX.), taking up the story at the crisis of midsummer, 1863, and carrying it forward to the cessation of hostilities in April, 1865. The political conditions from which the war came about and the objects for which the contest was waged are set forth in the previous volume, and in greater detail in Chadwick, *Causes of the Civil War* (*American Nation*, XIX.). The readjustment after the war is the subject of Dunning, *Reconstruction, Political and Economic* (*American Nation*, XXII.).

Interwoven with the narrative of military operations during 1863 are two chapters upon internal conditions: chapter i. on military law and war finance, and chapter iv. on life in war time. The remarkable campaigns on the Tennessee River in the second half of 1863 are described in chapters ii. and iii. Chapters v. and vi. are devoted to the reorganization of the eastern armies under Grant, and the terrible Virginia campaign of 1864. In chapter vii. the western campaign of that year is followed out from Chattanooga to Atlanta. The breathing space at the end of 1864, is utilized for a narrative of attempts at reconstruction (chapter vii.) and the presidential election of 1864 (chapter ix.). In chapter x. the blockade and naval campaigns during 1863 and 1864 are described. Chapters xi. and xii. are devoted to Sheridan's valley campaign and Sherman's march to the sea; chapters xiii. and xiv. to the renewal of plans of reconstruction, and to the vexed question of military severities both in the field and in the prisons. Chapters xv. and xvi. describe the life and experiences of non-combatants, North and South, in the last stages of the war. In chapter xvii. the last military campaigns appear. Chapter xviii. upon authorities includes a serviceable account of the official publications relating to the Civil War.

The purpose of the volume is not only to describe military movements and to characterize military commanders, but also to picture the Civil War as a national experience, in which public men, governing bodies, and the whole people on both sides, were intensely engaged. The war appears in its proper setting, as a contest, not between armies or governments, but between two social systems made up at bottom of the same kind of people, having the same traditions, and capable of reconstitution into one nation.

AUTHOR'S PREFACE

AS the Civil War approaches its end, the interest deepens rather than diminishes. To the student of the military art much more is offered worthy of attention than during the early period. On the side of the North, by relentless sifting the men come to the front who through natural endowment and painful training are adequate to the work to be done: on the side of the South the leaders, though the same as at the beginning, exhibit a developed power, and sway more absolutely the men and the resources committed to their direction. Campaigns, no longer ill-ordered and fortuitous, become examples of practised soldiership; while battles illustrate the struggle of opposing intellects, and are no longer a mere exchange of blows.

As a drama, the Civil War takes on as it proceeds, shadows new and ever gloomier. On both sides, the devotedness of the generation concerned, the sacrifice of comfort, of resources, of life, to what is believed to be the public good, becomes always more unusual and impressive. At last the combatants are locked in a struggle so intense and desperate that human strength and endurance can go no further. Here are the elements of colossal, all-absorbing tragedy.

For the most part, the battles described have been studied on the fields where they took place; the strategy of the generals, while traversing the lines of movement of the contending armies. Much has been gained from the stories of participants North and South, in stations high and low; while the author's own recollections tend to make definite the details of the picture. The present volume, like its predecessor, has been for the most part written in the Library of Congress, at Washington, and I desire to repeat here the acknowledgment of obligation already made to the accomplished staff of that institution for their politeness and skilled assistance.

JAMES K. HOSMER.

January 10, 1907.

OUTCOME OF
THE CIVIL WAR

OUTCOME OF
THE CIVIL WAR

CHAPTER I

MILITARY LAW AND WAR FINANCE
(1863)

IN 1863 the Fourth of July became trebly famous—
no longer the nation's birthday merely, but the
day also when through the fall of Vicksburg and
the retreat of Lee from Gettysburg the preservation of the nation grew likely. It was, indeed, high
time that, for the well-being of the Union, such a
day should dawn. During the spring the signs
were very unfavorable; that the war was likely soon
to take the North for its arena, as well as the South,
was plainly indicated. Every Federal disaster made
more numerous and more outspoken the advocates
of peace at any price. A bitter war of words broke
out, and in many places in the North seemed about
to pass into a war of weapons. Disaffection was
more acute and audacious in the West than in the
East, though not more deep-seated. Friends of the
South, looking on from Canada, believed a con-

federacy of the Northwest to be close at hand, which, when formed, would be hostile to the Lincoln government and ready to join hands with Jefferson Davis.

While in Indiana and Illinois the spirit of revolt abounded, its focus was in Ohio, where Clement L. Vallandigham, a bold and fluent irreconcilable, fomented the popular inflammation.[1] He had talked in opposition in Congress with no uncertain sound; on the stump he was still less restrained; and when Burnside, as commander of the department, issued a certain "Order No. 38," which in terms unusually plain forbade treasonable utterances, Vallandigham burst out with exceeding vehemence. On May 1, at Mount Vernon, in southern Ohio, a mass-meeting was held, the character of which was not concealed. The head of the Goddess of Liberty on the old-fashioned copper cent was cut out, and displayed generally as a badge upon the coat-lapel— a "copper - head." Many speakers of note were heard, among them Samuel S. Cox (better known as "Sunset" Cox), a man of brilliant gifts; but the voice of most authority was that of Vallandigham, who passed all previous bounds. Within a few feet of him stood officers of Burnside, in civilian dress, noting down the orator's sentences. He said "that it was not the intention of those in power to effect a restoration of the Union; that the government had rejected every overture of peace from the South,

[1] See *Am. Annual Cyclop.*, 1863, art. Habeas Corpus, for a good digest of contemporary accounts.

and every proposition of mediation from Europe;
that the war was for the liberation of the blacks
and the enslavement of the whites; that General
Order No. 38 was a base usurpation of arbitrary
power; that he despised it and spat upon it, and
trampled it under his feet; that people did not deserve to be freemen who would submit to the
conscription law. He called the president "King
Lincoln," and advised that at the ballot-box he
should be "hurled from his throne." Among the
cheers that followed, some one shouted that "Jeff
Davis was a gentleman, which was more than Lincoln was."

A few days later, a company of soldiers took Vallandigham out of bed at his home in Dayton,
Ohio, and conveyed him to Cincinnati, where forthwith was held a court-martial, presided over by
General Robert B. Potter. No part of American
liberty has been more jealously regarded than freedom of speech; had it come to such a pass in America
that a man could no longer say what he chose? And
if called to account, was it proper that the orator
delivering his criticism in a part of the country not
the seat of war should be seized by soldiers and
tried by a court-martial? Justification for Burnside's proceeding might be sought in Lincoln's
proclamation of September 24, 1862, which declared that "During the existing insurrection, and
as a necessary measure to suppressing the same, all
rebels and insurgents, their aiders and abettors,

within the United States, and all persons discouraging voluntary enlistments, resisting militia drafts, or guilty of any disloyal practice affording aid and comfort to rebels against the authority of the United States, shall be subject to martial law, and liable to trial and punishment by courts martial, or military commissions." [1]

This was certainly very definite; but the president's right to issue such a proclamation was gravely questioned, in particular by B. R. Curtis, who had been justice of the Supreme Court; [2] moreover, it had been superseded by an act of Congress of March 3, 1863, signed by the president, according to which the proceeding of Burnside was quite too summary. [3] Conceding that the arrest of Vallandigham was permissible (certainly in the arbitrary arrests which had taken place there was abundant precedent), the statute of March 3, 1863, made it necessary that the secretary of war should report the arrest to the Federal judge of that district; and if the grand jury found no indictment against him as giving aid and comfort to the enemy, the discharge of the prisoner was proper. In fact, the act of Burnside was an overstepping of his powers, which the administration should have discountenanced. In this crisis Lincoln showed vacillation. When, a few weeks later, Burnside suppressed the

---

[1] Lincoln, *Works* (ed. of 1894), II., 239.
[2] B. R. Curtis, Jr., *Life and Writings of B. R. Curtis*, II., 306 et seq.   [3] *U. S. Statutes at Large*, XII., 755.

Chicago Times, for an offence similar to that of
Vallandigham's, the president, under the pressure of
such good friends of his as Lyman Trumbull and
Isaac N. Arnold, and others, discountenanced the
proceeding. The trial of Vallandigham, May 11,
1863, was after Chancellorsville and before Gettysburg and Vicksburg, when the Union cause seemed
on the verge of ruin; and the mistaken prosecution
appeared about to precipitate a catastrophe.

At the court-martial, Vallandigham denied the
right of such a court to judge him, since he was a
member neither of the army nor navy. He produced witnesses, among them "Sunset" Cox, who
testified that he had said nothing treasonable,
though criticising the government severely. Un-
successful application for a writ of *habeas corpus*
was made to Federal Judge H. H. Leavitt, a War
Democrat, an appointee of Andrew Jackson. The
prisoner was duly found guilty and condemned to
Fort Warren, a sentence which Lincoln commuted
to banishment beyond the Federal lines into the
Confederacy.[1]

To the sorrow over Fredericksburg and the new
occasion for lamentation from Chancellorsville was
now added such a cry of indignation at the alleged
infringement of constitutional liberty that the tumult became appalling. In every quarter the peace
party mustered so formidably that to make head

[1] For a discussion of the legal and constitutional aspects, see
Rhodes, *United States*, IV., 245 et seq.

against it began to seem desperate. Mass-meetings poured out wrath in every part of the North; of especial note, among such demonstrations, were a series of conventions, one in Ohio, held June 11, by the friends of Vallandigham; one at Springfield, Illinois, the president's home; and one at Albany, New York, the ruling spirit of which was Governor Horatio Seymour. Of the three, probably the latter was the demonstration most threatening to the administration. Through dignity of character and high social position, the influence of Seymour was powerful. Lincoln had tried to win him over, but an interesting correspondence was the only result. The governor stood, with all whom he could sway, in angry opposition. Nor was the rage of the malcontents expressed in words alone. Vallandigham, who soon escaped from the South on a blockade-runner, and appeared at Niagara Falls, within a short distance of his constituents, was nominated by acclamation for governor by the peace party of Ohio,[1] who pushed the canvass with great vigor.

The enrolment and conscription act of March 3, 1863,[2] the execution of which was pressed by General James B. Fry, provost - marshal - general, met with wide disfavor. Forced enlistments seemed contrary to the spirit of American institutions. A provision intended to mitigate the situation, whereby on

[1] *Am. Annual Cyclop.*, 1863, art. Ohio.
[2] *U. S. Statutes at Large*, XII., 731.

payment of three hundred dollars a man drafted might purchase exemption, was interpreted to be a shielding of the rich, while the poor were left to suffer. The draft was met by scowls, which in many places developed into armed resistance. In particular, there began in the city of New York, July 11, 1863, a riot which exceeded in violence anything of the kind ever known in America. For several days the city was in the hands of a mob, who burned, pillaged, and murdered to an extent that suggested the excesses of the French Revolution. In the height of the trouble the conduct of prominent Democrats was discouraging and ominous. Archbishop Hughes seemed disposed to palliate the outrages, while Governor Seymour addressed a tumultuous assembly as his "friends." It was then asserted by Seymour that as many as a thousand lives, all told, were lost, an overestimate, possibly; but the number was large —unresisting negroes, men, women, and children, being especial objects of attack.[1]

Success came to the Federal arms in the nick of time. The New York riots occurred within less than a week of the fall of Port Hudson, which opened the Mississippi; Lee still stood threatening north of the Potomac; but great victories had been won, and were powerful in changing the face of things. A demonstration from troops, furloughed after Gettysburg, sufficed to put down the New York mob, though only by stern fighting. In Ohio, John

[1] *Am. Annual Cyclop.*, 1863, p. 811 et seq.

Brough, a sturdy War Democrat, took the field against Vallandigham, who in due time was "snowed under" by a majority of 101,000. New York also went Republican. In Pennsylvania, Andrew G. Curtin was triumphantly sustained; far and wide Union men plucked up heart and rallied about the administration.[1]

In all this crisis nothing is better worth noting than the bearing of Lincoln. If he tripped, it was only for a moment; he was intrepid, good-natured, ready with a reply in every emergency, and judged each case with sense and strength. He had misgivings as to Burnside's course with Vallandigham; but he stood by his agent, and parried the remonstrances as they came with tact and logic. "Must I shoot a simple-minded soldier-boy who deserts, while I must not touch a hair of a wily agitator who induces him to desert? This is not the less injurious when effected by getting a father, brother, or friend into a public meeting, and there working upon his feelings until he is persuaded to write the soldier-boy that he is fighting in a bad cause for a wicked administration of a contemptible government, too weak to arrest and punish him if he shall desert. I think that in such a case to silence the agitator and save the boy is not only constitutional, but, withal, a great mercy."

Stating his conviction that arbitrary measures, under ordinary circumstances harsh or unconstitu-

[1] *Am. Annual Cyclop.*, arts. Ohio, New York, Pennsylvania, etc.

tional, may be justified in the stress of a rebellion
or invasion, the president scouts the idea that the
people may become indifferent to arbitrary measures or perverted into a preference for such a polity.
He cannot believe it, "any more than I am able to
believe that a man could contract so strong a taste
for emetics during a temporary illness, as to insist
upon feeding upon them during the remainder of
his healthful life." [1]

Lincoln's frank admission to the Albany remon-
strants is interesting: "And yet let me say that
in my own discretion I do not know whether I
would have ordered the arrest of Mr. Vallandigham.
While I cannot shift the responsibility from myself,
I hold that as a general rule, the commander in the
field is the better judge of the necessity in any particular case. . . . It gave me pain when I learned that
Mr. Vallandigham had been arrested; . . . and it will
afford me great pleasure to discharge him as soon as
I can by any means believe the public safety will
not suffer by it. . . . Still I must continue to do so
much as may seem to be required by the public
safety." [2]

By way of counter-stroke to the earlier Copperhead mass-meeting at Springfield, Illinois, the supporters of the administration gathered at the same
place, at the beginning of September, in still greater
numbers. Lincoln was urged to be present, and
might have effected much by his presence. In our

[1] Lincoln, *Works* (ed. of 1894), II., 349–351.   [2] *Ibid.*, 351.

day, when the rear platform of the special train has become such a fulcrum of influence, and the president can place himself in distant New Orleans, Chicago, or San Francisco, while scarcely taking his hand from the Washington helm, an oratorical journey to Springfield would be easy. In 1863 the president felt that he could not leave his post. He wrote a letter, however, August 26, which perhaps did as well as a speech. It was an arrow shaped with beauty and grace, the finish of the shaft, however, not interfering with the keenness of the point or its unerring aim. One passage runs: "The signs look better. The Father of Waters again goes unvexed to the sea. Thanks to the great Northwest for it. Nor yet wholly to them. Three hundred miles up they met New England, Empire, Keystone, and Jersey, hewing their way right and left. The sunny South too, in more colors than one, also lent a hand. On the spot their history was jotted down in black and white. The job was a great national one, and let none be banned who bore an honorable part in it. . . . Nor must Uncle Sam's webfeet be forgotten. At all the watery margins they have been present. Thanks to all. For the great Republic, for the principle it lives by and keeps alive, for man's vast future,—thanks for all! Peace does not appear so distant as it did. I hope it will come soon, and come to stay. And there will be some black men who can remember that with silent tongue, clenched teeth, steady eye and well-poised bayonet, they have helped mankind on to this great consummation; while I fear there will be some white ones unable to forget that with malignant heart and deceitful speech they strove to hinder it." [1]

The signs looked better, as Lincoln said. The North was growing to the weight of sword and shield in the enemy's front, and learning also to manage the financial burden, good care of which was as necessary to successful warfare as first-rate soldiership. To be sure, there was a perilous prevalence of the greenback. The irredeemable paper money which Chase had so reluctantly brought himself to favor, and which all wise men, following our better traditions, had looked upon with misgivings, came in like a flood; but it was a device which men thought inevitable in a great crisis. The act of February 25, 1862, authorizing the issue of $150,000,000, was followed by acts of July 11, 1862, and of March 3, 1863, each act authorizing large amounts. [2] During the years of war there were outstanding, of legal-tenders, in 1861–1862, $96,620,000; in 1862–1863, $387,644,000; in 1863–1864, $431,179,000; in 1864–1865, $432,687,000. It should always be remembered to Chase's credit that he put forth this issue with hesitation, and that later, when chief-justice, he confessed he had committed an error. [3]

[1] Lincoln, *Works* (ed. of 1894), II., 398.
[2] *U. S. Statutes at Large*, XII., 345, 532, 710.
[3] Hart, *Chase*, 436; cf. Hosmer, *Appeal to Arms* (*Am. Nation*, XX.), 64, 167, 249; see also 12 Wallace, 576.

While paper money thus worked balefully, other financial expedients which the enterprising secretary and Congress had set on foot by the summer and fall of 1863 began to make impression. First, by an act approved March 3, 1863, the treasury had been authorized to contract loans of much greater volume than heretofore. Upon the second great loan, authorized February 25, 1862, for $500,-000,000, Chase secured two limitations which proved harmful—namely, that the interest should be only six per cent. and should be payable in gold; with interest so low the bonds would not sell at par on a specie basis; the price of his bonds was depressed to par in greenbacks, the fact that legal-tenders were convertible into bonds also having an influence. As regards the loan of March 3, 1863, Chase was not able to borrow anything like the amount authorized, but his work was successful and beneficent.[1] With the help of Jay Cooke & Co., he invited subscriptions in all quarters and from all classes, the securities being of such denominations that people of small means could take them, as well as capitalists. These were rapidly accepted, "coupon-bonds" becoming not only a hoard in every great financial institution, but a familiar possession in many households. An immense sum presently passed into this form of wealth, the favorite securities being the "five-twenties," the bonds whose holders could enforce their redemption in twenty

[1] Hart, *Chase*, 243, 288.

years, while the government could, if it chose, pay them after five years, the bonds meantime yielding an interest of six per cent. in gold, payable semiannually. Within two months after the adjournment of Congress, on March 3, 1863, the great deficit which had confronted it the preceding December quite disappeared. The soldiers were paid, and all necessary requisitions satisfied. More important than anything else, since the people thus showed their confidence in the triumph of the Union, and gave up their savings to its keeping, they proved their determination to sink or swim with it, committing themselves to its fortunes as never before.

The second vital financial measure, for direct taxation and internal revenue,[1] entered upon with many fears because counter to cherished American traditions, was received with few murmurs and soon yielded a large sum. George S. Boutwell, of Massachusetts, was made commissioner. The act was several times amended, and its operation at first was somewhat embarrassed, but its success increased year by year till, in 1866, the yield from this source was nearly three hundred and eleven millions. The country was divided into districts, corresponding generally with the congressional districts, in each of which were appointed an assessor and collector armed with adequate power for inspection and seizure. From domestic manufactures and productions, especially distilled spirits and fer-

[1] Act of July 1, 1862, *U. S. Statutes at Large*, XII., 432.

mented liquors, came the largest revenue. Tobacco was heavily taxed, but wool and cotton fabrics, boots and shoes, hardware, petroleum, everything into or over which passes human handiwork, paid its proportion. The well-to-do were assessed on their incomes; professions and branches of business in general could not be carried on without a license; and no formal paper—contract, receipt, check, or proprietary label—was valid without a stamp.[1] The country soon adapted itself good-naturedly to the situation, and among the perplexed shapers of the government policy the regret was general that the result could not have been foreseen and direct taxation applied more fully to the exigency rather than the irredeemable paper.

The third great gain to our financial well-being was a measure which, in the summer and fall of 1863, began first to find favor, though proposed by Chase in his first formal report as secretary of the treasury. This scheme, for a time neglected, but finally accepted, created a system of national banks. The popular loans and heavy taxes were temporary expedients; but the national-bank system was destined to supersede the old state banks, affording to the United States a system uniform, cheap, convenient, and as stable as the government itself. For this great achievement the credit belongs mainly to Chase,[2] and may be regarded as the supreme service he ren-

[1] Schouler, *United States*, VI., 386.
[2] Hart, *Chase*, 274 et seq.

dered to his country.   During the winter session of
1862–1863 the plan was freely debated, Eldridge G.
Spaulding and Samuel Hooper, in the House, and
John Sherman, in the Senate, sustaining the secretary's recommendation.   February 25, 1863, the bill
became a law, passing the Senate by a bare majority
of two, and almost as narrowly escaping defeat in
the House.[1]   Lincoln signed it gladly, and it went
into operation forthwith, receiving later amend-
ments as experience showed them necessary.   The
act provided for the charter of national banks under
the supervision of a new officer of the treasury, the
comptroller.   One-third of their capital must be in
United States bonds; and against the deposit of
bonds in the treasury, as a reserve, the comptroller
prepared for each bank circulating notes to the
amount of nine-tenths of the deposit.   By an act of
1865, on recommendation of Secretary Fessenden, a
tax of ten per cent. was levied on the circulation of
state banks, so that many of them hastened to
put themselves under the national arrangement.[2]
The benefits of the scheme to the country have been
immense.   In 1861 there were over sixteen hundred
state banks, scattered everywhere, varying infinitely as to solvency and as to wisdom of management.[3]   While the banks of New York and New

[1] U. S. Statutes at Large, XII., 665; John Sherman, Recollections, 231; Blaine, Twenty Years, I., 478.
[2] Dewey, Financial Hist. of the U. S., 328.
[3] Blaine, Twenty Years, I., 645.

England in good part maintained high credit, and some western states had legislated wisely, many banks were "wild-cat," practically unwatched in their transactions, and unpunished if they swindled. Bank-bills varied infinitely, and no expert was skilful enough to detect counterfeits. High rates of exchange prevailed, bills rarely passing at par except in their own locality. The confusion and loss were grave.

The new system brought order and security in money matters; but beyond that it knit the people to the government by a strong tie. The loans of currency to the banks from the treasury were part of the national indebtedness; hence every citizen became vitally concerned in the security and welfare of the Union. While in 1863 but sixty-six national banks were organized, the number rapidly grew. In 1864 there were five hundred and eight; a year later one thousand five hundred and seventy-three;[1] nor would it be possible to say, after forty years, to how large an extent the progress and welfare of the country has been due to this sagacious innovation.

While in the North there was a peace party, sometimes very vigorous, the South showed no toleration of any party or individual who opposed the war. Where such opposition was manifested, as in eastern Tennessee, it was straightway met by force of arms, the offenders being regarded no less as enemies than

[1] Blaine, *Twenty Years*, I., 644.

those who came from the North.   As to finance, in
the early part of 1863 the southern leaders had no
anxiety about the outcome: their victories were
overwhelming; intervention seemed certain; at the
breaking of the blockade, which could not be far
off, their accumulations of cotton, transferred to the
French and English mills, so long idle, would at once
make the Confederacy rich.   To anticipate this prosperity, before the first year of the war had ended
the government was irretrievably committed to a
paper-money policy.[1]

As to Confederate taxation, some money came
in through the small customs duties.   During 1863
a tithe of the agricultural products was exacted,
which for a time yielded much, a month's supply of
food for a million men coming in; but it was everywhere unpopular, and in North Carolina was rebelled
against.   April 24, 1863, was passed the Internal
Revenue Act of the Confederacy, from which, by
the end of 1864, about five million dollars in specie
value was obtained, apparently all a tax "in kind." [2]

Nor was there any large resort to bonds.   In
January, 1863, Emil Erlanger, a European financier,
appeared in Richmond to negotiate a loan of fifteen
million dollars, to be placed abroad.[3]   It was authorized January 29, and proved successful to all
but the unhappy subscribers.   It was taken up

---

[1] Schwab, *Confederate States*, chap. ii.
[2] *Ibid.*, 291 et seq.; for act, see *C. S. A. Statutes at Large*, 1
Cong., 3 Sess., 115.   [3] *Ibid.*, 30 et seq.

at 90, in great part in England. Erlanger & Co. made out of it a handsome sum; the Confederacy received about six million dollars, which was mostly spent in Europe; the subscribers lost ten million dollars, the bonds sinking ever lower after the Union victories, military and diplomatic, to final worthlessness. Professor Schwab believes this sum derived from the Erlanger loan, with fifteen million dollars derived from an earlier loan, taken by the southern banks, and the proceeds of seizures of United States funds and the customs duties, about five million five hundred thousand dollars (perhaps twenty-seven million dollars in all), to have been the entire amount of specie in the hands of the Richmond government during the war.[1]

The Confederacy was practically supported by paper money and from the proceeds of bonds purchased with paper money and paying interest in scrip. The people preferred notes to bonds, because the former circulated. Before the end of 1863, seven hundred million dollars in notes was in circulation, which sum in 1864 became a billion and more. Possibly the treasury itself had no definite knowledge of the amount afloat.[2] States, cities, banks — indeed, tradesmen, tobacconists, grocers, barbers — issued notes, these a fractional currency largely. February 17, 1864, the Confederate congress passed an act virtually repudiating earlier is-

[1] Schwab, *Confederate States*, 43.
[2] Rhodes, *United States*, V., 344.

sues of paper money. A scheme of compulsory funding was put in operation, recalling expedients of the American and French revolutions; holders of notes might exchange them for four-per-cent. bonds; an alternative for exchange into bonds was to receive new notes at a ratio of two to three; if the holder took neither the bonds nor the new notes, he must lose heavily, for by a provision of the act the old notes were to be taxed out of existence.[1]

A vivid picture of the "Time when Money was Easy" is given by George Cary Eggleston; the irredeemable paper fell ever lower, until it became scarcely an exaggeration to say that the householder must take his money to market in his basket and bring his purchases home in his pocket-book.[2] The funding act was a confession of bankruptcy on the part of the government. The resource of the produce loan was exhausted before the beginning of 1863. United States money became readily current, an incident so ominous that, February 6, 1864, an act was passed to prohibit its circulation.[3] Recourse was had to barter; and at the end of 1864 Kirby Smith wrote that only specie payments or barter prevailed in business in the trans-Mississippi.[4] The evidence is conclusive, remarks Schwab, "that

---

[1] *C. S. A. Statutes at Large*, 1 Cong., 4 Sess., 205; cf. Schwab, *Confederate States*, 64.

[2] Eggleston, *A Rebel's Recollections*, chap. iv.

[3] *C. S. A. Statutes at Large*, 1 Cong., 4 Sess., 183; also Schwab, *Confederate States*, 161.

[4] Rhodes, *United States*, V., 347.

at last public expenses were met, like those of a bankrupt corporation, by creating a huge floating debt represented by large arrears, four or five hundred million in the war department, and accumulated unpaid warrants in the Treasury." [1]

[1] Schwab, *Confederate States*, 83.

CHAPTER II

THE CHICKAMAUGA CAMPAIGN

(AUGUST, 1863–SEPTEMBER, 1863)

THE over-sanguine, who imagined after Vicksburg and Gettysburg that the South would now submit and that peace was in sight, were soon undeceived. From various parts of the wide arena came signs that the spirit of resistance was unbroken and the habit of victory not yet lost. During the closing acts of the Mississippi and Pennsylvania dramas, John H. Morgan, the bold raider, making his way with twenty-five hundred men from Tennessee through Kentucky, crossed the Ohio at Brandenburg, and entered upon a terrifying invasion of Indiana and Ohio. There were no trained troops at hand to oppose him; he passed rapidly from village to village, despatching companies right and left to create uncertainty as to his movements, replacing his horses as they gave out with fresh ones seized within the country, and taking booty as he chose in the well-to-do communities which he traversed. His troopers galloped long unharmed, the expedition apparently being a glorious "lark" for the youths who for the most part made up the

force.[1] But when, passing through the northern
suburbs of Cincinnati, they pressed eastward, their
career became disastrous. Had Lee carried Ceme-
tery Hill, things, no doubt, would have been different
with them; as it was, towards the end of July most
of them were captured on the upper Ohio and consigned, with their leader, to Federal prisons.[2]

A much graver affair than this brisk and futile
adventure was the renewed attempt of the navy, in
the same month, to reduce Charleston. After the
failure in April, General Quincy A. Gillmore succeeded to the place of Hunter, and Admiral Dahlgren to
that of Dupont. Both new commanders were brave
and capable men, the former an engineer of marked
ability. Nevertheless, their efforts were no more
successful than those of their predecessors; Beauregard was still at hand, and his defence was as successful as before.[3] July 18 an assault on Fort
Wagner, on Morris Island, a low-lying waste of sand
at the mouth of the harbor, was beaten back, a
pathetic incident of the event being the decimation,
at the head of the charging column, of the Fifty-
fourth Massachusetts, colored, the high-souled young
colonel, Robert G. Shaw, falling at the front. The
"swamp-angel," a powerful cannon planted with
much skill in a morass, hurled its balls five miles
into the streets of Charleston; and converging bat-

[1] Duke, *Morgan's Cavalry*, 437.
[2] *War Records*, Serial No. 34, pp. 632–817 (Morgan's Ohio
Raid).   [3] Roman, *Beauregard*, chap. xxxii.

teries from ship and shore reduced Fort Sumter to a heap of ruins. Neither city nor fortress fell before the assailants, however, until the last days of the war.[1]

Towards Tennessee, as the summer closed, all eyes began to turn. While the armies on the Mississippi and Potomac, west and east, were struggling so memorably, Rosecrans in the centre, with the Army of the Cumberland, was lying inactive at Murfreesboro. Though nearly six months had passed since Stone's River, no blow had been dealt. Rosecrans, whom Cox saw in April, 1861, quarrelling at Camp Dennison over the flooring of the tents,[2] though now a man of note, preserved the same characteristics. Though full of amiable traits, his shortcomings were marked,[3] none more so than a quickness of temper that burst out on occasions both slight and grave. He was constantly wrangling with Lincoln, Stanton, and Halleck. To their urgency that he should be active, he always complained that something was wrong that should be righted at Washington. If left to himself, he very probably would have struck during the spring; but under pressure he braced himself the other way, and lay idle even when his own judgment would have led him to act. Towards those below him his testiness, even to his generals, was equally manifest.

[1] *War Records*, Serial No. 46 (Operations at Charleston, June to December, 1863).
[2] Cox, *Military Reminiscences*, I., 24.	[3] *Ibid.*, 513.

A tentful of privates with their candles alight after taps would hear the flat of the general's sword on the canvas in token of displeasure, an exhibition which made him sometimes the victim of practical jokes.[1] Nevertheless, from Lincoln down through the rank and file, Rosecrans brought out affection, and none doubted that he was, in spite of his failings, a brave and able leader.

The stress at Vicksburg having caused Johnston to draw off a strong detachment from Bragg, that he might make head against Grant, a fine chance was offered Rosecrans to strike a blow at his weakened adversary. He started out, June 24, 1863, responding at last to the urgency from Washington, yet still protesting; but the campaign upon which he entered was conducted with the most satisfactory energy and skill. The weather, which through the spring and early summer had been favorable, changed to storms, through which Rosecrans drove on in his movements unremittingly. Feinting with his left while striking with his right, with faultless strategy he forced Bragg out of southern and central Tennessee, without a battle, bringing to naught the long labors by which Bragg had constructed at and near Tullahoma a series of strongholds.[2]

Chattanooga now lay not far off, the door into east Tennessee, which Lincoln was so eager to re-

---

[1] Cox, *Military Reminiscences*, I., 127.
[2] *War Records*, Serial No. 34, pp. 399–627 (Tullahoma Campaign).

lieve, and also the point commanding, above all
others, the Confederate communications east, west,
and south. Would not Rosecrans follow up his
success by seizing Chattanooga? But here came
more weeks of inaction, of chronic dispute with
Washington—angry demands which Halleck began
to find intolerable; there must be more men, horses,
mules, supplies; communications must be made
secure; other departments must co-operate. Stanton scrutinized keenly, sending a sharp-eyed agent,
Charles A. Dana, to report upon the spot; the patience of the president was sorely tried. But by
August 16 Rosecrans was again in motion, and so
effectively that some regard the resulting campaign
as the masterpiece of strategy during the Civil War.[1]
A disaster to the Confederacy scarcely less great
than those of July appeared imminent, to ward off
which the Richmond government brought to bear
all its resources.[2]

To study for a moment the situation, Burnside at
Cincinnati, after his work in quelling northern disaffection, was again assigned to the field, his especial
task being, with the so-called "Army of the Ohio,"
to advance through Cumberland Gap and capture
Knoxville, the citadel of east Tennessee; which he
accomplished, September 3, with no severe fighting.

[1] Nicolay and Hay, *Abraham Lincoln*, VIII., 71; Cist, *Army
of the Cumberland*, 174.
[2] *War Records*, Serial No. 50, pp. 3–1071 (Chickamauga Campaign).

From here Burnside was expected to reach a hand to Rosecrans, in the midst of the remarkable movement against Chattanooga. From Tullahoma, his conquest of June, and the posts adjacent, Rosecrans had pushed through the barrier of the Cumberland Mountains, and stood with his three corps, the Fourteenth, Thomas; the Twentieth, McCook; and the Twenty-first, Crittenden—not far from the Tennessee, a broad and deep stream, across which all bridges had been destroyed, protecting Chattanooga, where stood Bragg strongly fortified.

Like Rosecrans, Bragg, though unquestionably meritorious, had, as time went on, hardly made good his title to a high command. Fremantle, the intelligent British officer who traversed the Confederacy during the spring and early summer of 1863, portrays him as thin, sallow-faced, with bushy eyebrows meeting in a tuft over the nose, and keen, dark eyes.[1] General Taylor's order at Buena Vista: "A little more grape, Captain Bragg," had made his name more familiar, perhaps, before the Civil War, than that of any other southern leader; Davis held him in high regard; Johnston, who after Murfreesboro had been charged to investigate him, saw no reason for his removal;[2] but he had not at all won his subordinates—Polk, Hardee, D. H. Hill, and now Longstreet—who held him to be unequal to his place. Yet he was still retained, and

[1] Fremantle, *Three Months in the Southern States*, 145.
[2] Johnston, *Narrative*, 162.

was now very active. There was some excuse for
his ill-success at Tullahoma, his army having been
seriously weakened by demands from Vicksburg; but
now he was largely reinforced. Johnston sent back
the divisions that had not availed against Grant
and Sherman; Buckner came down from Knoxville after that city was lost; most important of all,
Longstreet set out from Virginia with the troops
who, on Lee's right at Gettysburg, had so nearly
carried the Round Tops, and, though not yet at
hand, arrived in time. It was a great loss to Bragg
that Hardee had been sent farther south, the defence of Mobile, which Grant appeared to threaten,
requiring a capable officer. But the Confederacy
had no better soldiers than remained to Bragg, and
the front which Rosecrans had to face was very
formidable.

The Federal beginning was brilliant.[1] It was
natural for Bragg to think that Rosecrans would
try first to connect with Burnside, strengthened by
whom his power of offence would be greatly increased. The eyes of Bragg, therefore, were turned
especially towards the northeast, over the region in
which the junction could most conveniently take
place, a region, too, presenting few difficulties to
marching armies. This idea Rosecrans encouraged,
despatching the Twenty-first Corps with much pa-
rade in that direction, up the Sequatchie Valley.
But meantime, with Thomas and McCook, the Four-

[1] *Battles and Leaders*, III., 638 et seq.

teenth and the Twentieth Corps, he crossed the river
farther down unopposed, striking out at once towards Bragg's communications with Atlanta. To
hold these unbroken was a vital matter to the Confederates: the loss of Knoxville interrupted the railroad line to Richmond and Virginia, and no route
remained but a roundabout line *via* Charleston and
Columbia, and through Georgia to Chattanooga.
Thomas and McCook were now in a difficult country
crossed by mountain ranges over which the roads
were few, poor, and quite unmapped. Nevertheless,
they made such progress that Bragg, in alarm, for-
sook his fastness, marching quickly southward in
a movement rashly interpreted to mean retreat;
whereupon Crittenden, with the Twenty-first Corps,
promptly crossed the Tennessee from the northern
side and occupied Chattanooga on September 9.
This was a great and bloodless conquest, and as a
piece of strategic work probably deserves all the
praise it has received.

Bragg was still further to be reckoned with. Full
of the idea that his adversary was retreating, Rosecrans pushed Thomas and McCook through the
mountains, hoping to strike his flank on the march
southward or make hot pursuit on his rear. McCook
went too far; or, at all events, the three Federal corps
became dangerously separated, an interval of three
difficult marches cutting off the Fourteenth Corps in
the centre from the Twentieth and Twenty-first on
either wing. In this situation it suddenly became

known to Rosecrans that Bragg was not in retreat, but had retired a short distance for a purpose, and was ready at Chickamauga to try conclusions. Had Bragg been a great commander, he might at this moment have brought things to a finish. While his own force, largely increased, was well in hand, the Federal army was badly scattered, and the three corps might have been destroyed one by one. This time fortune favored Rosecrans, for Bragg did not strike. In the respite the hard-marching Federals concentrated through a pass, Rossville Gap, over which ran the high-road from Chattanooga to Lafayette, and by September 18 stood backed by Missionary Ridge. In front of the Federal corps, after a broad interval of level, flowed Chickamauga Creek, in the woods behind which was now gathered the army of Bragg.

McLemore's Cove, in which the hosts were assembled, was a remote and secluded spot. It had been reached through difficult mountain-passes in regions sparsely inhabited; rock and forest everywhere prevailed, with now and then a settler's clearing. In the cove along the dark stream, bearing from some prehistoric slaughter the name Chickamauga, "river of death," broad meadows intervened between the ranges, which here and there had been taken up in farms; while on the stream was now and then a mill. These obscure and distant farms of Snodgrass, McAfee, Dyer, Kelly, the Widow Glenn, and Lee and Gordon's mills, lying in the September

sunlight, were about to be lifted into a lurid noto-
riety. Of the Union army, about fifty-eight thousand strong, Thomas, with the Fourteenth Corps, occupied the left; McCook, with the Twentieth, the
right; Crittenden holding the Twenty-first in reserve. The army of Bragg, amounting before the
battle ended to about sixty-six thousand,[1] had, at
the right, Polk; the left as yet awaited its leader.

Bragg, full of vigor, but impatient and unsyste-
matic, seized the initiative, his aim being to drive
back the Federal left, and, capturing Rossville Gap,
to cut Rosecrans off from Chattanooga. September
19 was throughout a day of fierce encounters, divisions from either side clashing with alternations
of fortune. Nothing was decided; but at night
Bragg had made no substantial progress. The
strengthened Union left held its own; and Polk,
who directed the Confederate assaults, found himself no nearer Rossville Gap than before. Yet the
Federals well understood that the fighting of the
day was but a preparation for a greater contest.

That night Bragg received a reinforcement of
value scarcely calculable, in the arrival of Longstreet from Virginia, by rail over the long circuit
through the Carolinas and Georgia. Longstreet, forsaking the train, was at once on horseback, riding
under the "quartering moon" through the wood-
roads to find Bragg and bring the weight of his
corps to bear upon the situation. Hurrying thus,

[1] Livermore, *Numbers and Losses*, 105.

he rode suddenly into a Federal outpost, escaping only by adroit management.[1] Bragg was found at last, and the dispositions for the morrow made. The right was again confided to Polk, who was expected to renew his attacks on the Federal left in the early morning. The left now received its leader in Longstreet, whose divisions were to wait until, by the gradual wheel of the Confederate line towards the west and south which Bragg hoped for, the convenient moment should arrive for an onset.

In the Federal camp neither alacrity nor vigilance was wanting. As the cannon cooled after the volleys of the 19th, Rosecrans gathered his generals in council at his headquarters at the Widow Glenn's.[2] Besides the corps commanders were some nine or ten of lower rank. The most interesting figure was Thomas, grave, undisturbed, deliberate, with a poise like that of Washington. He had borne through the day the brunt of Polk's assaults, and was physically exhausted. He fell asleep every minute, but when roused to give his opinion invariably answered, "I would strengthen the left." The mood of the participants was scarcely as grave as at the council after the second day at Gettysburg. Thus far there was nothing critical in the Federal situation. At the close McCook was called upon for a song, to which he responded with the "Hebrew Maiden."

[1] Longstreet, *Manassas to Appomattox*, 438.
[2] Described by Dana in his *Recollections*, 113.

3

At the dawn of September 20 Bragg was listening eagerly for sounds from his right, where Polk was expected to be at work betimes, and he subsequently brought accusations of neglect against that lieutenant; [1] but it is far easier to believe the statement of Polk, that the conditions made an early movement impossible. The forenoon was well advanced when his line at last charged; and the divisions of Breckinridge and Cleburne, directed by D. H. Hill, thrown by the general-bishop upon Thomas, made an unshrinking onslaught. Thomas had strengthened his front with the rude breastworks of earth, tree-trunks, and rails which at this stage in the war the soldiers of both armies had learned to throw up in a few minutes. Rosecrans perhaps went too far in following out Thomas's advice of the evening before, and in his hot way was depleting his right that the left might be sustained; Crittenden, in reserve, was practically stripped of his divisions, which were hurried off to act under Thomas,[2] and McCook's line grew thin from the heavy drafts despatched to the same point of attack. The forenoon was now nearing its end, and nothing had gone wrong; though the Federal right was dangerously weakened, Bragg's attack was firmly met; from general to private every man was on the alert. No one knew what lay behind the screen of woods before the Federal right wing, but probably under ordinary

[1] *War Records*, Serial No. 51, pp. 33, 47.
[2] *Ibid.*, Serial No. 50, p. 607.

circumstances Rosecrans could have successfully met danger from that quarter. The division at the extreme right was that of Sheridan, and the other commanders were scarcely inferior; there were no better men in the Union service.

Just here came the beginning of a disaster. The student of military history will recall how, on June 16, 1815, the corps of D'Erlon, twenty thousand men, by the mistake of an aide-de-camp, was sent to wander aimlessly between Quatre-Bras and Ligny, so that Ney, left short-handed, failed to defeat the English; and Napoleon, perplexed, gained only an incomplete victory over the Prussians, the upshot of all being that two days later the French lost Waterloo, which otherwise might perhaps have been won.[1] A similar stroke of ill-luck now befell Rosecrans. An aide of Thomas, passing along the line, thought he saw a gap between the divisions of Reynolds and Wood, where Brannan's division should have been. Brannan, indeed, was in his place, but with his line somewhat "refused" and so hidden by brushwood as to be not quite apparent. Forthwith the aide reported the oversight, and Rosecrans, who well understood the necessity of a perfect line in the circumstances, sent at 11 A.M. a hasty order to Wood "to close up on Reynolds."[2]   T. J. Wood, a veteran of the old army, one of the best of division-commanders, as was proved later on that day, and

---

[1] Ropes, *Campaign of Waterloo*, 174, 180, 184.
[2] *War Records*, Serial No. 50, p. 635.

on many another, saw plainly that there was a mistake. He could not close up on Reynolds without marching round behind Brannan, an utterly idle movement, which would at the same time create the gap that Rosecrans was so anxious to avoid. Why, then, did not Wood delay, it may well be asked, until there could be explanation? As luck would have it, Wood had just before been the object of an outbreak of temper from Rosecrans, who thought him slow in relieving certain troops to be detached to the left. Angry himself, from the general's reprimand, Wood was in no mood to risk another storm. He has been blamed for not delaying; [1] instead, with obedience too strict, he at once put his troops into motion, opening wide the dreaded gap in the line. To make the matter worse, Thomas now came up and told Wood that Reynolds did not need him, and took the responsibility of despatching Wood also to the left. [2]

An incident now ensued in the highest degree dramatic. Longstreet, just opposite, was listening impatiently, as the forenoon advanced, to the heavy battle on his right, eager for the time when, according to Bragg's plan, his turn should come. Learning now that, through oversight or discourtesy, his divisions were being ordered against the opposing

[1] Cist, *Army of the Cumberland*, 220 et seq.

[2] For criticism on Thomas for stripping McCook and Crittenden, see Livermore, *Some Federal and Confederate Commanders*, in the Military Hist. Soc. of Mass., *Papers*, X., 229.

enemy by Bragg without notice to him, he at once, with faultless tactics, threw into a column, by brigades, his Gettysburg veterans, with Hood in the lead.[1] Other troops not less brave were in the column. With a rush and a roar, the "rebel yell" mingling with the crash of the cannon, the column burst from its screen, poured through the gap so inopportunely left open by Wood, until eight brigades, the very pick of southern valor, had pierced the Federal formations through and through. Dana, who was near by, sleeping on the ground after great fatigue, was awakened by "the most infernal noise I ever heard." He saw Rosecrans, good Catholic that he was, crossing himself, and felt that a catastrophe had come.[2] The Union line once pierced, the assailants swept to the right. Hood had fallen dangerously wounded, but there were still good leaders, and there was no pause in the attack. Thirty minutes earlier Longstreet would have encountered a strong formation; thirty minutes later the movement so unfortunately in progress would have been concluded, and the Federal line would have met him in perfect array. As it was, all attempt to stay the onset seemed hopeless. In the midst of the wreck were Sheridan and plenty more as brave, but for a time even their prowess was of no avail. The flood of fighters surged towards the rear of Thomas, whom at the same time Polk as-

---

[1] Longstreet, *Manassas to Appomattox*, 447.
[2] Dana, *Recollections*, 115.

saulted in front. A *sauve qui peut* seemed the only Federal resource—let every man save himself.[1]

Borne back by the fugitives, Rosecrans and also Crittenden and McCook, whose troops had in great part gone to strengthen the left, were carried helpless into Rossville Gap. The general, feeling prematurely that all was lost on the field, pursued his retreat, with the two corps commanders, to Chattanooga, to make ready to receive within its fortifications the wreck of the army. Arriving at four o'clock, after the twelve-mile ride, spent with fatigue and anguish of mind, he was lifted from his saddle to the ground, and staggered nerveless. It would have been better for his fame if, like James A. Garfield, his chief of staff, he had forced his way from Rossville Gap back to the field, where, as the afternoon went forward, came a still louder tumult of battle, indicating that Thomas was holding his own.

The "horseshoe" which Thomas made his citadel is a rocky hillock rising steeply from the lower level before Rossville Gap. Concentrating his troops in a convex line around the crest of this hill, gathering in fragments from the broken corps to the southward, till he had in hand quite two-thirds of the army, with Baird, Palmer, Davis, Negley, Van Cleve, Reynolds, Brannan, and the too-obedient Wood, he refused to flee. Gordon Granger, posted in the morning as a reserve, marched without orders to

[1] Thruston, in *Southern Bivouac*, V., 412 (December, 1886).

the sound of the cannon, bringing a reinforcement of four thousand men. Against this "rock of Chickamauga," through the afternoon, the army of Bragg vainly dashed itself, till the dead lay in a wide-curving heap about the base of the horseshoe as the sun fell aslant. The general rode at a moderate pace just behind the line, with cool, encouraging words. The formation admitted of easy reinforcement, across the horseshoe, as now one point, now another, was threatened. The position was held till nightfall, when Thomas withdrew. In Rossville Gap, as the darkness gathered, two wearied, dust-covered horsemen met and dismounted. In the angle of a fence, the younger, taking a rail from the top, thrust it across the angle lower down for a seat.[1] Here the elder sank down in deep exhaustion, the younger at his side: they were Thomas and Sheridan. The latter had seen two-fifths of his command fall that day, among them two of his three brigadiers. He had been long without sleep or food. The wasted divisions lay about them exhausted like the generals. There was no pursuit; the foe were equally spent. Next day the wrecked army in a toilsome march fell back to Chattanooga, Sheridan with a remnant guarding the rear of the Twentieth Corps. From both armies 28,399 were left dead or wounded upon the field, of whom 16,986 were Confederates. The Federals lost nearly 5000 prisoners, against some 1500 on the other

[1] Sheridan, *Personal Memoirs*, I., 284.

side.[1] Nevertheless, neither army was destroyed; clearly neither had gained the object of its campaign. It was inevitable that another encounter must follow the indecisive battle.

[1] Livermore, *Numbers and Losses*, 105.

CHAPTER III

CHATTANOOGA AND KNOXVILLE
(September, 1863–December, 1863)

GRANT'S success at Vicksburg brought him recognition and deference. One of the first exercises of this newly won authority was the displacement of McClernand, so long to Grant a thorn in the flesh. His insubordination at Champion's Hill, and a foolish proclamation a few weeks later, in which, while arrogating to his own corps undeserved credit, he at the same time slurred his comrades of the other corps—a proceeding quite unmilitary and intolerable—furnished Grant occasion for superseding him, action in which the government acquiesced. In this incident Dana counted for much. As special commissioner of the war department at headquarters, an important part of his duty was to report to Stanton upon the men in responsible position. His estimates were so comprehensive as to include not only the chiefs, but even the brigadiers and staff-officers — a body of characterizations often severe, sometimes not just, but, on the whole, full of insight and intelligence, and of great help to the administration in selecting proper

instruments. As to McClernand, Dana's judgment
coincided with that of Grant, and in his place E. O.
C. Ord became commander of the Thirteenth Corps.

Grant's hands, however, were not yet quite free
to act. He counselled an immediate advance from
the north upon Mobile, which he believed might be
easily captured.[1] The plan was not approved; but
Joe Johnston's army was driven back to where it
could do no harm; the Thirteenth Corps was detached
southward to Louisiana, whence parts of it went afterwards to Texas; a division of the Fifteenth Corps
under Steele was despatched into Arkansas, and still
other troops into Mississippi; the Ninth Corps, sent
down by Burnside from Cincinnati during the siege,
was returned to him; with what remained, under
Sherman and McPherson, Grant lay at Vicksburg
as the summer closed.

The defeat at Chickamauga spurred the Federal
energies into vigorous action. At once the Eleventh
Corps, Howard, and the Twelfth Corps, Slocum, were
detached from the Army of the Potomac and sent
under Hooker to reinforce the defeated Rosecrans.
Full fifteen thousand men, with their equipments
and belongings, were in eight days transferred by
the northern railroads from Virginia to Alabama,
stepping out upon the western arena the first days of
October unfatigued and well appointed. This was
only one of numerous feats of the kind performed
by the departments of the quartermaster and com-

[1] Grant, *Personal Memoirs*, I., 484 et seq.

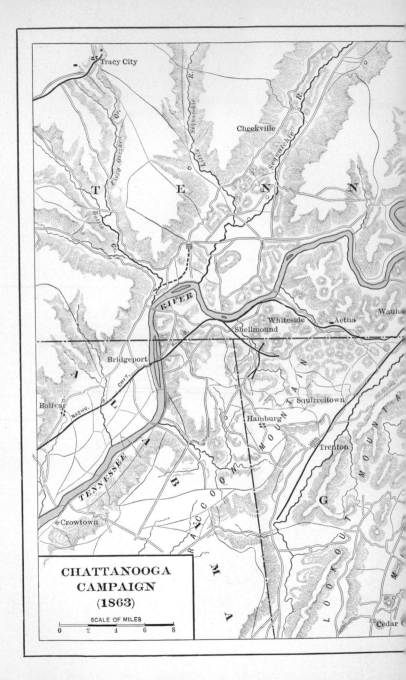

CHATTANOOGA
CAMPAIGN
(1863)

SCALE OF MILES

0   2   4   6   8

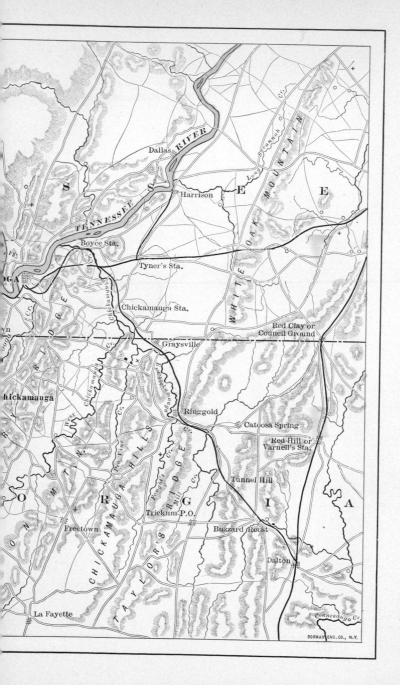

Dallas

RIVER

Harrison

Boyce Sta.

Tyner's Sta.

Chickamauga Sta.

Red Clay or
Council Ground

Graysville

Chickamauga

Ringgold

Catoosa Spring

Red Hill or
Varnell's Sta.

Tunnel Hill

Trickum P.O.

Freetown

Buzzard Roost

Dalton

La Fayette

Connesauga Cr.

BORMAY ENG. CO., N.Y.

missary generals, Montgomery C. Meigs and Rufus
Ingalls, officials in the background, but whose
mighty service in those years counted powerfully
towards the successful outcome.

Burnside, charged with the military occupation
of east Tennessee through Cumberland Gap, was
incited to do his best. Grant, too, was instructed to
report at the earliest possible moment at Cairo.
Proceeding thither at speed, he was ordered to
Louisville, and met on the way no less a personage
than Secretary Stanton himself, who had hurried
west to concert with him proper measures for the
crisis. He was assigned at once to the command of
a new department, that of the Mississippi, comprising the country west of the Alleghanies, and involving the control of not only the Army of the Tennessee at Vicksburg, but also of the Army of the
Cumberland and the Army of the Ohio, the latter
being the force of Burnside. He acquiesced in the
superseding of Rosecrans, whose military inadequacy had been plain to him since the battles of
Iuka and Corinth.[1] Rosecrans, also McCook and
Crittenden, thereupon joined the company, now becoming numerous, of commanders found wanting,
often rather through ill-luck than ill-desert, and
consigned to shelves more or less honorable, with
little part thenceforth in the great drama. Thomas
was made commander of the Army of the Cumberland. No sooner were these dispositions made than

[1] Grant, *Personal Memoirs*, I., 490.

they were definitely announced by telegraph. Grant
at once proceeded to Chattanooga, meeting on the
way Rosecrans coming north, from whom he received excellent suggestions as to a campaign, "if
he had only carried them out." [1] A day or two
later he was in Chattanooga, where the situation
demanded all his power.

The Army of the Cumberland lay intrenched
within the town, dependent for its supplies upon
a single long and imperfect road across the mountains. The Tennessee, broad and deep, was a barrier on the north. Just east of the town began
Bragg's intrenchments, on the river, running thence
southward along the high crest of Missionary Ridge,
then westward across the valley to Lookout Ridge,
there connecting again with the river; the outpost
here occupied a famous landmark, Lookout Mountain, which, rising twenty-four hundred feet, domi-
nates the region far and near.

Though diminished and disorganized at Chickamauga, the Army of the Cumberland was by no
means beaten or discouraged. Two-thirds of it, indeed, had been held by Thomas to gallant work in
the battle, retiring in good order at last. It is perhaps not too much to claim that had Rosecrans
gone back with Garfield from Rossville to the field,
and shown the force and fertility that he showed in
the crisis at Stone's River, a victory might have
been gained in spite of the rout of the right. The

[1] Grant, *Personal Memoirs*, I., 498.

Federals in Chattanooga stood quite undismayed
under a leader whom they thoroughly trusted, on
short rations, to be sure, but cheerfully biding their
time.　Meanwhile, Hooker was already at hand with
two corps; and Sherman, who now succeeded to the
command of the Army of the Tennessee, was ordered,
September 23, to march with all speed with the
Fifteenth Corps to Chattanooga, leaving McPherson
at Vicksburg and Hurlbut at Memphis.[1]

The powerful blow delivered by the Confederacy
at Chickamauga, though to some extent an offset
to the Federal successes of the summer, did not
really balance them, and had a sequence full of
disappointment to the South.　Longstreet believed
that on the field the tactics of the afternoon of
September 20 were gravely at fault, and that the
advantage gained was not properly pushed home.[2]
Chattanooga was only partially invested, whereas,
in the opinion of this strong commander of the left
wing, the Federal communications might and should
have been entirely cut.　Fortunately for the Federals, the camp of their adversaries was a scene
of contention, Bragg having no friends among his
higher officers, and on his part criticising and denouncing them in unmeasured terms.　Polk was removed from his command; D. H. Hill, too, was now
forced out of service, not to draw his sword again
until the last days of the war.　Though Hardee was

[1] W. T. Sherman, *Memoirs*, I., 372 et seq.
[2] Longstreet, *Manassas to Appomattox*, 452, 461 et seq.

recalled from the South and given Polk's place, his
relations with Bragg were scarcely more friendly;
while every line of Longstreet's memoirs implies
disgust at what he regards as the mismanagement
of his chief.

Into this scene of dissension suddenly dropped
Jefferson Davis, and it is impossible to feel that his
visit helped his cause. No testimony could shake
his faith in Bragg, though he was so far moved by
the general dissatisfaction as to offer the command
to Longstreet, then to Hardee. Both refused, depressed with hopelessness as to success under the
prevailing conditions.[1]   Longstreet urged that Johnston, already in nominal command of the department, should be trusted, stating his own willingness
to serve under him. When Davis manifested displeasure, Longstreet begged to resign. This request
was refused, and Bragg was retained, with memorable results.

John C. Pemberton, captured at Vicksburg, but
later exchanged, was with Davis at Chattanooga.
In spite of his strong fight at Champion's Hill and
his stubborn defence of Vicksburg, he was, on account of his northern birth and ill-success, in a high
degree unpopular. When Davis, therefore, sustaining Bragg's action in removing Polk, suggested Pemberton to command the corps, he was met by disapproval, which he was forced to respect, so that
Hardee was appointed.[2] The ineffective invest-

[1] Longstreet, *Manassas to Appomattox*, 466.   [2] *Ibid.*, 469.

ment with which Bragg's lieutenants were so dis-
satisfied, but which they were powerless to change,
soon came to a disastrous end.

. Grant arrived in Chattanooga October 23, finding that Thomas had omitted nothing that it was
possible to accomplish.[1] The intrenchments were
strong, the army in good spirits, the demoralization
from Chickamauga a thing of the past. To be sure,
rations were short, and animals were dying by hundreds of starvation. A scheme was on foot, however, for opening a better and shorter route for
communicating with the North, planned by an
able engineer, General W. F. Smith, which Grant at
once approved and carried out.[2] In the operation
the Army of the Cumberland was well supported
by the corps of Hooker.[3] Longstreet, who held the
Confederate left, was eluded and beaten back, and
by the brilliant night capture of Brown's Ferry, a
well-protected road was opened to the town from
Bridgeport, which point the railroad reached. In
the Federal host hope now rose to the highest. They
lived in plenty; the corps of the Army of the Potomac
were good comrades; and now, by Grant's order,
Sherman was hurrying the Fifteenth Corps from
Memphis across Tennessee to their relief.

Bragg now took a most unfortunate step.[4] Burn-

---

[1] *Battles and Leaders*, III., 679.
[2] *War Records*, Serial No. 54, pp. 39–234 (Reopening of the
Tennessee River).   [3] Dana, *Recollections*, 134.
[4] *War Records*, Serial No. 54, pp. 255–550 (Knoxville Campaign).

side, with the newly constituted Army of the Ohio, made up of the Ninth and Twenty-third Corps, was lying in east Tennessee, making glad, at last, the heart of Lincoln by bringing succor to the greatly suffering Unionists of that region. At no time in his career did Burnside bear himself so well as during this campaign.[1] The man vanquished at Fredericksburg rarely referred to the past; much less did he spend time in bewailing misfortunes or in criticism; he faced his new work with skill and a manly heart. As he approached, Buckner, the Confederate commander, retired before him, and, as has been noted, he occupied Knoxville, September 3. His detachments spreading thence through the valleys, enjoyed what to a Federal army was a most unusual experience, a warm welcome from the people to whom they came.

During the visit of Jefferson Davis at Chattanooga, a plan was concerted for a quick disposing of Burnside in east Tennessee, by an expedition from Bragg's army that should return in time for the new battle, which it was now plain the Federals were determined upon. For this work Longstreet was selected; he showed no reluctance, but insisted upon despatch as vital to success. Accordingly, Longstreet, with the division of McLaws, and the former division of Hood, now under Jenkins, together with Wheeler's cavalry, entered early in November upon an operation marked with disaster;

[1] Cox, *Military Reminiscences*, I., 520 et seq.

while Bragg, meantime, his best troops at a distance, was obliged to meet a peril which he had not rightly measured.

Sherman, in answer to Grant's summons, marched eastward from Memphis with all the speed possible. Going himself in advance of the troops, he narrowly escaped capture by raiding cavalry near Corinth.[1] The Army of the Tennessee at this time performed other feats than those of arms: General G. M. Dodge, with eight thousand men, making their own tools, built railroads, boats, mills, bridges, with an industry and skill that repaired in a brief time the ravages of war.[2] Word soon came from Grant to drop all work not bearing directly upon the quickest possible advance to Chattanooga; and, obeying to the letter, on November 14, 1863, Sherman rode into the threatened town, as usual in advance of his divisions. The columns arrived a week later, prepared for work that was at once assigned them.

The Confederate line before Chattanooga, except on the left, had changed little since the first investment immediately after Chickamauga.[3] Hardee's corps held the right, where at the north Missionary Ridge came to an end, with the Tennessee, just below the junction with the Chickamauga, near its base. Thence southward to Rossville Gap the line followed the crest, which was often narrow, the

[1] W. T. Sherman, *Memoirs*, I., 379.
[2] Grant, *Personal Memoirs*, 513 et seq.
[3] *War Records*, Serial No. 55 (Chattanooga Campaign).

4

slope on either hand descending steeply to the
lower level. Bragg had his headquarters here in
a central position, the troops of Breckinridge holding the highland from Hardee's position as far as
Rossville Gap. Crossing the Chattanooga Valley to
Lookout Range, the line southwestward to the river
again was now but weakly garrisoned, for from this
post Longstreet's divisions had just departed for
Knoxville. Here Bragg's position was notably less
advantageous than when the siege began. Before
Longstreet's departure, the advance of Hooker in
connection with the opening of the "cracker-line,"
the convenient road for supplies so cleverly made
available by W. F. Smith, established a powerful
force threateningly near the weakened Confederate
left.

Opposed to Bragg, Grant, in the lower ground to
the west, appreciating fully the value of promptness, now ranged his zealous and hopeful army.
Sherman held the left, for the moment lying on the
north of the river opposite Hardee. Thomas, with
the Army of the Cumberland, reorganized and reinforced since its disaster, fronted the line of Breckinridge on Missionary Ridge immediately before the
town; Hooker, as mentioned, stood at the right, on
ground won since the siege began. To about fifty-
six thousand Federals stood opposed forty-six thousand Confederates.[1] Any one who has beheld the
theatre of operations will believe that the advan-

[1] Livermore, *Numbers and Losses*, 106.

tage of the Confederate position was fully equal to
the difference in numbers. Grant's plan was that
Sherman should make the main attack on the left,
while Thomas and Hooker were to make demonstrations in their fronts designed to prevent the
reinforcement of Hardee against Sherman from the
line farther south; but their feints, should a chance
offer, were to be turned into real assaults.

Accordingly, on November 23, 1863, Thomas began offensive operations by marching out from the
forts near the town, with Grant in his company, and
seizing advanced ground which included Orchard
Knob, a rocky hill in front of the Confederate line;
Thomas stood prepared to assault from Orchard
Knob, while Hooker, at the right, attacked the
slope of Lookout. The air on the next morning,
November 24, was charged with coolness, mists
from the river obscuring the lowlands, while clouds
drifted about the heights. Long before light the
corps of Sherman threw off concealment and made
its way by pontoons across the river against the
north end of Missionary Ridge. This was quickly
carried and the ridge surmounted, whereupon Sherman encountered a great disappointment: the height
upon which he stood was isolated, a gorge which
had quite escaped his reconnoissance intervening between it and the ridge proper, on the steep opposite
side of which Hardee was posted; but there was no
abatement of the vigor of the attack, which was met
with equal spirit, the armies clashing in eager battle.

It was at the south that the Union success first began. The ardor of Hooker's men, impelling them beyond the lower acclivities of Lookout Mountain, soon carried them to the highest points, till at last the battalions, fighting as they climbed, reached Pulpit Rock, a height of twenty-four hundred feet. Nor did Hooker pause here. Though delayed somewhat in the low ground by Chattanooga Creek, he soon crossed, the Confederates retiring, and was in good time at Rossville; whence, pressing northward along Missionary Ridge, with a division in either valley east and west, and still another advancing on the crest between, he threw back Breckinridge, who was thus brought into a strait.

Ere this Thomas was in motion. The feat of Hooker's men, lifted as they were high in air, had been distinctly visible and audible to the Army of the Cumberland, who, standing impatient in battle array on the afternoon of the 25th, received the order to take the rifle-pits which Bragg had contrived at the foot of the ridge. That proved an easy task, after which the men, without orders, stung by their late humiliation at Chickamauga, and beholding the chance which fortune opened, surged in a wave of blue up the almost precipitous ascent. A second line of rifle-pits half-way up offered an obstacle even less embarrassing than that at the base. Soon the panting ranks were at the summit, four hundred feet above the plain. The hostile line was at once broken through, and, turn-

ing right and left, the assailants in a few moments
overpowered all resistance, whether of infantry or
of artillery, barely missing the capture of Bragg
himself, who galloped eastward down the height.
In this impetuous and happy exploit many were
brave, but the figure of special interest perhaps was
Sheridan, who reached the top among the first.
Afire with the battle-glow, lavish it is to be feared
of imprecations, mounted upon a cannon that his
short stature might be properly pedestalled, he
swayed the throng of stormers.

Sherman, who as yet had made no headway, must
be succored at the northern end of the ridge.   The
division of Baird, therefore, which among the troops
of Thomas was farthest to the left, fell hotly upon
Hardee's rear.   Struck thus before and behind, even
that skilful soldier was without recourse.   He withdrew defeated to the Chickamauga Valley, as did
also Breckinridge at the south.   Every position was
captured, the entire ridge cleared of the foe, and
through the night, that fell as the battle closed, the
beaten Bragg fled southward into Georgia.

To the Federals the loss in killed was 753; wounded,
4722; to the Confederates, in killed, 361; wounded,
2160;[1] the latter lost many guns and more than
4000 prisoners.   The victory of Chattanooga, though
attended with small comparative loss, was more important in results than many bloodier fields; and
as regards elements of impressiveness perhaps sur-

[1] Livermore, *Numbers and Losses*, 106.

passes every other battle of the war. East and West
fought side by side in earnest emulation. It was
the Army of the Tennessee, Vicksburg men, that
struck at the north; the Army of the Potomac,
Gettysburg men, that scaled Lookout; the Army
of the Cumberland, Chickamauga men, that carried
Missionary Ridge. To these last, since they had
suffered most, it fell appropriately to administer
the *coup de grâce*. Here, too, for the only time, contended side by side the four supreme Federal leaders
—Grant, Sherman, Sheridan, and Thomas. For the
striving of these champions nature provided a ma-
jestic theatre, and rarely indeed has a battle been
attended by circumstances so picturesque.

The charge of the Army of the Cumberland, without orders, up the beetling Missionary Ridge, before
Grant and Thomas, astounded and anxious on
Orchard Knob, was such a spectacle as human eyes
have rarely seen. Hooker's achievement on Lookout Mountain, beheld among and above the drifting
clouds by both hosts, was a worthy drama, worthily
witnessed. Sheridan, in intense interest, followed
with his glass a color-bearer, who in front of the
line waved his flag dauntlessly in the charge till
the mountain was carried.[1] As the evening deepened, the full moon rose magnified at the horizon
line by atmospheric refraction. While it hung for
a few moments behind an eastern ridge, a charging
column passed across its disk, weirdly silhouetted

[1] Sheridan, *Personal Memoirs*, I., 306.

before the beholders, the brandished weapons and frenzied figures wild and strange as in a march of goblins.[1]

How fared Longstreet meantime, detached with the best troops of the Confederate army for the Knoxville expedition? From the first things went wrong. Delayed at the start, they found themselves on arriving among a hostile people, and were met everywhere by Burnside with vigor and skill. The Federal chief had able lieutenants, especially Potter and Hartranft of the Ninth Corps,[2] who, as colonels at Antietam, carried the stone bridge on the left; and also Sanders, a young cavalry general, whose promise was cut off untimely in this campaign. The southern officers and men appear to have gone to work only half-heartedly. Of the brigadiers, the conduct of Robertson was bad; while Law, jealous of Jenkins, who had been preferred to him as leader of a division in place of the wounded Hood, wilfully held back in his duty, believing that a success would go to the credit of his rival.[3] Even the true and tried McLaws, who in capturing the garrison of Harper's Ferry before Antietam did perhaps as much as Stonewall Jackson, and at Fredericksburg repulsed from the sunken road the Federal right, was now accused of slackness and court-martialled.[4]

[1] Sheridan, *Personal Memoirs*, I., 315.
[2] *War Records*, Serial No. 54, p. 332.
[3] Longstreet, *Manassas to Appomattox*, 495–548.
[4] *War Records*, Serial No. 54, pp. 503 et seq.

The doughty Longstreet himself, without faith in the enterprise and disheartened by the behavior of both superiors and subordinates, acknowledges a letting down of his own energies. In an assault, November 29, upon Fort Sanders, at Knoxville, where he was beaten back with a loss of a thousand men, he admits that he too credulously accepted an exaggerated account of the strength of the Federal works, and drew off when he ought to have struck again.[1] For the Confederates all came to naught. As Bragg had been driven south of the Georgia border, so Longstreet, after a trying winter experience in the unfriendly highlands, at last made his way back through southwest Virginia to the side of Lee. When the year 1864 opened, Tennessee throughout was almost wrested from the Confederate grasp; a party of guerillas now and then might threaten a bridge or rob a train, but as to regular and formal resistance in that state, the war for the time was over.

[1] Longstreet, *Manassas to Appomattox*, 507.

CHAPTER IV

LIFE IN WAR-TIME NORTH AND SOUTH
(1863)

AT the end of 1863 the North had reason to feel that, in spite of many a rough stroke received, she had inflicted more than she had suffered: the Confederacy was now cleft apart, and the patrol of the Union gun-boats up and down the Mississippi was constant and vigilant. Not only was it out of the question for armies to cross, but it was a risk for individuals to attempt a passage in a skiff; much more so to attempt to ferry over a herd of cattle, a load of cotton, or provisions of any kind: unlucky furloughed soldiers from the trans-Mississippi could not get home.[1] Resistance was practically quelled in both the divided parts north of the Gulf states. West of that river, Kirby Smith and Dick Taylor were soon to strike a last telling blow for the Confederacy on the Red River; but, as regards the trans-Mississippi country, the Richmond government had little to contemplate but a series of reverses, as a result of which its cause was prostrate. East of the river the war was

[1] Hague, *A Blockaded Family*, 130.

practically at an end in Kentucky and throughout
Tennessee, except one last spasmodic convulsion to
be described ere long. Alabama remained to be
subdued, and also the great region from Florida
northward; though in each Atlantic state the sea-
coast was dominated, if not actually occupied, by
Federal armies and fleets, with the exception of a
harbor here and there into which the blockade-
runners still continued to penetrate.

This wide subjugation, with the desperate effort
to fight it off, profoundly modified the life of the
southern people. Men of the arms-bearing age were
in the field, and those who stayed at home, the
women, old men, and children, were greatly affected in their conditions. The modification was not
always of a melancholy kind. Miss Parthenia A.
Hague, living in southern Alabama, author of an
interesting record,[1] gives a pleasant picture of the
days passed on the plantations. The vigorous men
were in arms, the plantations tilled by the negroes,
whose fidelity to their old masters was largely unshaken. The blockade, cutting off as it did everything that came from the outside, threw the people
upon their own resources. Instead of the unvarying cotton, crops became diversified, producing, so
far as possible, what could no longer be imported.
Domestic industries, long obsolete, were plied again:
the women spun, wove, and dyed, making fabrics
which they turned into garments; candles were

[1] Hague, *A Blockaded Family*, passim.

moulded, baskets and furniture contrived of wicker-
work, hats from wool, and shoes from leather, which
had never before been so well tanned. Flocks of
goats were introduced with great benefit, in the
idea that they might tempt the cupidity of possible
invaders less than horses and beeves. Communities
grew self-reliant as never before. It seems plain
that the harsh circumstances tended to bring about
a healthier life than when the planter and his wife
superintended the slave-raised cotton, while meantime from the outside came in a stream of supplies
that removed the need of work of brain or hand.
But hardship and affliction constantly grew deeper;
privation pinched ever more acutely; death deso-
lated every household; the fear of the foe was constant, until they came, and came to crush.

The suffering on the plantations was small as
compared with that in the besieged towns. One
may still see in Vicksburg two or three of the caves
into which the people were driven—damp burrows
into the heart of the hills, the crumbling roofs and
sides propped up by timbers, the ravines into which
they opened never out of reach of the far-penetrat-
ing shells of the Federals. Of the constant terror,
the pressing want, the wounds, and death with
which each day was attended, there are pathetic
recitals.[1]

Of the high life of the South in war-times, the
aristocracy under the old régime being scarcely less

[1] *My Cave Life in Vicksburg, by a Lady.*

a class apart than in the midst of feudal conditions, there is no more vivid picture than that of Mrs. James Chesnut, wife of a former United States senator from South Carolina who became a Confederate general and an aide of Jefferson Davis.[1] She was in middle age, full of vitality, good-hearted, well schooled and travelled, possessed, too, of a cheery humor, at times so breezy and robust as to recall the Wife of Bath. Flitting from point to point—Montgomery, Richmond, Columbia, Charleston, or at this or that country seat—her familiars were Jefferson Davis, Lee, and many other men of the hour and their families, whom she depicts in her panorama in lively colors. At first her narrative effervesces with high spirits, reflecting merrily a cheerful environment; but gloom deepens as the months proceed; in place of buoyancy come wrath and depression, while laughter ceases in the frequent shadow of death. After a battle in 1863 she limns a sober picture of a communion service in St. Paul's Church in Richmond, during which the sexton hurries at short intervals up the aisle with a whispered summons to the families whose sons, brothers, or husbands are brought in from the fields in their coffins. He goes at last to the minister in the chancel, who, leaving the distribution of the bread and wine to his assistant, departs with the others to meet his sorrow.[2]

Yet Mrs. Chesnut cannot long be sad. In a De-

---

[1] Mrs. Chesnut, *Diary from Dixie*.   [2] *Ibid.*, 245.

cember record of this year she tells a merry story of an excursion down the river in the flag-of-truce boat to a French frigate which had come up through Hampton Roads. The party, in much-fractured French, tried to establish an *entente cordiale*. "Vieff l'Emperor!" cries one. "A la santé de l'Emperor!" cries another, with raised glass. But the Frenchmen, of course under orders to be cautious, are unresponsive. The good lady may be excused for saying that the frigate was "a dirty little thing," and her officers unattractive. "They can't help not being good-looking, but with all the world open to them, to wear such shabby clothes!"

That the Confederacy, shut off from the world by the ever-tightening blockade, was by this time badly out at the elbows there is much evidence. In the spring of 1863 there were bread riots; in November flour sold at over a hundred dollars a barrel, and suffering more acute was impending.[1] The painful lack in the Confederacy of all supplies except food and the raw materials for fabrics was a source of weakness which could not be overcome. Clothes, shoes, medicines, machinery, arms, paper, powder—the thousand appliances of civilized life in peace and the means for making war—came to the South only in blockade-runners from Europe or were captured by her armies from her northern foes. There was grievous dearth of workshops, skilled labor, and scientific accomplishment which could

[1] Jones, *Rebel War Clerk's Diary*, II., 90, 284.

be turned to practical account in such an exigency. Nevertheless, there were men who coped as they could with a situation which ever grew more serious, and the story requires mention of work often as important as that of generals in the field.

John M. Brooke, a naval officer of ingenious turn, while attached to the Naval Observatory at Washington, had attracted notice as the inventor of an apparatus for deep-sea sounding[1] and otherwise furthering the study of the physical geography of the sea, which about the middle of the nineteenth century was engaging attention. Taking sides with the South, he was soon put in charge of the Tredegar Works, at Richmond, and here developed into a skilful mechanical engineer, creating with small means a vast forge and machine-shop, and educating a numerous body of mechanics. His principal achievement was the devising of the ram *Virginia*, a remarkable feat in view of his limited means.[2] His plans were so marked by originality as to place him in the class with Eads, Ericsson, and other great Tubal Cains who in these latter days have equipped the world with marvellous tools. On shore as well as sea Brooke continued to supply machines; and he kept in some sort of order the hard-worked railroads; while shot and shell and

[1] Corbin, *Maury*, 99.
[2] Scharf, *Confederate States Navy*, 145; *Battles and Leaders*, I., 715.

the cannon that hurled them came abundantly out
of the Tredegar furnaces.

Matthew Fontaine Maury, of an old Huguenot
family in Spottsylvania County, Virginia, was in
1861 probably the most distinguished scientific man
who held a commission in the navy.[1]   At the head
of the Naval Observatory in Washington, his reputation was especially that of an hydrographer.   His
work in mapping the ocean-currents, in meteorology,
in studying marine phenomena in general, from the
bed of the sea to the winds that blew above its sur-
face, in devising and properly laying the first ocean
cables, was recognized as of value by the sailors of
every land.   When at the outbreak he resigned his
commission, Constantine, grand-admiral of Russia,
offered him high position.   But he went with the
South, serving the Confederacy first as chief of sea-
coast, harbor, and river defences, and later in Europe.
His service was especially noteworthy in contriving
instruments for submarine warfare—mines and torpedoes, which the Federal ships found formidable
long after the southern navy at home had practically
ceased to exist.

Of southern scientists of that time none were more
interesting than the brothers John and Joseph Le
Conte.[2]   Like Maury, of Huguenot strain, they were
born in Georgia, men of genius in several directions,
before the war accomplished chemists.   From Jo-

[1] Corbin, *Maury*, passim.
[2] Joseph Le Conte, *Autobiography*.

seph's autobiography it appears that he was in youth a favorite pupil of Agassiz. He hesitated in regard to secession, but at last, when the University of South Carolina (where both brothers were professors) was broken up by the enlistment of all the students, they were swept away in the current, becoming active workers and severe sufferers for their cause. The Le Contes established laboratories at Columbia, South Carolina, which became the main source of supply for medicines and hospital requirements. Through them also the South was able to utilize its nitre-beds; in the manufacture of powder the Le Contes became indispensable.[1] Joseph, whom we know best, was an amiable teacher and scholar, who later as a geologist, in the University of California, of which John became president, established a fame among the first. His autobiography, written late in life, narrates in calm and unembittered terms many painful experiences in the war time. With manly candor he writes:

"I am not blaming anybody on either side. It was evidently an honest difference of opinion as to the nature of our government; it was honestly fought out to a finish, and the result frankly accepted. But let it be distinctly understood that there never was a war in which were more thoroughly enlisted the hearts of the whole people—men, women, and children—than were those of the South in this. To us it was literally a life and death struggle for national

[1] Mrs. Chesnut, *Diary from Dixie*, 187.

existence; and doubtless the feeling was equally honest and earnest on the other side."[1]

The aspect of the North at the end of 1863 was in marked contrast to that of the South. In politics it was an "off year," the elections being for state officers only; but the results indicated better things for the Union, particularly the overwhelming defeat of Vallandigham in Ohio. As regards loss of men, the suffering in both sections was similar. The homes were few which had not sent out at least one soldier, and very many had sent more, from whom the grave gathered a heavy tribute. But excepting this desolation, there was little sign of bad times at the North. It was prosperity that one beheld. The energetic government supplied every need with prompt liberality; every forge was making weapons and ammunition; every factory turning out tents, clothes, equipments, supplies of every kind. Whatever the land could produce, crops, horses, cattle, found a ready market; there was labor for all, and the pay was sure and ample; to the adroit and rapacious, extraordinary opportunities opened for amassing fortunes; to many wealth came almost without an effort. The merchants who happened to have on their shelves a stock of cotton cloth, the farmers who had raised good crops of onions or tobacco, the lumbermen who had beams and boards on hand, sold their merchandise at unexpected prices. A public debt, to be sure, was rolling up, surpassing

[1] Joseph Le Conte, *Autobiography*, 181.

5

everything the world had previously known, and the cautious apprehended a dismal reckoning in the future; but the mass of the people had few fears. They bought with alacrity the government securities and paid with few murmurs the internal revenue taxes, which by this time furnished an abundant return. The rising price of gold was ominous; the disappearance, too, of specie from the currency was startling; but in its place the people accepted the greenbacks, of which there were in circulation,[1] January 1, 1864, $444,825,022, thereby submitting to a forced loan in addition to the "kewpon bonds," which in thousands of plain households now gave evidence of the confidence in the government. Of the resolute cheerfulness of the northern people, no better or more representative utterance can be found than a passage from the pen of one of the best and ablest Americans, Dr. Asa Gray, in his letters to Darwin and others at this time.

"Oh foolish people! When will you see that there is only one end to all this, and that the North never dreams of any other. . . . Wait a year longer and you may return to a country in which slavery having tried to get more has lost all, and as a system, is defunct. The November elections show a united North. Peace Democracy has made its issue and is dead. The re-election of Lincoln by acclamation seems probable, supported by moderate men of all sorts, the extremes of the opposing par-

[1] Blaine, *Twenty Years*, I., 643.

ties alone going against him. Merry Christmas to you!"[1]

A noteworthy feature of the Civil War was the organized charity.   In the wars of past times, up to the middle of the nineteenth century, the comfort of the soldier depended upon what his government could give him. The suffering in the Crimea, making plain as it did the inadequacy of the authorities to cope with the needs of the troops, developed agencies with which the name of Florence Nightingale is forever bound.   Proceeding upon this precedent, at the outset of the Civil War the Sanitary Commission was organized.[2] Its purpose was to supplement the work of the government, in the field, in camps, and in hospitals, supplying to the troops such mitigations of pain and privation as are possible. June 9, 1861, formal organization was effected by an order of the secretary of war.   The president of the commission was Henry Whitney Bellows, a New York clergyman of great energy and eloquence, who had initiated the movement; and its able secretary was Frederick Law Olmstead. With them were associated men of distinction in law, business, above all in the medical profession; at once a beginning was made of organized philanthropy.

Everywhere there was zeal; the suffering to be relieved was that of sons and brothers. Money was ready to flow; especially the hearts of women were

[1] Asa Gray, *Letters*, II., 511–517.
[2] Stillé, *Hist. of the Sanitary Commission*.

moved; whatever their brains could suggest, or their
hands contrive, came in overflowing measure. This
offering needed direction, which the Sanitary Commission undertook to furnish. That its work was
wisely done was questioned by few that saw it; and
its record is an interesting chapter in the history of
the war. The service rendered by its managers,
though unpaid, was constant and able. Through
its channels at least twenty-five million dollars flowed
out in relief.[1] The commission possessed the confidence of the soldiers who were ministered to, and
of the people who ministered. Since the war it
has been the model upon which the "Red Cross"
work in various lands has been planned.

Affiliated with the Sanitary Commission was the
Western Sanitary Commission, organized in St. Louis
for work in the Mississippi Valley.[2] A brother organization was the Christian Commission, supported
by people of evangelical religious belief, whose effort
was, besides physical relief, to reinforce the work of
the chaplains in the care of souls.

While in these great societies all was done with
the best purpose and the warmest zeal, they did not
escape criticism. Stillé speaks of a lack of sympathy on the part of the government departments;[3]
and General Sherman, with his usual frankness,
while admitting great usefulness, declares that the

---

[1] Stillé, *Hist. of the Sanitary Commission*, 490.
[2] Mrs. Charlotte Eliot, *W. G. Eliot*, 212.
[3] Stillé, *Hist. of the Sanitary Commission*, 510.

ministrations of such societies should be in the rear
of fighting armies and not on the field of battle.[1]
Their creation, however, was undoubtedly a step in
advance, and henceforth no civilized country will
array armies without studying carefully this American experience.

A word or two should be said as to the work of the
public press in the war. The newspaper, which in
quiet times is the universal informant and counsellor, becomes in war-times more than ever a necessity
of life. "Bread and the newspaper," one is scarcely
less essential than the other. The work of the press
during the Civil War was performed by men often
of the highest character and ability. Horace Greeley, Henry J. Raymond, Charles A. Dana, A. K.
McClure, Murat Halstead, Whitelaw Reid, George
W. Smalley, Joseph Medill, Samuel Bowles, and
many more most capable writers—the list is a brilliant one of those who in editorial chairs or as correspondents in the field furnished news and moulded
opinion.

Nevertheless, throughout the war, there was never
a time when in either North or South the relations
were entirely easy and cordial between commanders
and newspaper-men, and they often were at swords'
points. Lee is said to have spoken of newspapers
in general with great severity.[2] He impugned their
patriotism, instancing particularly their conduct

---

[1] W. T. Sherman, *Memoirs*, II., 392.
[2] R. E. Lee, Jr., *Recollections and Letters of Lee*, 416.

when, in 1863, Longstreet was sent west before Chickamauga; it was vital to keep the movement secret, but the newspapers insisted on making it public. Grant's disposition towards the correspondents was no kinder;[1] and Cox tells stories of jarring and ill-accord between generals and correspondents which probably all generals at the front could have paralleled.[2] These writers, no doubt, were often inconsiderate, tactless, and perhaps worse. The general was sometimes browbeaten in his headquarters by a correspondent who told him that his paper every day made and unmade greater men than he was. One writer of note, William Swinton, was accused by both Grant and Cox of being an eavesdropper, a presumptuous hector, and a calumniator.

Perhaps there is a deep-seated reason why soldiers and newspaper-men should be unfriendly. If "war is hell," as a high military authority states, it is no more infernal in the devastation and homicide which results, than in the deception which war makes no less necessary. From the time of the Trojan horse, at the outset of history, to the capture of Aguinaldo, in our day, the course of human warfare is marked no more by bloodshed than by strategy. There can be no warfare without strategy, and strategy is the art of making feints. The great strategist is he who can best hoodwink his adversary, and strike his blow while the adversary is in error. Such a course

[1] Grant, *Personal Memoirs*, II., 68.
[2] Cox, *Military Reminiscences*, I., 172.

once entered upon, is liable soon to become bald treachery and lying. To make war is of necessity to produce devastation, man-slaying, untruth—a thing only justifiable as the sole means of averting what is worse. The world believes that the time is not yet come when it can dispense with the soldier, and while he exists, the soldier apparently must deceive as well as burn and kill.

Now, while it is essential in the soldier's trade that he go furtively to work, the very air in which the press lives is publicity. It exists to tell the truth fully and accurately; and if a suspicion arises that the press comes short here, it is straightway discredited, loses influence, and may be thrust aside. When, therefore, the journalist, the man who must tell the truth or fail, faces the soldier, who must deceive or fail, a natural antagonism develops between the two; unfriendliness is inevitable. The agent of publicity can never be welcome in a campaign.

CHAPTER V

CONCENTRATION UNDER GRANT
(DECEMBER, 1863–APRIL, 1864)

THE military events of the summer and fall of
1863 brought to the front the great commanders
who were thenceforth to take responsibility and
achieve victory. In civil life also new men pushed
to the front. The thirty-eighth Congress (elected
in 1862), which met December 7, 1863, organized
by choosing as speaker Schuyler Colfax, of Indiana,
the party vote standing 101 to 81, the majority indicating accurately the Republican strength, though
there were besides a few Democrats who usually sustained the administration.[1] Colfax, who thus came
forward into high position, was by trade a printer,
a man active-minded and industrious, who since his
appearance in public life had been marked as an
able debater, and now confirmed a reputation as a
skilful parliamentarian.[2] Several of the prominent
men of the thirty-seventh Congress were missed:
Elbridge G. Spaulding and Roscoe Conkling, of New
York; John A. Bingham and Samuel Shellabarger,

[1] Blaine, *Twenty Years*, I., 497 et seq.
[2] Riddle, *Recollections*, 249.

of Ohio; Galusha A. Grow, of Pennsylvania, and still others. Of the new men, perhaps the most brilliant was Henry Winter Davis, of Maryland, whose ardent Unionism had operated powerfully to save his state from secession, and who, though before the war a supporter of John Bell, was opposed to the conservatives and a promoter of the war. His powers were conspicuous, and the highest anticipations were entertained of his eminence as a statesman, blasted two years later by his premature death. Another interesting figure was the brave soldier, Major-General Robert C. Schenck, who, severely wounded at the second Bull Run, resumed a political career which he had earlier followed with distinction, and was chosen from Ohio as the successor of Vallandigham. He became chairman at once of the committee on military affairs, and soon succeeded Thaddeus Stevens at the head of the committee of ways and means, always showing a grasp of mind and a capacity for effective statement which won admiration. At this time, too, entered James A. Garfield, also a major-general, who had earned his promotion at Chickamauga. His health was breaking under the hardships of campaigning, and he now chose a field of service no less arduous if less dangerous. William B. Allison, John A. Kasson, Samuel J. Randall, and a young man of thirty-three, James G. Blaine, were also among the new members. Into the Senate came a representation of the loyal war governors, Morgan, of New

York; Sprague, of Rhode Island; and Ramsey, of
Minnesota; while among the Democratic accessions
were Reverdy Johnson, of Maryland, and Thomas
A. Hendricks, of Indiana.

The work of the thirty-seventh Congress had been
one of path-breaking, in framing a military policy,
devising ways and means to meet vast expenditures,
and undermining slavery as the root of all the
political evils. What was begun, the thirty-eighth
Congress must continue. The proposition for an
amendment of the Constitution making slavery
thenceforth impossible will be discussed further on.[1]

On the first day of the session, E. B. Washburne,
of Illinois, moved a restoration of the grade of lieutenant-general, and supported his motion in a most
earnest and picturesque speech, making no secret
of the fact that he had Grant in view for the revived
dignity. In spite of some reasonable opposition
(Garfield, for instance, thought the movement premature), both Houses voted favorably, and on
February 29, 1864, the bill was signed.[2] The mod-
est hero appeared in Washington, stammering and
abashed before plaudits, as he had never been before batteries. No one paints more vividly the
homeliness of the rather shabby, unimpressive figure than Richard H. Dana, who saw him at Wil-
lard's as he started out under his new responsibilities. "I suppose you don't mean to breakfast

---

[1] See below, chaps. viii. and xiii.
[2] *U. S. Statutes at Large*, XIII., 11.

again till the war is over," remarked Mr. Dana,
jocosely. "Not here I sha'n't," said Grant, han-
dling his English as cavalierly as if it were a rebel
position.[1]

With his new rank was imposed upon Grant the
entire command of the Union armies, both East and
West. Sherman took the department of the Mississippi, McPherson succeeding him as commander
of the Army of the Tennessee. Halleck lost his
prominence, though still on duty as "chief-of-
staff," near the secretary of war. No incident connected with these changes is more interesting than
the interchange of letters between Grant and Sherman.[2] The general-in-chief accords to Sherman and
McPherson, and to his other lieutenants, the fullest
credit for their help in winning his successes, showing in every simple phase a warm affection for these
friends and aids; to all which the impetuous Sherman responds with affecting heartiness: the two
manly spirits, long working together, now stood in
a conjunction, the fruit of which was to be the saving of the nation.

As long as the national arms enjoyed a reasonable
success, it was certain that the support of Congress
would not fail. Vigorous means, as we have seen,
had been taken to keep up the number of the troops.
Those whose terms were about to expire were encouraged to "veteranize," or re-enlist, by an offer

[1] Adams, *R. H. Dana*, II., 272.
[2] W. T. Sherman, *Memoirs*, I., 426.

of a month's furlough; the draft was firmly en-
forced, the people acquiescing quietly in what had
at first seemed to many an outrage. The money
commutation allowed brought many millions into
the treasury. By this time the enlistment of
negroes had become a settled policy, no longer
objected to by soldiers in the field or conservatives
at home. Massachusetts sent two regiments of her
own colored citizens well equipped and officered,[1]
and in other northern states negroes were enlisted;
but the great body of colored troops were recruited
among the freedmen of the South. These did excellent service on military works, in garrison duty,
and often among fighters at the front: Lincoln
stated in his message, December 8, 1863, that there
were a hundred thousand colored men in the government service, fifty thousand of whom had borne
arms in battle.[2]

It was natural and inevitable that there should
no longer be any such rush to the ranks as in 1861:
the country was sadly familiar with the grimness of
war's visage; and the opportunities at home for
well-paid work were such as had rarely before been
known. The privilege of hiring substitutes sent
some very poor material into the ranks: but the
gaps were filled, and as spring drew near, a vast
multitude, on the whole patriotic, brave, well
trained, and well equipped, stood ready to force the

---

[1] Pearson, *John A. Andrew*, II., 69 et seq.
[2] Lincoln, *Works* (ed. of 1894), II., 454.

struggle to a finish, too fondly believed to be within easy reach.

After Vicksburg, the capture of Mobile seemed a natural and feasible sequence, but Grant and Sherman were diverted, as has been seen, to Chattanooga. Banks, in Louisiana, also would willingly have gone eastward against the only Confederate port left between Florida and Texas, but the government formed another plan. A French army was making progress in Mexico, and French intrigues were already on foot designed to affect Texas. To thwart Napoleon III., a firm hold on Texas seemed necessary; yet at the moment the North held nothing in that state.[1] Banks was therefore ordered to Texas, where, in the fall of 1863, after a failure at Sabine Pass, he made important lodgments along the coast at Brownsville on the Mexican border, and at Matagorda Bay. It was thought in Washington that a more satisfactory point of occupation would be found in the interior, to be approached by the Red River. Banks accordingly, in 1864, much against his will, made preparations for such a campaign as the spring approached, the only season when the Red River is navigable.

Meantime, the programme of the year's battles opened elsewhere. The important towns on the Atlantic coast of Florida had for some time been in the Federal grasp. With the false idea that a Union sentiment existed in the interior, which

[1] Nicolay and Hay, *Abraham Lincoln*, VIII., 285.

might be encouraged by the advance of an army thither, Gillmore, commanding the department at Charleston, was allowed to despatch such an expedition.   General Truman Seymour, a brave and experienced officer, was put in charge; he entered upon the task with misgivings, and soon met with misfortune.   Florida was not ripe for a Union movement; and at Olustee, February 20, 1864, Seymour was repulsed, losing eighteen hundred and sixty men[1] in his vain effort.[2]

Grant's policy was to avoid wasting strength in outskirt operations, and concentrate upon two main lines of effort.   The campaign of Olustee came before he was in charge; and Banks's expedition up the Red River could not well be checked in March, when Grant assumed his wider duty.   Divisions from the Thirteenth and Nineteenth Corps were detailed, all that could be spared after making secure the widely extended Federal conquests in Louisiana and Texas; and in addition a fine body of ten thousand men under A. J. Smith was sent down from Vicksburg.   Steele, also commanding in Arkansas, was ordered southward to co-operate; while Porter's fleet of gun-boats was to ascend the stream on the flank of the advancing army.

Though the effort was great, the signs from the

---

[1] T. W. Higginson, *Army Life in a Black Regiment*, 240.
[2] *War Records*, Serial No. 65, pp. 274–356 (Florida Expedition).

outset were unfavorable.[1] The Vicksburg troops were lent with strict directions that they must be returned in a month: the water in the Red River, though it was the season of flood, was almost too low for navigation: Banks's statement of requirements necessary to success was neglected: he was delayed while inaugurating, under the president's orders, the new state government of Louisiana. His lieutenants, among them W. B. Franklin, in the background since Fredericksburg, were West Point men, and recognized with no good grace the authority of a superior from civil life, who, however brave, had gained little credit in the field. Fortunately for the Federals, conditions were no better in the camp of their foes. Dick Taylor, an able officer, who had sustained the Confederate cause in Louisiana as well as circumstances allowed during the trying year of 1863, was still on the ground, but ranked by Kirby Smith, to whom had been committed the whole trans-Mississippi. Both generals, with their forces, came together below Shreveport, high up on the Red River, and discord began at once.[2] Had Taylor's hands been free, the Federal experience would probably have been rougher than it was.

Banks pushed forward close to Shreveport, having the fleet on his right. While advancing through

[1] *War Records*, Serial No. 61, pp. 162–638 (Red River Campaign).
[2] Taylor, *Destruction and Reconstruction*, 148 et seq.

pine barrens, in a region almost waterless, on a single narrow road, his head of column was heavily assailed at Sabine Cross Roads, April 8, 1864, his advance being routed and driven back. Next day, at Pleasant Hill, the Federal fortunes were better, but the army grew constantly more demoralized. The losses were great, and dissensions paralyzed the leadership. The river fell when by all precedents it should have risen. Porter, apprehensive that his ships would be caught in the shallows, hurried down stream, and the army followed, maintaining a severe running battle, as far as Alexandria. The month having expired, the ten thousand men lent from Vicksburg were now recalled by peremptory orders from Grant: a serious crisis confronted the Federal force.

The one man who in this disastrous campaign earned great credit was a Wisconsin lieutenant-colonel, Joseph Bailey, whose feat was not one of arms, but of engineering. The Red River at Alexandria is broken for a mile by rapids, passable by steamers only at high water. When Porter reached the falls with the fleet, he found only three feet and four inches of water, whereas his larger vessels with their heavy armament required at least seven feet. Bailey, acting as engineer on Franklin's staff, was a lumberman, and, recalling his experiences, proposed a plan which met with opposition,[1] but which he was allowed to try. Finding skilled helpers in regi-

[1] Mahan, *Gulf and Inland Waters*, 204 et seq.

ments from Maine and the Northwest, he raised the
river to an adequate level by means of ingenious
"wing dams." On May 13, the ten great gun-boats
and the smaller craft were brought off in safety, for
Bailey's engineering raised the river six and a half
feet; this, with what the channel before contained,
was ample for the purpose. While the worst was
in this way happily averted, Banks's campaign
badly failed. The recrimination between the "political general" and his West Point subordinates
was unusually bitter, only surpassed by the violent
quarrel between the Confederate leaders. The com-
ponents of the forces on both sides were soon absorbed elsewhere, and no serious engagement took
place afterwards in the trans-Mississippi.[1]

The Red River was practically the end of Banks,
who had been more unfortunate than blameworthy;
for although retained in nominal command in
Louisiana, he was really superseded by E. R. Canby,
appointed to superintend a new department to
include the whole trans-Mississippi.

The lieutenant-general appointed the beginning
of May, 1864, as the moment for advance both in
the East and West. The probable Confederate
strength at that date is put at 477,233 men "present
for duty"; to whom Grant opposed 662,345. The
statement of the adjutant-general as to Federals
"present equipped for duty," April 30, is 533,447:

[1] See Committee on the Conduct of the War, *Report*, 1864–
1865, pt. ii., 3–401.

a corresponding deduction from the Confederate
estimate so as to state the relative numbers in
commensurate terms, would make the total number
of southern combatants actually ready for battle
about four hundred thousand.[1]

Though Grant was concentrating as none of his
predecessors had done, a considerable dispersion of
force was unavoidable. In the North, thousands of
prisoners must be guarded, and much local disaffection must be watched: Canada also, when misfortune befell, showed a spirit semi-hostile, harbor-
ing many active enemies of the North. At the
Northwest and West, the Sioux and other Indian
tribes must be held in check, while the great areas
of conquered country both east and west of the
Mississippi, could not be left ungarrisoned. A number of small armies, therefore, aggregating a considerable force, were scattered about. Dix commanded the troops in New York and New England,
Couch in Pennsylvania, Lew Wallace in Maryland,
Augur at Washington, Heintzelman the central
West, Pope in Minnesota, Rosecrans in Missouri,
Wright on the Pacific, Carleton in New Mexico.
Steele, who was charged with holding the trans-
Mississippi against Kirby Smith, had a large force;
as did also Banks (soon to be superseded by Canby),
who, it was hoped, might move against Mobile.
But for the most part the Federals were massed for
two main operations, which Grant designed should

[1] Badeau, *Military Hist. of Grant*, II., 555, 556.

be merged into one. Sherman confronted Johnston
on the northern border of Georgia, his force comprising the Army of the Cumberland under Thomas,
reinforced by the Army of the Tennessee under
McPherson and the Army of the Ohio now under
J. M. Schofield. Meade, with the Army of the
Potomac, faced Lee in Virginia, having on his left,
about Fortress Monroe, a force gathered from the
Carolinas and southeastern Virginia, which it was
hoped would support him powerfully, and on his
right still another force in the Shenandoah Valley,
which was expected also to lend an effective hand.[1]

Where best among such conditions could the
commander-in-chief take his place? After the experience with Halleck, it was quite plain that he
should be somewhere in the field. "Do not stay
in Washington," wrote Sherman, March 10. "Halleck is better qualified than you to stand the buffets
of intrigue and policy. Come out West. . . . For
God's sake, and your country's sake, come out of
Washington! I foretold to General Halleck before
he left Corinth the inevitable result to him, and
now I exhort you to come out West. Here lies the
seat of the coming empire, and from the West when
our task is done, we will make short work of Charleston and Richmond, and the impoverished coast of
the Atlantic." [2] Grant did not stay in Washington,
neither did he go West. Recognizing the heaviest

[1] Badeau, *Military Hist. of Grant*, II., 29, etc.
[2] W. T. Sherman, *Memoirs*, I., 428.

and most important task to be the destruction of
Lee and the Army of Northern Virginia, he established himself at the side of Meade.

Meade, since Gettysburg, while perhaps over-
cautious, had done nothing to forfeit the respect
and confidence of his countrymen.[1] He followed
Lee as he retired southward, in the summer of 1863,
and was ready to try conclusions for a second time.
In September came the departure of Longstreet for
Chickamauga, and his absence made Lee wary;
before the month ended the departure of the two
Federal corps under Hooker, in the same direction,
restrained Meade.   A contest of manœuvres ensued,
in which Meade showed skill,[2] with now and then a
flash of battle, the most serious being an affair at
Bristoe Station, October 14, 1863, where Warren, commanding the Federal rear-guard, struck effectively
at A. P. Hill, and an affair at Rappahannock Station, November 7, much to the credit of the Sixth
Corps.   A general engagement was imminent near
the Chancellorsville battle-ground, at Mine Run,
but the moment passed unused and both armies
went into winter quarters.   Lee was depressed after
Gettysburg and wished to retire, to which neither
his government nor army would listen.   The failure
of Meade to secure marked success in his fall campaign was perhaps due more to inefficient subordinates than to his own defects: in particular the

---

[1] *War Records*, Serial No. 48, passim.
[2] Pennypacker, *Meade*, chaps. xiv., xv.

loss of Reynolds and the temporary disabling of Hancock could not be made good.[1] When the lieutenant-general appeared, in March, 1864, in the camp of Meade, the latter begged to be allowed to retire in favor of some commander tested and trained under Grant's own eye, magnanimously offering to serve in a lower place: this Grant refused to permit, ascribing to Meade all honor, and retaining him in his high command. To Meade's high-minded conduct the course of Buell was in contrast. When offered by Grant the command of a corps with Sherman or Canby, he declined to serve under men whom he had once outranked, and was soon after mustered out.[2]

[1] General Warren before the Committee on the Conduct of the War, *Report*, 1865, pt. i., 387.
[2] Grant, *Personal Memoirs*, II., 50.

CHAPTER VI

ON TO RICHMOND

(MAY, 1864–JUNE, 1864)

WHEN the Army of the Potomac stood ready for its campaign of 1864, on April 30, it counted ninety-two thousand men and two hundred and seventy-four guns. The Eleventh and Twelfth Corps were still in the West; the First and Third Corps had been incorporated with others. There remained the Second Corps under Hancock, now recovered from his wounds, the Fifth under Warren, and the Sixth under Sedgwick. Close by, but for a time not combined with the others, was the Ninth Corps, under Burnside, about twenty thousand strong. Farther away, but expected to co-operate immediately with the Army of the Potomac, were the two wings, the Army of the James, comprising the Tenth and Eighteenth Corps, about forty thousand men, and the force in the Shenandoah Valley and West Virginia, of about twenty - six thousand men. By great misfortune both wings were inefficiently commanded—the Shenandoah force by Sigel, whom it was necessary to consider on account of his supposed influence with the Germans—the Army of the

James, by Benjamin F. Butler, the War Democrat, whose capacity for working ill, should he be thrust aside, was dreaded.[1] Of both these men Grant had no personal knowledge, and the responsibility for their appointment must rest mainly with the administration. To the short-comings of Butler, especially, the disappointments of the campaign now about to begin are largely due.

To this great Federal army Lee opposed in the immediate front but sixty thousand men, with two hundred and twenty-four guns, under Longstreet, Ewell, and A. P. Hill; but Beauregard was hastening to his aid, bringing all the strength that could be gathered in the Carolinas and along the coast. Lee's inferiority in numbers was to some extent balanced by the advantage that his work was to be defensive, on interior lines, within a country friendly, and with which he was familiar. He was thoroughly known and idolized by his army, which he had led for two years, and which from the corps commanders to the rank and file was the selected strength of the Confederacy—as admirable a body of troops, perhaps, as the world has ever known.

Grant, a complete stranger to his men, and also to his officers, except as he had encountered here and there a few in the old army, planned an advance which would make it possible to receive supplies from the Potomac and the Chesapeake, inlets from which ran far into Virginia to points near his pro-

[1] Badeau, *Military Hist. of Grant*, II., 44.

posed line of movement. His campaign was to be aggressive and unremitting: "I propose to fight it out on this line if it takes all summer," was his grim announcement. It was to be a warfare of the hammer, of unceasing attrition.[1]

On the night of May 3, the Army of the Potomac crossed the Rapidan, the Fifth Corps at Germanna Ford, followed at once by the Sixth; the Second Corps crossed farther east at Ely's Ford; the great train of five thousand wagons was divided between the two fords; the Ninth Corps advanced in rear of the others, but all were south of the river in good time on the 4th. All orders were issued through Meade, though Grant was at hand and supreme. The two commanders were and remained in harmony, but the arrangement was unsatisfactory, causing a division of authority which sometimes proved unfortunate.[2]

Once across, the army was on familiar ground. Warren, followed by Sedgwick, was presently at the scene of Stonewall Jackson's last exploit, just a year before; while Hancock stood at Chancellorsville. It was again the old tangle of the Wilderness, a barren country, stripped at an earlier time of its forests to feed long-abandoned furnaces and mines, now covered with a second growth of thicket almost

[1] Grant's report in *War Records*, Serial No. 67, p. 13 (From the Rapidan to the James).

[2] Ropes, "Grant's Campaign in Va. in 1864," Military Hist. Soc. of Mass., *Papers*, IV., 377 et seq.

impenetrable. Through the tract, worthless for
farming, with clearings only here and there, narrow
roads accommodated the infrequent travel. The
line of the Union advance was southward along a
track crossed by roads from the southwest, first a
turnpike, then a mile or two south a plank-road,
both leading from Orange Court House, the headquarters of Lee, towards Fredericksburg.

Grant would have been glad before fighting to
push through the Wilderness into the more open
country southward, where his superior numbers
would give him an advantage; but Lee saw plainly
his opportunity, and struck at once, May 5. Ewell
marched down the turnpike upon Warren and Sedgwick, while A. P. Hill advanced by the plank-road
against Hancock, who, pushing on from Chancellorsville, had reached a point south of his colleagues.
Burnside, too, hastened forward, the design being to
place him between the turnpike and the plank-road;
while on the other side Longstreet, whom Lee had
retained at Gordonsville, in view of a possible crossing by the Federals farther up the Rapidan, forced
his march eastward, arriving opportunely.

The conflict from the first was almost hand to
hand. The Army of the Potomac, aware that the
new general believed they had never been made to
do their best in action, sought close quarters, which
their adversaries were not slow to grant. The battle
of Sedgwick and Warren against Ewell on the turnpike was quite distinct from that of Hancock against

Hill, and later Longstreet on the plank-road. Both
fights, however, were alike heavy and indecisive—
alternations of advance and retreat on either side,
the encompassing thickets making regular formations impossible: companies and squads breasted
one another — fragments into which brigades and
regiments were necessarily torn. The persistency on
both sides was thorough, the bloodshed unstinted.
It was on the plank-road that the combat came nearest to a decision. At the junction here with a wood-
track called the Brock Road, Sedgwick, proceeding
with most of the Sixth Corps to the support of Warren, had left the division of Getty, who, when Hancock arrived, pressed hotly, supported by him,
upon A. P. Hill. Success for a time seemed likely.
Hill was forced back upon the path by which he
came; but Longstreet was at hand—the best of
troops and leadership at the critical moment.[1] Lee
was in the front, and could with difficulty be induced to retire to a less threatened station, after
a pledge from Longstreet to restore the day.

Guided by the sheriff of the county, who knew
every by-path, Longstreet, making a détour with
certain divisions, from the concealment of the brush
assailed Hancock's flank, and almost brought about
a crushing of the Federal wing as complete as that
in Hooker's battle of the previous year. A strange
coincidence now befell. As Stonewall Jackson, at
the critical moment, fell by the fire of his own

[1] Longstreet, *Manassas to Appomattox*, 559 et seq.

men, so now, Longstreet with his party, hurrying
along the plank-road, his impetuous columns disordered as they charged, were mistaken for Federal
cavalry; whereupon the Twelfth Virginia fired a
volley, prostrating many. A Minié ball passed
through Longstreet's right shoulder and neck; he
was borne off the field, waving his hat feebly with
his left hand that his disconsolate columns might
see he was yet alive. It has been claimed that a
Confederate victory might have been won but for
the striking down of Longstreet; but the strength
of the Army of the Potomac was there, and undismayed. No successor could on the instant carry
out the complicated manœuvre which was in progress, not even Lee, who presently assumed command. The opportunity passed, and Hancock's
men were soon rallied.[1]

Thus May 5 and 6 passed in ineffective struggle. The Federal loss was 17.3 per cent. of their
number engaged, the Confederate loss 18.1 per
cent.[2] Besides the disabling of Longstreet, the Confederates lost other generals, among them Micah
Jenkins, who since the wounding of Hood at Chickamauga had ably led his division. The Federals lost
Wadsworth, and on May 9, the able and experienced Sedgwick. May 7, Grant set out for Spottsylvania Court-House, hoping to pass round his adver-

[1] Longstreet, *Manassas to Appomattox*, 562; Sorrel, *Recollections of a Confed. Staff Officer*, 240.

sary's right: but Lee was there before him. Longstreet's corps, driven out of its bivouac by a forestfire, marched some hours earlier than the orders required, and by good luck was able to bar the Federal advance; whereupon ensued a series of combats as determined and as sanguinary as those of the Wilderness. At this stage of the war, every position was at once intrenched, the troops contriving marvellously, in the briefest time, out of rails, stones, earth, whatever might be at hand, a shelter from assault, rude but answering the purpose. Lee, acting on the defensive, employed to the utmost this warfare of the axe and spade. At Spottsylvania, Grant found his adversary everywhere protected; and though he did not hesitate to assault, gained no lasting advantage.

Two attempts of this kind were especially brilliant, and promised at first success. On May 10, Emory Upton, a young colonel of the Sixth Corps, gained a lodgment within the enemy's works which failed of results by not being supported. On May 12, Hancock's first division, under Francis C. Barlow, performed a feat of extraordinary gallantry. Barlow charged near daybreak a point where the Confederate line was thrust forward in a salient. The crest was surmounted and crossed: the defenders were captured right and left within the parapet: twenty cannon, thirty standards, four thousand men, the "best division in the Confederate army,"[1]

[1] Henderson, *Science of War*, 325 (Wilderness Campaign).

with two generals, were in Federal hands. It
was, in fact, the Stonewall division, with its commander, Edward Johnson. The Confederate centre
appeared fairly broken; a few rods more and the
Army of Northern Virginia would be cut in two.
But a second line of works rose before the stormers,
well defended. The Federal supports, instead of
failing to come up, this time came up too soon and
too numerously: the crowd of men, disordered by
success, failed to make the best application of their
strength:[1] Lee was at hand, putting himself in the
front to repel the danger. The men of Gordon's
division turned his horse backward, while a shout
arose from the ranks, "General Lee to the rear!"
They refused to advance till Lee retired out of
danger.[2]

Then throughout the day raged a conflict surpassing in its terrors. The assailants clinging to one
side of the works they had captured faced the
defenders on the other: captures were made back
and forth by hauling men over the intervening
breastworks. Meantime a volleying went forward
so incessant and deadly that oak-trees, their trunks
severed by the balls, fell to the earth.[3] With thousands more added to his losses, the Confederate list
being still larger,[4] Grant again, May 19, swept round

[1] Barlow, in Military Hist. Soc. of Mass., *Papers*, IV., 254.
[2] Gordon, *Reminiscences of Civil War*, 278.
[3] Such a trunk nearly two feet thick is preserved in the National
Museum at Washington.
[4] Livermore, *Numbers and Losses*, 112.

the Confederate right, only to confront his adversary fixed in new strongholds.

A fortnight had now elapsed since the Army of the Potomac crossed the Rapidan, and we must look at the work of the other armies, which set out at the same time, co-operation with which was an essential part of Grant's campaign.   In the Army of the Valley, the force under Sigel, and a smaller body under Crook and Averell farther west, advanced as ordered.   Crook accomplished results, reaching southwest Virginia, destroying supplies, and breaking the railroad connection with Tennessee.   Sigel's operations were feeble: encountering opposition, he was presently heard from in retreat, and soon after was relieved of command.[1]

A much greater disappointment befell Grant in the case of the Army of the James.   Here Butler was in command for reasons other than military.   Grant went to Fortress Monroe to make Butler's acquaintance, and, we may believe, to form some conclusion as to his capacity.   Apparently, Butler impressed him as clear-headed and forceful.[2]   At any rate, Grant acquiesced in the selection, and thought to make things secure by placing at the heads of the Tenth and Eighteenth Corps, which together made up the Army of the James, Q. A. Gillmore and W. F. (Baldy) Smith, accomplished and experienced engineer officers of the regular army.   Smith, in par-

[1] Grant, *Personal Memoirs*, II., 72, 142.
[2] *Butler's Book*, chap. xiv.

ticular, had Grant's confidence, having served under his own eye with brilliant efficiency at Chattanooga, and Grant brought him east believing that there was no officer better fitted than he to command a corps. It was expected that Butler would administer his department, which included southeastern Virginia and North Carolina, leaving the field operations to Smith's guidance.[1] But Butler had no thought of being anywhere except in the foreground and actively directed the movements.

Charles Francis Adams, who as a cavalry officer took part in this campaign, compares Grant's campaign of 1864 to that of Napoleon in 1815. While Napoleon advanced upon Wellington, it was essential that Grouchy should detain Blücher: so while Grant engaged Lee, Butler was expected to defeat or at least neutralize Beauregard,[2] for to that able soldier Jefferson Davis, after hesitation, assigned the preservation of Lee's communications, and the defence of Richmond from the south and east. As to Grouchy so to Butler, the orders were vague, much being necessarily left to the discretion of the lieutenant. Beauregard did not arrive upon the scene till May 10,[3] and Butler, who had struck out with great vigor, was on the verge of success. May 4, after a feint towards the York River, his two

[1] Grant to Butler, April 2, 1864, *War Records*, Serial No. 67, p. 16.
[2] Adams, *Some Phases of the Civil War*, 36 (pamphlet, 1905).
[3] Roman, *Beauregard*, II., 199.

corps were transferred to City Point on the James, occupying immediately Bermuda Hundred, a strong position within a few miles of Richmond.

Here the fair beginning, a surprise to the Richmond authorities, was frustrated by unwisdom. The relation of the general to his lieutenants had become in a high degree unpleasant; he held them to be insubordinate West-Pointers who would injure, if they could, a volunteer; they held him to be headstrong, inexperienced, and incapable.[1] Disapproving of his scheme of operations, they united in recommending an advance upon Petersburg, a city twenty-two miles south of Richmond and commanding its southern connections, which at the time was unfortified and ungarrisoned. "The Grouchy of the Wilderness Campaign," though his troops were within three miles of Petersburg, May 9, rejected the advice in an angry letter,[2] ordering a movement in another direction, which he claimed his orders favored. Had the advice of Smith and Gillmore been followed, apparently nothing could have prevented the capture of Petersburg. To avoid the loss of the three great southern roads (to Danville, to Weldon, and the south-side road), and the loss of Richmond, Lee would have been forced to break up from before Grant and march at once southward. The chance was missed; the demonstration of Butler failed; Beauregard arrived with an army, and soon

[1] *Butler's Book*, 649; for W. F. Smith's opinion, see *Battles and Leaders*, IV., 206.   [2] *War Records*, Serial No. 68, p. 35.

attacked successfully at Drewry's Bluff.   The Army
of the James, instead of affording the help upon
which Grant had counted, was presently "bottled
up"[1] at Bermuda Hundred, as Grant later put it,
quite safe, but also quite unable to trouble the
peace of Richmond.

Meanwhile, Grant, struggling in his dreadful grap-
ple with Lee, reached out as it were to the south,
hoping to grasp the help for which he had made
provision.   As campaign followed campaign, the
cavalry of the Army of the Potomac had constantly
grown in usefulness, until now it was a formidable
arm.   Though Pleasonton, who had led it with
credit, and Buford, who had done so well at Gettysburg, had now disappeared, Averell was doing good
service with Crook in southwestern Virginia; and
Kilpatrick was soon to distinguish himself in Georgia.   Several forceful young officers worked to the
front—D. M. Gregg, Wesley Merritt, James H. Wilson, and George A. Custer.   Grant was bent upon
having his troopers under the best leadership, and
placed Sheridan in command here, the only com-
rade from the West (except Rawlins) whom he had
at his side in any prominent position in the Army
of the Potomac.   Meade's army remained entirely
under its old generals, except that at the head of
the cavalry rode Philip H. Sheridan, last seen by us
mounted upon the cannon at the climax of the battle of Missionary Ridge.

[1] Grant, *Personal Memoirs*, II., 75.

7

As Grant, among almost total strangers, found his environment not altogether congenial or fortunate, so Sheridan at first was ill at ease and not quite well received. He had in the Wilderness a quarrel with Meade, in the heat of which he threw up his command, but Grant interfered to prevent.[1] In the woods the cavalry found small opportunity. The embarrassing thickets, filled with infantry, army wagons, and guns, left little scope for horsemen along the encumbered tracks; but at Todd's Tavern, near where Hancock received the blow from Longstreet, Sheridan measured swords with Stuart to some purpose. The latter was a factor whom Grant was anxious to eliminate from the game; great harm, too, would come to Lee if the railroad between him and Richmond could be out; above all, it was important to connect with Butler, who was relied upon to encircle Richmond on the south about this time.

All this Sheridan must do, and May 9, eluding the divisions of Lee as they manœuvred for the defence of Spottsylvania Court House, he was soon far on his way. Reaching the Virginia Central Railroad, Custer tore up ten miles of track, wrecking at the same time locomotives, cars, stations, and supplies; and soon after, in like fashion, the road from Richmond to Fredericksburg was broken up. Sheridan now hastened towards Richmond, within six miles of which, at Yellow Tavern, he encountered Stuart,

[1] Sheridan, *Personal Memoirs*, I., 368.

prompt and bold in his defence. A hard battle ensued, in which, while the skill and gallantry were
equal, the Federal superiority in numbers told
powerfully. The Confederates were defeated, Stuart
himself being among the slain, a loss to the South
hardly less than that of Stonewall Jackson.[1]

The battle over, Sheridan pursued the division
of Fitzhugh Lee nearly to Richmond, pausing only
when the inner intrenchments were reached. Had
the Army of the James enveloped the city on the
south, as it might so easily have done, the hand extended by Grant would have met here a friendly
clasp. As it was, Sheridan could do nothing more
than elude his many foes, on the battle - fields of
two years before, coming down at last by devious
paths to Harrison's Landing, McClellan's old camps
on the James, with Butler opposite at Bermuda
Hundred. A week had passed since the raid began;
in another week the cavalry returned, Sheridan reporting to his chief May 24.

In the interval Grant was marching and ma-
noeuvring widely. Another move about the flank
of Lee brought the Army of the Potomac to the
North Anna, where its great adversary with faultless management, May 23, blocked its path once
more behind impregnable defences. Yet another
march brought Grant to the Chickahominy, with
Richmond almost in sight, but still unattainable.
The ground now occupied was precisely that of the

[1] McClellan, *J. E. B. Stuart*, chap. xx.

early operations of the "Seven Days," but the two
armies had exchanged positions: while Lee held the
neighborhood of Gaines's Mill, and the line which
Meade, as a brigadier in the Pennsylvania reserves,
had then maintained against A. P. Hill, Meade
now ranged the Army of the Potomac near Cold
Harbor, on an area over which Stonewall Jackson
and D. H. Hill had advanced to attack Fitz-John
Porter.[1]

The scene awoke sombre memories in the minds
of those much-tried veterans, whose associations
with this region were of the darkest.   Lee stood at
Cold Harbor, intrenched more firmly than ever.
Since May 4, when the campaign began, the Federals
had made almost as many desperate assaults upon
impregnable positions as there were days; and all
to no purpose.   It is probably Grant's worst mistake, one that always hung heavy upon his heart,
that he here resolved upon still another attack in
front.[2]   The Eighteenth Corps, under W. F. Smith,
lying idle at Bermuda Hundred after Butler's failure, had been transferred to the Army of the Potomac, now badly in need of reinforcements.   As the
Federals reconnoitred, no sign appeared that the
confronting works were assailable: but with mad
recklessness, on June 3 an assault was ordered "all
along the line."   The obedience and gallantry were
unhesitating, the soldiers sometimes pathetically

[1] Hosmer, *Appeal to Arms* (*Am. Nation*, XX.), 58.
[2] Grant, *Personal Memoirs*, II., 171.

pinning papers inscribed with their names to their clothes that their bodies might later be identified. The failure was utter. Barlow, with the first division of the now more than decimated Second Corps, effected a lodgement, as he had within the Spottsylvania salient three weeks before: but it was only for a moment; the line recoiled, leaving upon the earth about twelve thousand dead and wounded men.[1] Grant, with determination almost insane, would once more have applied the hammer, whose smiting head was not of steel, but flesh and blood; his second thought was better and he desisted. The Army of the Potomac lost in killed, wounded, or captured, in the interval from the crossing of the Rapidan to its arrival in June, near the James, 54,926 men. That Grant showed inhumanity towards his wounded at Cold Harbor is an accusation without good foundation.[2] During the week after the assault of Cold Harbor, Grant and his men, baffled and depressed, marched once more southward by the left, crossing the James, June 14, at City Point.

June 6, Hunter, who succeeded Sigel in the Shenandoah Valley, won a victory at Piedmont, which made him master of the valley. June 8, he made a junction at Staunton with Crook and Averell,

---

[1] Livermore, *Numbers and Losses*, 114.
[2] *War Records*, Serial No. 67, p. 188; see correspondence between Grant and Lee, *War Records*, Serial No. 69, pp. 638, 639, 666, 667; discussion by Colonel T. L. Livermore, Military Hist. Soc. of Mass., *Papers*, IV., 457.

from southwestern Virginia, marching thence with promptness by Lexington to Lynchburg, before which city he arrived on the 16th. The hope of its capture, however, failed; for Lee, alarmed, sent Breckinridge in haste back to the valley; and, more important, despatched Ewell's corps, twelve thousand of his best men, under Early, to meet Hunter. Grant, too, was watchful, sending off Sheridan with two divisions towards Charlottesville to succor Hunter, whose whereabouts was uncertain. Sheridan was forced to return without finding him, but damaged as he could the Virginia Central Railroad, and fought a sharp cavalry battle with Wade Hampton and Fitzhugh Lee, June 11, at Trevilian's Station. Hunter, unsupported, living off the country, and out of ammunition, retired to the Ohio River; whereupon Early set forth on an enterprise to be mentioned presently.[1]

The Eighteenth Corps was no sooner back at City Point, after Cold Harbor, than it was sent against the defences of Petersburg, believed to be not strongly held. W. F. Smith attacked June 15, but not boldly; Hancock, who brought up the Second Corps to his aid, through some oversight of Meade not being informed what he was to do, failed to carry out Grant's purpose.[2] Petersburg might easily have been captured. On the 16th, however, the

[1] *War Records*, Serial Nos. 70, 71.
[2] Grant, *Personal Memoirs*, II., 189; but see Pennypacker, *Meade*, 322, and Bache, *Meade*, 467.

works were manned, and when the Federal onset at last came it was beaten back. Nor was Grant more successful in his efforts to capture the railroads. On the Weldon road, June 22, A. P. Hill foiled an attempt at seizure, defeating badly the Second Corps, for the time without the leadership of Hancock, whose Gettysburg wound had opened afresh. Wilson, with the cavalry, was not more fortunate, for though he tore up many miles of track on both the South Side and Danville railroads, the damage was soon repaired, and the expedition got back only through hard fighting with serious loss.[1]

Drought set in, during which the roads grew heavy with dust, and the marching columns could scarcely find water: but this put no bar upon the warfare. Down the valley turnpike, Early with his twelve thousand men marched, crossing the Potomac and throwing Washington and the North into panic after the old fashion of Stonewall Jackson. Grant hastily despatched the Sixth Corps on transports from the James; and the Nineteenth Corps just arrived at Fortress Monroe from Louisiana. July 8, Lew Wallace, with one division of the Sixth Corps and an improvised army of militia, clerks, convalescents, whatever could be gathered about Baltimore at a day's notice, made a brave stand at the Monocacy near Frederick. He was defeated, but Grant declared the defeat was worth many victories, for Early

[1] *War Records*, Serial Nos. 80–82.

there lost a day, which saved the capital.[1]   July 11,
Early was in the northern suburbs of Washington, but
as he hesitated before the bold front of the handful
that manned the works, the Sixth and Nineteenth
Corps, just arrived, occupied the lines.   It was the
last, and also the worst, scare which the city underwent. Early retired to the valley, but not to inaction.[2]

One more mortification occurred for Grant and
the Army of the Potomac in this gloomy midsummer. A regiment of Pennsylvania coal-miners,
directed by their lieutenant-colonel, Henry Pleasants,
constructed a mine under a part of the Petersburg
intrenchments, which, July 30, was ready for explosion. Grant declares that most careful directions were laid down, which, if followed, would have
made sure the capture of the city through the
breach, during the resulting panic.   The mismanagement, for which Burnside was mainly accused, was
almost incredible: the preparations ordered were
neglected: for the storming column inferior troops
with an incapable general were selected.   The mine
exploded with an effect of which even to-day, after
forty years, the so-called crater is an appalling
evidence, and the way was clear to the heart of the
city.   But the stormers, instead of advancing, huddled into the crater, while the appointed leader
sheltered himself in a bomb-proof in the rear.   The

[1] Grant, *Personal Memoirs*, II., 196, 197.
[2] *War Records*, Serial No. 70 (Lynchburg and Shenandoah
Valley Campaigns).

defenders soon recovered spirit, the division of
Mahone being in the front. About four thousand
Federals were sacrificed and no advantage gained.[1]

The Federals had now sacrificed, before and
about Petersburg, more than fifteen thousand men,
and it was sadly significant that the loss in prisoners
was sometimes very large as compared with the
casualties. It meant that the Army of the Potomac
had deteriorated: the fighters of the Wilderness and
Spottsylvania were slain or crushed in spirit; while
the flood of recruits that kept the numbers full, men
obtained by the draft, and substitutes gained by
high bounties, were not the stuff for soldiers. When
discouragement was deepest, Sheridan was appointed, August 7, to command the army in the valley of
Virginia, a new military division being constituted.
The stifling and melancholy summer approached its
end; but as to Virginia there was no lifting of the
anxiety. Many causes might be assigned for the
Federal failures, but the chief one was the devotion
and bravery of the southern troops and the extraordinary ability with which they were directed.

[1] Grant, *Personal Memoirs*, II., 202; *War Records*, Serial Nos.
81, 82 (Court of Inquiry); Committee on the Conduct of the War,
Report, 1864–1865, pt. i., 525. For the controversy over Grant's
campaign of 1864, see Ropes, "Grant's Campaign in Va. in 1864,":
Military Hist. Soc. of Mass., *Papers*, IV., 363; McClellan, *Grant
versus the Record;* Badeau, *Military Hist. of Grant*, II.; Liver-
more, "Grant's Campaign against Lee," Military Hist. Soc. of
Mass., *Papers*, IV., 407; C. F. Adams, *Some Phases of the Civil
War*, 32–46; Humphreys, *Virginia Campaign of '64 and '65;*
Henderson, *Science of War*, chap. xi.; Long, *Lee*, chap. xvii.

CHAPTER VII

THE ATLANTA CAMPAIGN

(MAY, 1864–AUGUST, 1864)

SHERMAN, in 1864, was early active. February 3 he marched from Vicksburg with twenty thousand men for Meridian, in eastern Mississippi, where the Mobile and Ohio railroad crosses the line from Jackson eastward, forming an important strategic point which Polk had been set to guard. Sherman directed matters with characteristic energy, destroying the roads and the Confederate resources in a region till then not reached by Federal power; but he failed in his attempt to dispose of Forrest, who frustrated the efforts of a cavalry column from Tennessee.[1] The elevation of Grant to supreme command brought promotion to Sherman: March 18 he assumed his large responsibilities—the control of four great western armies, with headquarters at Chattanooga.[2]

The Confederate leaders were in anxious consultation over plans for retrieving the disasters of 1863, no one of which plans seemed so promising as a

[1] W. T. Sherman, *Memoirs*, I., 418 et seq.
[2] *Ibid.*, II., 5.

combined and rapid movement northward towards the Ohio River. In this, Bragg's old "Army of Tennessee," uniting with Longstreet, and receiving other reinforcement, it was believed might occupy middle Tennessee and Kentucky, and draw northward the Federal armies whose range in the South had become so wide. Davis and his new chief of staff, Bragg, as well as Lee, Longstreet, Hood, and other energetic spirits, regarded such an enterprise as hopeful: [1] but it was never entered upon, probably because Johnston, who succeeded Bragg in the command in the Mississippi Valley, was too cautious to make a rash movement. Many obstacles must be removed before such a scheme could be prudently undertaken. While the consultation progressed, the initiative went to the Federals, and the campaign took place in the South and not in the North. Longstreet, as we have seen, returned to Lee: while Johnston concentrated to meet what stood before him.

The Confederacy had been sundered the previous year by the capture of the Mississippi River; the new Federal scheme was to sunder it once more by driving a line of conquest southward to the important city of Atlanta, and thence still farther into the Confederacy.[2] To accomplish this task, to Sherman

---

[1] Hood, *Advance and Retreat*, 88 et seq.; Longstreet, *From Manassas to Appomattox*, 544; Johnston, *Narrative*, chap. x.; Davis, *Confed. Government*, II., 548.

[2] *War Records*, Serial No. 72, p. 3 (Grant's Report).

were assigned nearly a hundred thousand infantry, comprising the Army of the Cumberland, under Thomas, of sixty thousand; the army of the Tennessee, under McPherson (who now succeeded Sherman in that post), of twenty-five thousand; and the Army of the Ohio, of fifteen thousand; besides cavalry and 254 guns.[1] The Army of the Ohio was under John M. Schofield, a new commander who now comes into the foreground. He was of the West Point class of 1853, in which McPherson had been first scholar, Schofield sixth, Sheridan thirty-fourth, and Hood forty-fourth.[2] He had filled a post which was full of trouble in administering the Department of Missouri, where the enemy was scarcely more annoying than the jarring local factions. This work he had gladly given up shortly before, to accept command in east Tennessee; and now he led his army to Sherman's side, where he was to prove himself a good soldier.

Johnston stood some thirty miles south, with Dalton for a centre, his army in two corps under Hardee and Hood: early in the campaign the number was raised to seventy-five thousand by the arrival of the corps of Polk from Mississippi, and by other reinforcements.[3] He had an efficient force of cavalry under Wheeler. Both armies were made up for the most part of seasoned veterans: the corps

---

[1] Livermore, *Numbers and Losses*, 119.
[2] Cullum, *Register of U. S. Mil. Acad.*, arts. Schofield, etc.
[3] *Battles and Leaders*, IV., 247 et seq.

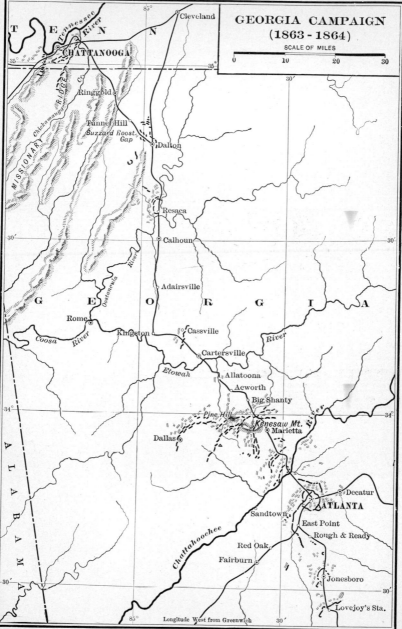

GEORGIA CAMPAIGN
(1863 - 1864)

SCALE OF MILES

0   10   20   30

TENNESSEE

Cleveland

Tennessee River

CHATTANOOGA

Ringgold

Tunnel Hill
Buzzard Roost Gap

Dalton

Resaca

Calhoun

Adairsville

GEORGIA

Rome

Kingston   Cassville

Coosa River

Cartersville

Etowah

Allatoona

Acworth

Big Shanty

Pine Hill   Kenesaw Mt.

Dallas   Marietta

ALABAMA

Decatur

ATLANTA

Sandtown   East Point

Rough & Ready

Red Oak

Fairburn

Chattahoochee

Jonesboro

Lovejoy's Sta.

Longitude West from Greenwich

BORMAY ENGRAVING CO., N.Y.

commanders on both sides were men sifted out for their positions through the severest experience: in the subordinate ranks the rawness of the earlier years disappeared. The proportion of the Confederates to the Federals was about seven to ten. Operating, as the Confederates did, in a familiar and friendly country, on interior lines, on the defensive, against a foe hundreds of miles from his base, in a hostile country and always the assailant, their inferiority in numbers was balanced by the advantages of position.

Sherman and Johnston had already proved themselves great leaders, but as they stood now face to face, they were in some ways strongly contrasted. Sherman was forty-four years old, tall, lithe, erect, thrilling with vitality, quick to impatience, but genial, every sentence and gesture indicating alertness of mind and soundness of judgment. Aggressiveness was very apparent in him—the qualities of an offensive leader. Johnston, whose mother was a niece of Patrick Henry, was fifty-seven years old, below the middle height, compact in build, cold in manner, of measured, accurate speech, a dark, firm face surmounted by an intellectual forehead. He was quite at ease under his high responsibilities.[1] The wounds received at Fair Oaks were now thoroughly healed, and he was in full vigor. As Sherman was in temperament very sanguine, Johnston by nature and through experience was cautious

[1] Freemantle, *Three Months in the Southern States*, 116.

and wary. While dominating his environment by ability and weight of character, he did not invite friendships; he exacted deference and a recognition of his authority, and when these were withheld became disputatious. He was always at cross-purposes with some one, and his *Narrative* is one long controversy, on the one hand with Jefferson Davis and the Richmond superiors, on the other with subordinates who ventured to dispute the wisdom of his methods. With so much wariness a defensive attitude would be the natural outcome; and this campaign was destined to secure for Johnston a high place as a Fabian.

While the Federal army was numerous and well equipped, it had in truth enormous difficulties to face. The region in which it operated, northern Georgia, was wooded and mountainous, in great part thinly settled, and quite unsurveyed and unmapped. The hundred thousand men, with thirty or forty thousand animals, must be supplied mostly from the Ohio River, by a single track of railroad running from Louisville to a great permanent depot at Nashville; thence to Chattanooga to a secondary depot; thence on towards Atlanta. Up to the very precincts of Louisville, these communications were exposed to the enemy, even while Sherman was preparing to start. Forrest, now developed into a matchless commander of cavalry, appeared at Paducah on the Ohio River; this time he was beaten off, his troopers capturing Fort Pillow as they re-

tired, April 13, and refusing quarter to the negro
soldiers in its garrison.[1]   His return even thus far
north was to be feared; while as regards the more
southern stretches, the line between Nashville and
Chattanooga was certain to be often attacked, and
below Chattanooga might be broken any day.

Along this thread of connection, one hundred and
thirty cars, carrying ten tons each, must proceed
every day, in order that Sherman's army might be
fed and clothed; a still larger service must be provided if supplies were to be accumulated against a
blockade. To preserve this vital cord every possible
arrangement was made; heavy detachments were
stationed in the important towns; guards sheltered
in block-houses watched every important bridge
and culvert.[2] Two men from civil life, carefully
selected, were appointed to superintend. Since the
work of these men was quite as important as that
of generals in the field, they should be honored in
the record. W. W. Wright was a constructing engineer, to whom the rank of colonel was given for
convenience, together with a force of two thousand
men. His task was to keep the road in repair, a
duty thoroughly performed. The destruction from
natural wear and tear, in track and rolling-stock,
necessarily great in view of the demands, was made
good without delay; while the wreck made by raiders
and the retiring enemy, of bridges, rails, tanks, and

[1] *War Records*, Serial No. 57, p. 518 et seq.
[2] W. T. Sherman, *Memoirs*, II., 10.

locomotives, was repaired as if by magic, from duplicate material kept on hand. The telegraph followed the army even to the battle-field, the electricians carrying wire and insulators in wagons up to the firing-line. Along the road thus held open by Colonel Wright, a skilled railroad operator, Colonel Adna Anderson, directed the passage of thousands of tons demanded for every day's consumption, with such promptness that the army was never in a strait.[1]

The beginning of May, 1864, came before the many absent troops (furloughed for a month, it will be remembered, on condition that they should "veteranize") were fully returned to the ranks; but Sherman set forth[2] on the day appointed in conference with Grant, May 3. Two days later he faced Johnston, intrenched at Dalton, the Army of the Cumberland in the centre and the Army of the Ohio to the east, while to the Army of the Tennessee was assigned the work of flanking the Confederate left, the first manœuvre of the campaign.

The enemy was much too strong to be attacked in front; but when it presently appeared that his position might be turned, McPherson made his way through Snake Creek Gap towards Johnston's rear, threatening his communications at Resaca and opening a path for the whole Federal army about the Confederate left. Johnston thereupon aban-

[1] Cox, *Military Reminiscences*, II., 106.
[2] *War Records*, Serial Nos. 72–76 (Atlanta Campaign).

doned Dalton, retiring southward to Resaca, where
he occupied strong works previously constructed,
and faced his foe again. Such was the procedure
during nearly two months, Johnston slowly falling
back from position to position, each a stronghold
skilfully selected and fortified beforehand; out of
each one of which in turn he was flanked by Sherman. Two months of such fighting brought the
army, after a progress of more than a hundred miles,
in sight of Atlanta. Let it be noted that in the con-
temporaneous Virginia campaign, though Lee once,
in the battle of the Wilderness, attacked fiercely,
almost recklessly, he afterwards, like Johnston, retired and fortified, while Grant outflanked him until
Richmond was at hand. The two campaigns were
essentially alike.

Sherman believed that McPherson made an error
in not attacking Resaca. That point on his approach was but weakly held, and might have been
captured.[1] As it was, the Federals gained small advantage: here, too, Johnston was still further favored,
for Polk reinforced him from the west.

Two streams large enough to obstruct an army,
the Oostanaula and the Etowah, now crossed Sherman's path; running southwest the streams unite to
form the Coosa River, at which point stands Rome,
a Confederate centre for supplies and manufactures.
Sherman crossing the Oostanaula, May 15, captured
Rome, and through the country eastward, more

---

[1] W. T. Sherman, *Memoirs*, II., 34.

open than the Dalton neighborhood, again threatened Johnston's line of supply.   The latter fell back
as before, yielding Calhoun, Adairsville, and Kingston, and giving no opportunity for attack.[1]   Sherman, most anxious for a battle on open ground,
where his superior numbers would tell, ran risks to
invite an encounter.   May 18, at Cassville, his corps
became somewhat perilously separated as they
marched; and Johnston, who was eagerly watching
for a false step, prepared to attack.   Polk and Hood,
who felt their troops were ill-placed, dissuaded him,
preventing a stroke that might have been successful.[2]
A week after, at New Hope Church, Howard with
the Fourth Corps, and Hooker with the Twentieth
(into which had been consolidated the old Eleventh
and Twelfth), assaulted unsuccessfully the strongly
intrenched Confederates.   May 28, Hardee attacked
the Federals with no better success.[3]   In the manœuvres which followed, Sherman seized the railroad
to Atlanta, crossing the Etowah, and establishing a
depot at Acworth.   Johnston withdrew to the neighborhood of Marietta.

In the almost constant skirmishing and battles of
this first month of the campaign, the Federal loss in
killed, wounded, and missing, was little short of
twelve thousand, while that of the Confederates ap-

[1] Cox, *Atlanta*, chap. vi.
[2] W. T. Sherman, *Memoirs*, II., 65; Johnston, *Narrative*, 323;
Hood, *Advance and Retreat*, chaps. v., vi.
[3] Cox, *Atlanta*, 84.

proached ten thousand. The Federal number was
kept up by the arrival of the Seventeenth Corps,
under Frank P. Blair. While Sherman had gained
much ground, as yet he had won no permanent advantage, and his operations seemed no more effective
than did those of Grant at the same moment in Virginia. Meantime his connection with the Ohio,
maintained by the slender line of railroad through
Georgia, Tennessee, and Kentucky, grew more precarious with each advance.

The prudent Johnston had the fact well in view,
that the halting progress of the Federal armies both
in East and West was powerfully stimulating disaffection throughout the North; he believed if he
could hold his own for a while longer, he might do
much to bring about the downfall of the Lincoln
administration in the presidential campaign now at
hand.[1] In June, severe rains prevailed, during which
the streams became floods and the country a morass.
While Sherman with his mired corps was prohibited
from action, Johnston stood before Marietta on Kenesaw Mountain and heights adjoining. As heretofore, his engineers planned well, and having at
command the Georgia militia and thousands of impressed negroes, he had prepared in advance a shelter for the Confederate army. The respite gained
through the storms was used to make the works
more than ever formidable. Sherman, fuming at
delay, apprehending attacks upon his communica-

[1] Johnston, *Narrative*, 363.

tions by Johnston's unemployed men, or, indeed, the detachment of a force to Lee in Virginia, which he was especially charged to prevent, resolved upon a direct assault.

At this moment disappears from the stage Lieutenant-general Leonidas Polk. While a cadet at West Point, he was converted under the influence of the chaplain, Reverend C. P. McIlvaine, afterwards bishop of Ohio, taking orders after graduation in the Protestant Episcopal Church, and becoming bishop of Louisiana.[1] He early took up arms for the South, not relinquishing his sacred office. It throws an interesting light upon the men with whom we are dealing to read that a few days before his death, as they were riding together, the bishop was told by his fellow lieutenant-general, Hood, that he had never been received into the communion of the church, and he begged that the rite might be performed.[2] The bishop arranged for the ceremony at once — at Hood's headquarters, a tallow candle giving light, the font a tin basin on the mess-table. The staff were there as witnesses; Hood, "with a face like that of an old crusader,"[3] stood before the bishop. Crippled by wounds received at Gaines's Mill, at Gettysburg, and at Chickamauga, the warrior could not kneel, but bent forward on his crutches. The bishop, not robed, but girt with his

[1] Cullum, *Register of U. S. Military Acad.*, art. Polk.
[2] W. M. Polk, *Leonidas Polk*, II., 329, 330.
[3] Mrs. Chesnut, *Diary from Dixie*, 230.

soldier's belt, administered the rite. A few days
later Johnston was baptized in the same simple
way. Now the bishop's time had come: June 14,
while reconnoitring on Pine Mountain, a Federal
cannon-ball struck him full upon the breast and
his life of devotion was ended.

As June drew near its end, the sun shone out, the
roads dried, and Sherman resumed activity. Rest-
lessly reconnoitring the hostile lines, he fixed upon
the point which seemed weakest, and on June 27,
1864, the assault was delivered with a loss of two
thousand;[1] the failure was complete; whereupon
Sherman, making the best of the roads now becoming firm, returned to his former methods. Manœu-
vring again by the right, he presently crossed the
Chattahoochee, a considerable stream, and now had
Atlanta in full view. But the unconquered Johnston anticipated him; withdrawing as before, he
occupied previously prepared lines more formidable
than ever.

During the second month of this campaign, the
tale of Sherman's loss in killed, wounded, and missing was seven thousand five hundred; for the Confederates, probably seven thousand.[2] Aside from
the great battle at Kenesaw, the skirmishing in the
rain had been constant; and although at this stage of
the war even the skirmish-line was elaborately fortified as soon as occupied, so close and deadly was the
conflict that a daily average of two hundred went

[1] Livermore, *Numbers and Losses*, 121.   [2] Cox, *Atlanta*, 351.

to grave and hospital. Yet the temper of both armies remained buoyant; neither entertained the thought of failure; each followed its general with confidence unshaken.

The weight of authority favors the view that the retreat of Johnston before Sherman was a master-stroke of military art, and that his removal from command, which now took place, was a grave calamity to the Confederacy, and one of the worst of many blunders committed by Jefferson Davis in his delusion that he possessed good military judgment.[1] Hood, who was appointed to succeed Johnston, criticised this policy severely, and Davis presents his side with dignity and force.[2]   In truth, the course of the Richmond government can be palliated; Johnston, estranged from them, while serving them ably and with perfect fidelity, maintained always an attitude sullen and unfriendly. While reporting with exactness what happened, he was silent as to his expectations and purposes—a reticence which irritated and embarrassed. A little frankness and sympathy on his part towards Bragg and Davis, whom he left in doubt as to whether or not he meant to defend Atlanta, would probably have kept him in his place.[3]

[1] See Wood and Edmonds, *Civil War in U. S.*, 392; testimony of Hardee and Stewart, corps commanders, in Johnston, *Narrative*, 365 et seq.; Pollard, *Lost Cause*, 543.

[2] Hood, *Advance and Retreat*, chaps. iv.–ix.; Davis, *Confed. Government*, II., chap. xlviii.

[3] Cox, *Military Reminiscences*, II., 275.

From Sherman down, there was not a man in the
Federal army who did not hear with joy that Johnston was no longer in command; and it is impossible
to read his *Narrative* without feeling that the cause
of the Union escaped a great peril. Four hundred
miles now stretched between Sherman's hundred
thousand men and their base at Louisville, the line
throughout open to attack, with troopers like Forrest sure to be let loose upon the communications.
Johnston was displaced for doing in Georgia precisely what in Virginia had added to the fame of
Lee—falling back upon the post he was set to defend, while his adversary with enormous waste of
life and resources was no nearer beating the army
or capturing the city. Johnston insisted upon the
wisdom of protracting the campaign with reference
to its effect upon the northern presidential election.
Had Atlanta been held during the fall by a con-
tinuance of this Fabian policy, probably the party
which at the North declared the war to be a failure would have come into power, and the cause
of the South might have secured a new consideration.[1]

Johnston's policy was not purely defensive. He
hoped and watched from the first for a moment
when his adversary would lay himself open and he
might strike with effect. At Cassville came this opportunity, missed through the reluctance of his lieutenants to run the risk. A second chance opened

[1] Johnston, *Narrative*, 355 et seq.

before Atlanta, in the very moment of his dismissal, and Johnston confided his plan to Hood, as the latter stepped into his place. Sherman's three armies now immediately before the city, advancing near Peach-Tree Creek, became separated, a wide gap opening between Thomas and McPherson. Hood, assuming command on July 18, 1864, following his predecessor's suggestion, on the 20th threw his army into the opening, to the great peril of Sherman. Hood had courage, but never great skill, and was beaten off by severe fighting; Johnston would have done better. July 22, Hood tried again in the northern suburbs of Atlanta. Hardee, getting into the rear of the Army of the Tennessee, made an attack of which the issue was for a time doubtful. McPherson, in the moment of surprise, rode into the skirmish-line of Cleburne's advancing division. They called to him to surrender; but raising his hat as if in salute, he turned his horse to gallop away, but fell with a mortal wound.

This was the worst calamity of the day, but there was a heavy sacrifice of less important lives before the battle ended. A week later, July 28, while Sherman, reaching out to the southwest, attempted to seize the railroads on which Atlanta depended, Hood delivered a third blow at Ezra Church—but like the rest it was manfully encountered and turned aside, again by the Army of the Tennessee, with Howard at the head in place of McPherson. Hood's aggressive policy was not resulting well, his own losses for July being larger than those he inflicted. August, like July, was a month of severe fighting. Stoneman, despatched southward with cavalry, in the hope that besides injuring the enemy he might reach Andersonville and set free the thirty-two thousand prisoners whose condition was a matter of great concern to the North, quite failed of large results. To save his main force, he sacrificed himself with a few followers, facing imprisonment— a chivalrous act, which did not make impression when it afterwards appeared that the surrender was to an inferior force, and quite needless.[1] At the end of the month there were severe encounters about Jonesboro, Sherman struggling as before to cut off Hood from Macon and Montgomery as he had already done from Augusta. September 1, Atlanta was still holding out; Lincoln's anxiety had not ceased, and the people feared that the outpour of blood and treasure in Georgia, as well as in Virginia, would lead to no result. Since the advance from Chattanooga, Sherman had lost thirty-five thousand men, while inflicting upon his enemy a loss as heavy. It was a time of great darkness, and the country knew not that it was the darkness that precedes the dawn. On August 31, the Democratic convention at Chicago adjourned after proclaiming that the war was a failure,[2] and on that day it seemed to the world that neither Grant nor

[1] Cox, *Atlanta*, 189.
[2] McPherson, *Polit. Hist. of the Great Rebellion*, 417.

Sherman had accomplished anything to prove the declaration false.   Just in time, September 2, came the sunburst: Hood evacuated Atlanta, and the Twentieth Federal Corps took possession.

CHAPTER VIII

ATTEMPTS AT RECONSTRUCTION
(1863-1864)

WHEN once the country was involved in war, debate became secondary to the wielding of weapons: but from the first there were underlying difficulties which must come up if the Federal government finally asserted its supremacy. Was the arbitrary control of individuals in the North, away from the scene of hostilities, to have the ultimate sanction of the supreme court and of public opinion? Were those engaged in making war on the United States ultimately to be put on civil trial for treason? Were the enactments and executive acts against slavery, forged in the heat of contest, to stand after peace should be restored? Were the states, as fast as they acknowledged the impossibility of getting out of the Union, to be restored at once to their former status?

The extent of the war powers of the government was a question warmly discussed in Congress and outside. One writer on the subject gravely claimed that, "It was intended by . . . the Constitution . . . that the powers of Government in dealing with civil rights in time of peace should be defined and limited: but the powers to provide for the general welfare and the common defence in time of war should be unlimited." [1]   During 1863 the suspension of the *habeas corpus*, and other invasions of ordinary private rights, were regulated by statute and by practice; the president's earlier acts were covered by a kind of statute of indemnity, his authority to suspend the *habeas corpus* definitely admitted: but the sentiment of the country was against arrest and confinement without some specific charge.   Nevertheless, conduct in the government, which at first appeared arbitrary, thenceforth passed unchallenged. [2]

As for slavery, the Republican majority in the House in 1863–1864, though only twenty, was radical and energetic.   Not satisfied even with the Proclamation of Emancipation, on December 14, 1863, James M. Ashley, of Ohio, like Lincoln tall and uncouth, but possessed of political shrewdness and moral earnestness, introduced a momentous measure —namely, to submit to the states in proper constitutional fashion, with the approval of two-thirds in each House of Congress, a thirteenth amendment to the Constitution abolishing slavery in the United States. [3]

[1] Whiting, *War Powers and the Constitution*, 27.

[2] Dunning, *Essays on the Civil War*, 62.

[3] *Cong. Globe*, 38 Cong., 1 Sess., 19; John Sherman, *Recollections*, 277 et seq.

When the war began, not one-tenth of the people of the country would have favored immediate and unconditional abolition; but in the three years' struggle sentiment ripened rapidly.[1] Congress was throughout much in advance of the people; while the president held in check the legislature, he also counselled and led the country, which in the school of events was learning that he was the main agent to bring about a happy consummation. The measure of Ashley was referred to the judiciary committee, which at a later date recommended its substance as a thirteenth amendment: a test vote on a resolution to table stood 79 for the amendment and 58 against it, an evidence that a two-thirds vote in favor of such a measure could not be secured in the House.

January 13, 1864, Senator John B. Henderson, of Missouri, proposed in the Senate a joint resolution to abolish slavery throughout the United States by a thirteenth amendment to the Constitution, which February 10 was reported by Lyman Trumbull, of Illinois, in these words: "Neither slavery nor involuntary servitude, except as a punishment for crime whereof the party shall have been duly convicted, shall exist in the United States or any place subject to their jurisdiction." The spokesman of the opposition was Garrett Davis, of Kentucky, who proposed to amend by excluding the descendants of negroes on the maternal side from all places of

[1] Blaine, *Twenty Years*, I., 504 et seq.

office and trust under the government of the United States. He proposed at the same time an amendment (a slap at the section from which so much originated of which he disapproved) consolidating the six New England states into two, to be called East and West New England. In the debate that followed, Trumbull ascribed to slavery the present misfortunes of the country, and earnestly pleaded for its removal. Clark, of New Hampshire, criticised the Constitution, lamenting its recognition of slavery, to which he also traced the public woe. On the other hand, Saulsbury, of Delaware, justified slavery from history and Scripture, citing both Old and New Testament authority in its sanction; while Hendricks, of Indiana, objected to amending the Constitution while eleven states were unable to make themselves heard in the matter. The debate lasted from March 28 to April 8, when a vote of 38 to 6 in favor of the measure was taken.[1]

When Henderson's resolution was submitted to the House, issue was again joined, and the test vote stood 76 to 55, the necessary two-thirds still wanting. It was, however, vigorously debated, Morris, of New York, Ingersoll and Arnold, of Illinois, and George S. Boutwell, of Massachusetts, standing out among the Republicans; while among the Democrats Samuel J. Randall, of Pennsylvania, and George H. Pendleton, of Ohio, were especially able.

[1] *Cong. Globe*, 38 Cong., 1 Sess., 1313 et seq.; Blaine, *Twenty Years*, I., 506.

Randall exclaimed that the policy pursued was uniting the South and dividing the North, which could not be gainsaid;[1] while Pendleton argued with acuteness that three-fourths of the states could not by any technical process either establish or abolish slavery in all the states; that the power to amend meant not the power to revolutionize, and it was nothing less than a revolution which was under discussion.

The vote on the passage of the amendment, taken June 15, 1864, stood 93 to 65: the bill was evidently growing in favor, but did not yet command the necessary two-thirds. Ashley, who from the first had steered the measure, by an adroit manœuvre made sure of its thorough discussion by the people: he voted with the opposition; then, after the announcement, using his parliamentary privilege, entered upon the Journal a motion to reconsider the vote, and declared that the question should go before the country, and that he would bring it up in the following December, at the next session.[2] The matter thus became a live issue in the presidential canvass just beginning.[3]

The financial situation of the government at the opening of the session, December 7, 1863, was decidedly improved. The amended national bank act was in operation; taxation was beginning to be productive; the successes at Gettysburg and Vicksburg

---

[1] *Cong. Globe*, 38 Cong., 1 Sess., 2991.
[2] *Ibid.*, 3357.   [3] Blaine, *Twenty Years*, I., 507.

caused gold to drop, and the five-twenty bonds were rapidly taken. The customs duties were producing all that had been hoped for: though the returns from the internal revenue caused some disappointment. But there was no thought in Congress, or in the mind of the secretary of the treasury, other than to press forward on the lines already laid down. Seven hundred and fifty - five million dollars was the estimate of what would be required before the end of the fiscal year, June 30, 1864; Chase expected to provide $594,000,000 from further loans: additions to the internal revenue taxes were expected to yield $150,000,000; $161,-500,000 was anticipated from customs duties and other ordinary sources.[1] To Chase's demand for authority to act, Congress responded liberally, as John Sherman says, "placing in the power of the Government almost unlimited sources of revenue, and all necessary expedients for borrowing"[2] On March 3, 1864, a new loan act was passed providing for an issue of $200,000,000 in bonds:[3] the minimum period of redemption was placed at ten years and the maximum at forty, which gave them the name of "ten-forties." Through an error of Chase, who set the interest at five instead of six per cent., this issue of bonds proved less successful than the five-twenties: the total amount sold up to June 30 was

[1] Dewey, *Financial Hist. of U. S.*, 312 et seq.
[2] John Sherman, *Recollections*, 279.
[3] *U. S. Statutes at Large*, XIII., 13.

only $73,337,000. Chase tided over the strait by issuing, as he had before, short-term six-per-cent. notes, the interest to be compounded, which investors took easily, an expedient which caused continued anxiety and embarrassment, for these loans rapidly matured and had to be renewed.[1]

Not only did the laws relating to loans engage the serious attention of Congress, but also those relating to currency, customs duties, and internal taxes. For such legislation the foundation was laid by the preceding Congress, but numerous supplementing and correcting acts were passed. The internal revenue bill now enacted, June 30, was far more comprehensive and searching than its predecessor: "Indeed, every instrument or article to which a stamp could be attached "[2] was counted in; all incomes above six hundred dollars must pay ten per cent.; while licenses were exacted for every calling, with a minute care that nothing could escape. A special income tax of five per cent., in addition to the previous tax, was levied to provide bounties for enlisting soldiers, but the measure passed only after long debate and hesitation, for discontent was feared among the people. The tax, however, met with little objection; and in general the internal revenue was cheerfully paid, pouring a handsome contribution into the national coffers. It was a time of

[1] Dewey, *Financial Hist. of U. S.*, 313.
[2] *U. S. Statutes at Large*, XIII., 223-306; John Sherman, *Recollections*, 278.

prosperity; the market was good for everything
that could be grown or manufactured; labor was in
demand.

The customs duties were carefully revised and
much increased by a statute of June 3, 1864, the
consideration of protection to home industries being
ignored in the immediate need of a heavy revenue.
Many articles heretofore free became dutiable, and
a large increase of income at once resulted.[1]

June 3, 1864, Congress carefully went over and
re-enacted in a new form the national bank legislation of 1863,[2] still with a comptroller of the
currency in charge of this branch of the treasury.
Whereas in 1863 sixty-six state banks underwent
conversion into national banks, in 1864 the number
was five hundred and eight. In subsequent years
the number rapidly increased with the stimulus of
an act of March 3, 1865, by which state bank issues
were legislated out of existence by a ten-per-cent.
annual tax. It was no hardship for any honest institution to comply with the conditions, and make
secure the payment of its circulating notes by a
deposit with the government. Probably in our
whole financial history no more beneficent change
has ever taken place. If, as has been suggested, it
could not have been brought about except under
the pressure of war,[3] the establishment of the national banking system is a make-weight worth men-

[1] *U. S. Statutes at Large*, XIII., 202.   [2] *Ibid.*, 99.
[3] Dewey, *Financial Hist. of U. S.*, 323.

tioning even against the loss and distress of the evil time.

It is well to note that the financial managers in this session were turning to less objectionable methods than the issue of irredeemable paper money. By the acts of February 25 and July 11, 1862, and January 17, 1863, $450,000,000 greenbacks had been authorized, of which $431,000,000 were outstanding. As all forms of gold and silver had disappeared, small notes, "fractional currency," in denominations running as low as three cents, were authorized, March 3, 1863, the amount rising at last to $50,-000,000.[1] The greenback pervaded life, but no more were issued after the summer of 1864.[2] It was becoming apparent that sounder expedients were possible, and Congress was adopting them.

The quotation of gold rose during the summer to 286, indicating a depreciation of paper money to about thirty-five per cent. of its face value. The best heads were at fault as to what ought to be done. A piece of financial legislation which completely failed of its end was the gold bill of June 17, 1864,[3] intended to correct the abuses in the buying and selling of gold. The law proved to be worse than useless, gold rising in price as never before. The best financiers became urgent for its repeal, and fortunately there was time for reconsideration before the session closed. The fluctuations in gold, at the time

---

[1] Dewey, *Financial Hist. of U. S.*, 310. [2] *Ibid.*, 288.
[3] *U. S. Statutes at Large*, XIII., 132.

so much misunderstood, are regarded now as the
symptoms of the public depression and anxiety:
when success came, people were no longer alarmed
lest the greenbacks should become imperilled.[1]

John Sherman declares the devising of the great
financial schemes, sometimes mistaken but often
successful, to have been the work of the ways and
means committee in the House and the finance
committee in the Senate.   "They occupied the principal attention of both Houses, and may fairly be
claimed as successful measures of the highest importance.   "I was deeply interested in all of them,
took an active part in their preparation in committee and their conduct in the Senate, and feel
that the measures adopted contributed largely to
the triumph of the Union cause." [2]   The veteran
statesman, writing thirty years later, does not claim
too much.   The financiering of the Civil War period
may properly excite our admiration and gratitude.
Mistakes were inevitable; but the tremendous temporary exigency was met, and in some ways the
financial condition of the country was vastly and
permanently bettered.

Of the acts not relating to slavery or finance,
passed at this session, the more important[3] were
those looking towards greater military efficiency,
including a new enrolment act, and one creating the

[1] Dewey, *Financial Hist. of U. S.*, 297.
[2] John Sherman, *Recollections*, 281.
[3] *U. S. Statutes at Large*, XIII., 6, 11, 30, 32, 47, 385.

office of lieutenant-general, already referred to; enabling acts for statehood for Nevada (March 21, 1864) and Nebraska (April 14, 1864); an act to encourage immigration (April 19, 1864), which John Sherman thinks was justifiable only under the extraordinary circumstances prevailing:[1] and acts relating to Pacific railroads. More liberal grants were bestowed upon the roads authorized the previous year; and a new enterprise, the Northern Pacific Railroad, to connect Lake Superior with Puget Sound, was sanctioned, and most liberally endowed from the public lands.[2]

The most exciting discussion in Congress in the session of 1863–1864 was upon the status of the rebellious states, and resulted in a disagreement between the executive and legislative branches of the government that threatened at first to wreck the administration. The origin of this controversy must be traced back to the beginning of the war. As a provisional arrangement, to remain in force only until the formalities of reorganization could be completed, the administration appointed "military governors," "with authority to establish all necessary officers and tribunals, and suspend the writ of *habeas corpus*, during the pleasure of the president, or until the loyal inhabitants of the state shall organize a civil government in conformity with the constitution of the United States."[3]

[1] John Sherman, *Recollections*, 280.
[2] *U. S. Statutes at Large*, XIII., 356, 365.
[3] Nicolay and Hay, *Abraham Lincoln*, VI., 345.

No military governor was necessary in Virginia, for a minority, after the secession of the state in 1861, organized a loyal state government, with Francis H. Peirpoint at the head; and the senators and representatives chosen under this government were duly recognized by Congress. Soon after, steps were taken for the setting off of the western counties, and in 1862 was organized the new state of West Virginia, with Wheeling for a capital; June 19, 1863, it was formally admitted to the Union, on the fiction that the Peirpoint government was competent to give the necessary assent of "Virginia." Peirpoint's shadowy commonwealth, often called the "vest-pocket government," with Alexandria for a capital, was also represented for a time in Congress.[1]

By the end of 1863 five of the seceding states, Virginia, North Carolina, Tennessee, Arkansas, and Louisiana, were in whole or in part nominally subjugated: and some steps needed to be taken with reference to their relations to the Union. March 5, 1862, Andrew Johnson was confirmed as military governor of Tennessee, Albert Sidney Johnston having just retired as far south as Murfreesboro after the Confederate defeats at Forts Henry and Donelson. Here, although there were two representatives in Congress, the provisional arrangement was not replaced by any state government until a period later than that to which we have arrived.[2]

---

[1] *Am. Annual Cyclop.*, 1863, art. Virginia.
[2] McCarthy, *Lincoln's Plan of Reconstruction*, 1 et seq.

May 2, 1862, Edward Stanley was made military governor of North Carolina; but for a long time there was no great development of Union sentiment. In Louisiana, August, 1862, General George F. Shepley, who had been made by Butler mayor of New Orleans, was appointed military governor; and by his authority, December 3, 1862, a state election was held at which 7760 votes were cast, resulting in the choice of two Federal representatives, who were duly admitted to seats at Washington. No attempt to reorganize the state government was made in 1863.[1] In Arkansas, though Federal success in the field and wide-spread Union sentiment induced Lincoln as early as March, 1862, to appoint a military governor, reconstruction remained in abeyance[2] until 1864, when a free-state organization came into existence.

December 8, 1863, Lincoln took the portentous step of sending to Congress a special message containing a copy of a proclamation already issued, irrevocably committing the executive to a general plan of reconstruction. He announced as the conditions necessary for the recognition of a state, three preliminaries: "(1) The completion of an organization by persons who (2) have subscribed to the Constitution of the United States, and (3) who have pledged themselves to support the acts and proclamations promulgated during the war with reference to slavery." [3]

---

[1] McCarthy, *Lincoln's Plan of Reconstruction*, 36 et seq.
[2] *Ibid.*, 77 et seq.   [3] Dunning, *Essays on the Civil War*, 77.

The president further dealt with the status of individuals by prescribing an oath to be used in states lately in rebellion, pledging the person taking it to support the Constitution of the United States and all acts and proclamations put forth during the rebellion relating to slavery, except such as had been formally repealed: this oath might be taken by all men except high military and civil officers of the Confederacy, and others who had resigned civil or military positions in the United States to take part in the rebellion, or who had unlawfully treated colored men in the United States service who had been taken prisoners. To all persons taking this oath, full amnesty for past offences was granted. Moreover, whenever, in any rebellious state, a number not less than one-tenth of the voters at the presidential election of 1860 should desire, having taken the oath, to reconstitute their state, they should have power to do so, and thereupon return to the old relations with the Union. The proclamation further declared that any temporary provision made for the freedmen of a state, recognizing their freedom and looking towards their education, would not be objected to by the national executive: it suggested that as regards name, constitution, laws, boundaries, etc., there should be as little departure as possible from what had been established before: it recognized that the admission to seats in the Federal Congress, of persons elected as senators and representatives, rested entirely with Congress, being outside of executive control. The proclamation concludes by stating that while thus laying down for rebellious states a method for returning to their allegiance, it must not be understood that no other possible mode would be acceptable.[1]

In the message, the president in his usual clear and straightforward way reviewed the situation, citing the acceptance which the Emancipation Proclamation had met at last, the justification and growing approval of the employment of negro soldiers, the lessening of pro-slavery sentiment in the border states, the favorable change in the feeling of Europe. He maintained that his action was authorized by the Constitution or by statutes. "The proposed acquiescence of the national executive in any reasonable state temporary arrangement for the freed people" is made with the hope "that the already deeply afflicted people of those states may be somewhat more ready to give up the cause of their affliction, if to this extent this vital matter be left to themselves"; while at the same time the president retained power to correct abuses. He dwelt on the possibility of other acceptable plans for reconstruction, and urged Congress to help forward the great consummation.[2]

John Hay, who was on the floor of Congress when the message was received, recorded in his diary that the approval seemed unanimous. In the Senate, not only Chandler, Sumner, and Wilson spoke of it

[1] Lincoln, *Works* (ed. of 1894), II., 444.   [2] *Ibid.*, 454.

with delight, but Dixon, of Connecticut, a strong
conservative, and Reverdy Johnson, the Democrat,
of Maryland, also approved. In the House the
sentiment was similar, George S. Boutwell, James A.
Garfield, Henry T. Blow, of Missouri, all men of
radical views, were full of enthusiasm. One member went shouting through the lobbies: "The President is the only man. There is none like him in the
world!" Reverend Owen Lovejoy exclaimed: "How
beautiful upon the mountains are the feet of him
that bringeth good tidings!" while Horace Greeley,
who was on the floor of the House, less devout but
not less hearty, declared the message "devilish good."
In congratulating Lincoln, conservatives vied with
radicals. The president was greatly cheered, and
with good reason: to devise a settlement of this most
difficult matter in a way almost universally acceptable among loyal men was an achievement indeed [1]

The judiciary eventually sustained fully the view
of the executive regarding reconstruction, the supreme court unanimously showing in its opinions
that, like the president, it never doubted the constitutional existence of the states. "Circumstances
had disarranged their relations with the Federal
Government, but with the correction of the disturbance the former conditions could be resumed." [2]

[1] Nicolay and Hay, *Abraham Lincoln*, IX., 109.
[2] Dunning, *Essays on the Civil War*, 72; see opinion of supreme court in the Prize Cases, December term, 1862, 2 Black,
668; also case of the *Venice*, 2 Wallace, 278.

As to the legislative branch of the government, however, a want of harmony began to appear which brought momentous consequences. While at one with the executive and the judiciary, in according to the states a being incapable of destruction by any unconstitutional organization of the inhabitants, Congress shrank from the steps towards restoration announced in the president's message of December 8, 1863. It was feared that Lincoln would be lax in exacting satisfactory guarantees of continued loyalty.

The change in the temper of Congress soon manifested itself. Henry Winter Davis, of Maryland, moved at once in the House that the part of the message relating to reconstruction be referred to a special committee "on the rebellious states," of which he was made chairman; and on February 15, 1864, he reported a plan of reconstruction quite different from Lincoln's.[1] Davis, able and of high personal character, a cousin of David Davis, of Illinois, Lincoln's intimate friend, had won the admiration of the president, who greatly desired his friendship and support; but Davis had taken a dislike to Lincoln, perhaps because the latter favored the Blairs,[2] which developed into hostility extreme and vindictive. In spite of the bitterness, Lincoln's all-abounding magnanimity wrapped Davis within his regard; the president could not win him, but he steadfastly endured, striking no return blow.

[1] *Cong. Globe*, 38 Cong., 1 Sess., 668 (February 15, 1864).
[2] Nicolay and Hay, *Abraham Lincoln*, IX., 113.

In opposition to Lincoln's idea, declared in his inaugural and repeatedly reaffirmed, that no state had power to secede from the Union, Davis maintained that the seceding states were out of the Union—a proposition so vehemently announced in the preamble that the House rejected it, but the same idea pervaded the resolutions which followed.[1] The work already begun in states wholly or partly conquered[2] was to be set aside as invalid, and nothing more of the kind attempted. The incompetency of the executive to act in the case being thus assumed, the bill laid down as a "Congressional plan" a scheme much more severe and difficult than the one rejected; in any state which might have succumbed to the Federal arms, under a provisional governor a census of white men was to be taken, a majority of whom must take the oath of allegiance, after which delegates might be elected to a convention to establish a state government. In the new state constitution three provisions must appear: (1) disfranchising practically all high civil or military officers of the Confederacy; (2) abolishing slavery; (3) repudiating all debts and obligations created by or under the sanction of the usurping power. Such a constitution having been adopted and ratified, the provisional governor was to certify the same to the president, who after having been authorized by Congress to do so, should recog-

[1] *Cong. Globe*, 38 Cong., 1 Sess., 2107 (February 22, 1864).
[2] See chap. viii., above.

nize the state; after which recognition congressmen and presidential electors might be chosen.[1]

Davis supported his bill in a speech of unusual power,[2] in which, while denouncing the amnesty oath suggested by the president as utterly inadequate, and rejecting contemptuously any plan for a scheme based upon the votes of only one-tenth of the former voting population, he strongly urged the passage of his bill. He argued that the proclamation recognized slavery; that reconstruction belonged to Congress alone, and should go to the root of things. Rarely in the history of the United States has eloquence produced so marked a result. Whereas among the Republicans opinion had at first been almost unanimous in favor of the president's plan, the ablest and most cautious being among the heartiest in their approval, when the matter after much debate came to a vote, March 22, the Davis bill passed by 73 to 59.

It was brought up in the Senate by B. F. Wade, who sustained the measure in a strain similar to that of Davis. It is evident that the Republican leaders had made up their minds to set Congress athwart the president's plans. Hence the vote was favorable in the Senate, and the bill, usually called the "Davis-Wade bill," went to the president for his signature on the closing day of the session.

The diary of John Hay, who was at the presi-

[1] McPherson, *Polit. Hist. of Great Rebellion*, 317.
[2] *Cong. Globe*, 38 Cong., 1 Sess., App. (March 22, 1864).

dent's elbow, is here again most interesting. Lincoln sat in the president's room at the Capitol, July 4, at noon of which day Congress was to adjourn. Members intensely excited stood at hand as the bills were one after another disposed of. When the reconstruction measure came at last, Lincoln laid it aside, whereupon in the general tension of the group, Zachariah Chandler sharply interrogated Lincoln as to his intentions. "As to prohibiting slavery in the reconstructed states," said Lincoln, "that is the point on which I doubt the power of Congress to act." "It is no more than you have done yourself," said Chandler. "I conceive," said Lincoln, "that I may in an emergency do things on military grounds which cannot be done constitutionally by Congress." Mr. Chandler, not concealing his anger, went out; while Lincoln, turning to the cabinet who sat at hand, said: "I do not see how any of us now can deny and contradict what we have always said, that Congress has no constitutional power over slavery in the states." One senator present, Fessenden, of Maine, expressed his entire agreement with this view. The president continued: "the position of these gentlemen, that the insurrectionary states are no longer in the Union, seems to me to make the fatal admission that states whenever they please may of their own motion dissolve their connection with the Union. Now we cannot survive that admission, I am convinced." [1]

[1] Nicolay and Hay, *Abraham Lincoln*, IX., 120.

Congress adjourned in great excitement, and Lincoln followed up his action in "pocketing" the bill, without signature or veto, by issuing, July 8, a proclamation to the people, in which after reciting the circumstances, he declared his unpreparedness to commit himself to any one plan of reconstruction, and also his unpreparedness to set aside as naught the action of Louisiana, Arkansas, or any lately insurrectionary state whose people began to show a desire to return to the Union.   He expressed his strong hope that the thirteenth amendment, for the time held up, would within a few months be adopted, and his earnest desire to aid any state desiring to return to the Union, and his approval of the congressional scheme as "one very proper plan for the loyal people of any state choosing to adopt it."[1]

To this Wade and Davis replied, August 5, by a manifesto in the *New York Tribune*, "To the Supporters of the Government," the severest attack ever made upon Lincoln within his own party. Every line of the proclamation was traversed and sharply criticised, especial emphasis being laid upon the usurpations of the executive.   "This rash and fatal act of the president—a blow at the friends of his administration, at the rights of humanity and at the principles of republican government. . . . But he must understand that our support is of a cause and not of a man; that the authority of Congress is paramount and must be respected; . . . he must

[1] Lincoln, *Works* (ed. of 1894), II., 545.

confine himself to his executive duties,—to obey and to execute, not make the laws, and leave political reorganization to Congress."[1] Yet it clearly appeared ere long that Lincoln, before the people, had received no harm from this attempt to wound him in the house of his friends.

[1] McPherson, *Polit. Hist. of Great Rebellion*, 332.

CHAPTER IX

LINCOLN'S SECOND ELECTION
(1864)

THROUGHOUT the first three years of the war
the determined champions of the Union saw
that it was as imperative to keep control of the
political as of the military organization. Hence,
politicians watched with eagerness the state elections from year to year, and the congressional
elections of 1862; the intense conviction of the
necessity of maintaining a fighting majority in
Congress caused the people to shut their eyes to
the drastic methods by which the border states
were led to return a solid Republican delegation
to the House in the election of 1862, thus barely
saving the war government from paralysis. The
attitude of the War Democrats was of great significance in this crisis, and to placate them and make
common political action easier, the name Union
party was in many states taken up instead of
Republican, and even came to be the official title
of the national organization in the presidential campaign of 1864. Nevertheless, those wise in forecast-
ing felt that Republican success depended upon con-

tinued victories by Union armies; and in the Union
party itself were elements not satisfied with Lincoln.

Lincoln's most formidable rival was Chase, a
man whose ability, worth, and weakness have had
in our narrative full illustration. He was discon-
tented with the president and with his colleagues in
the cabinet; he desired intensely for himself the
highest place, of his adequacy for which he was
serenely sure; he so misunderstood the situation
as to imagine that he had a great popular following. He wrote, January 24, 1864: "Had there been
here an Administration in the true sense of the
word—a president conferring with his cabinet and
taking their united judgments and with their aid
enforcing activity, economy, energy, in all departments of the public service, we could have spoken
boldly and defied the world. But our condition
here has always been very different. I preside
over the funnel; everybody else, and especially the
Secretaries of War and the Navy, over the spigots
—and keep them well open, too. Mr. Seward con-
ducts the Foreign Relations with very little let or
help from anybody. There is no unity and no
system except so far as it is departmental. There
is progress, but it is slow and involuntary—just what
is coerced by the irresistible pressure of the vast
force of the people. How under such circumstances
can anybody announce a policy which can only be
made respectable by union, wisdom, and courage!"[1]

[1] Warden, *Chase*, 562.

How Lincoln felt towards Chase is shown by a
deliverance recorded in John Hay's diary, October
16, 1863: "Mr. Chase makes a good Secretary and
I shall keep him where he is.   If he becomes president, all right.   I hope we may never have a worse
man.   I have observed with regret his plan of
strengthening himself.   Whenever he sees that an
important matter is troubling me, if I am compelled
to decide in a way to give offence to a man of some
importance, he always ranges himself in opposition
to me, and persuades the victim that he has been
hardly dealt with, and that he would have arranged
it very differently. . . . I am entirely indifferent
as to his success or failure in these schemes so long
as he does his duty at the head of the Treasury
Department." [1]

The two great men, associated very closely, both
desired the nomination — an honorable ambition.
Lincoln was justly confident that he had done well,
and was anxious to continue until he had brought
the country out of its strait.   Chase misjudged
the crisis, the feeling of the country, his immediate
environment, most of all, perhaps, himself: he had
no strength with the people, nor was there a single
public man of prominence who actively favored his
candidacy.   A Chase organization, however, more
or less formal, came into existence, at the head of
which was Samuel C. Pomeroy, of Kansas, a senator
of no large significance, who, unknown to Chase,

[1] Nicolay and Hay, *Abraham Lincoln*, VIII., 316.

issued a confidential circular that went broadcast through the country. This asserted the impossibility of Lincoln's re-election, and criticised what it termed Lincoln's temporizing and hesitating disposition, which would be certain to manifest itself more strongly during a second administration; asserted the inexpediency of allowing to any president a second term in the then existing condition of the Union; and finally pointed out the combination in Chase of the qualities requisite for a chief magistrate.[1]

February 22, 1864, the circular appeared in the newspapers, whereupon Chase wrote Lincoln that he had not known of the existence of such a letter: he admitted that at the urgent solicitations of his friends he had become a candidate, and asked that he might be allowed to resign his post, should his position, in the judgment of the president, prejudice the public interest. To this Lincoln responded goodnaturedly, stating at the end that he "perceived no occasion for a change."[2] The candidacy of Chase speedily collapsed. Not only was there no response, but those on whom he particularly counted ranged themselves with Lincoln. When the Republican members of the Ohio legislature in full caucus nominated Lincoln, February 25, Chase at once withdrew.

Besides Chase, some of the Republicans thought of Grant, but he would not listen to the idea of his

[1] Hart, *Chase*, 312.
[2] Nicolay and Hay, *Abraham Lincoln*, VIII., 321 et seq.

nomination. Quite a different case was that of Frémont; though discredited both as the administrator of a department and as a soldier in the field, he still had a following, and a meeting was held, May 31, 1864, at Cleveland, Ohio, in his interest. The gathering was in no sense representative; a company of two hundred or so, mostly from St. Louis and New York, without credentials from any body of the people, came together of their own accord. No figure of prominence was present, though Horace Greeley had been, without reason, expected. A letter was read from Wendell Phillips, who made a comparison between Frémont and Lincoln to the disadvantage of the latter, and suggested for the convention a radical platform, providing for the confiscation and distribution of the conquered South, and for universal suffrage. Frémont was finally nominated for the presidency by this irresponsible party, with John Cochrane, of New York, for vice-president. Frémont accepted, declaring at the time, among other things, his belief that the work of Lincoln was "politically, militarily, and financially a failure." The Democratic press, eager to foment a division in the Republican ranks, sought to make much of it, but the Cleveland convention was soon looked upon as an event of no importance.[1]

The Republican convention was appointed for June 7, 1864,[2] a date unusually early, but the leaders desired to settle upon the candidate, and pre-

[1] McPherson, *Polit. Hist. of Great Rebellion*, 410.   [2] *Ibid.*, 403.

sent at once to the opposition a front as nearly
united as possible. From the beginning of January, throughout the winter and spring, indications
abounded that the only candidate was Lincoln,
loyal men from the states east and west making
manifest their enthusiasm for the great chief. When
the convention assembled at Baltimore, ex - Governor E. D. Morgan, of New York, called it to
order, his brief speech being marked especially by
the declaration that the thirteenth amendment, then
pending in Congress, was fundamental to Repub-
licanism, a key-note echoed back in heavy and long-
continued applause.

The temporary chairman, Reverend Robert J.
Breckinridge, D.D., of Kentucky, a patriarchal and
dignified figure, whose kinsmen were among the
most strenuous insurgents, came out of the hot
border battle with the smell of fire, as it were, in
his garments, to bear his testimony. His speech
was as fervid as the utterance of a prophet of old.
Disregarding what was usual, he forestalled the
action of the convention by announcing Lincoln as
the only possible candidate. With passion almost
ferocious, he declared "the only enduring cement
of free institutions to be the blood of traitors. It
is a fearful truth, but we had as well avow it at once;
and every blow you strike, and every rebel you kill,
you are adding it may be centuries to the life of the
government and to the freedom of your children."
He declared himself to be absolutely aloof from

politics. "As a Union party I will follow you to the gates of death; as Republican or Democrat, I will not follow you one foot." The address was especially impressive when Dr. Breckinridge indorsed Morgan's approval of the abolition of slavery. "I join myself with those who say, away with it forever!"

For permanent chairman, Governor William Dennison, of Ohio, was announced, whose excellent speech enforcing eloquently Breckinridge's doctrine produced scarcely the same effect; for he came from and would return to the security of a northern state, whereas the boldness of the Kentuckian might consign him to a bloody grave.

When the convention began to work, its task was easy. Of delegations applying for admission none were rejected except that claiming to be from South Carolina; those of Virginia and Florida were admitted to the floor without the right to vote; all others had full privileges; as to Missouri, where among loyal men there had been a fierce dispute of factions, two delegations appeared, of which the one representing the more radical men was selected.

The issues involved in the contest were set forth in the platform,[1] presented by Henry J. Raymond, editor of the *New York Times*, chairman of the committee on resolutions. This able appeal to the country insisted upon the duty to maintain the integrity of the Union, and the Constitution and laws

[1] McPherson, *Polit. Hist. of Great Rebellion*, 406.

of the United States; and as Union men pledged
everything in the party's power to aid the government in quelling the rebellion and in bringing to
the punishment due to their crimes, the rebels and
traitors arrayed against it. The platform further
approved the determination of the government not
to compromise with rebels, and to prosecute the war
with the utmost possible vigor.

Slavery was denounced as the cause and the
strength of the rebellion, and the platform explicitly
called for such an amendment to the Constitution,
to be made by the people in conformity with its
provisions, as shall terminate and forever prohibit
its existence within the jurisdiction of the United
States.

The president's policy and administration received
ungrudging support in an eulogium on Abraham Lincoln, and the convention approved as essential to the
preservation of the nation, and as within the provisions of the Constitution, " the measures which he
has adopted to defend the nation against its open
and secret foes . . . especially the Proclamation of
Emancipation."   The only thing resembling censure
was " a resolution looking towards changes in the cabinet so that harmony should prevail in the national
councils, and only those remain who cordially indorsed
the principles proclaimed in these resolutions."   In
view of the French invasion of Mexico, the platform
declared that " The people of the United States view
with extreme jealousy, as menacing to the peace

and independence of their own country, the efforts
of any European power to obtain new foot-holds for
monarchical governments, sustained by foreign military force, in near proximity to the United States." [1]

The chairman of the Illinois delegation named
for the presidency, in the briefest terms, "Abraham
Lincoln, God bless him." The ensuing vote stood,
for Lincoln, 484; the Missouri delegation, following
strict instructions, cast their votes for Grant, but
they at once fell in with the rest to make the vote
unanimous.

For vice-president the selection was more diffi-
cult. No dissatisfaction existed as regards Hanni-
bal Hamlin; but the feeling prevailed that a War
Democrat would give strength to the ticket: Daniel
S. Dickinson, of New York; Lovell H. Rousseau and
Joseph Holt, of Kentucky; Benjamin F. Butler, of
Massachusetts, and Andrew Johnson, of Tennessee,
were names suggested. In the balloting Andrew
Johnson received two hundred votes, after which
all united in declaring his nomination unanimous.
Thus the Tennesseean, crude, headstrong, preju-
diced, but full of courage and devotedly patriotic, came to the front. Lincoln, who had rigidly
abstained from making any suggestions as to the
action or declarations of the convention, heard the
result calmly, but did not conceal his gratification.
He did not understand, he said, that he was held
to be the best and wisest man in America; but

[1] McPherson, *Polit. Hist. of Great Rebellion*, 406, 407.

simply that it was a bad plan "to swap horses while crossing the river." [1]

The Baltimore convention took place while the North was still buoyant with the hope that Grant and Sherman would soon do great things: but while it was in session the details of the dreadful repulse at Cold Harbor were arriving; and before the month ended Sherman was beaten back at Kenesaw Mountain. The situation in the two main armies grew worse during July and August, Richmond and Atlanta baffling every Federal attempt. Even Lincoln became depressed, while his stanchest supporters quite lost heart. The president, to whom the success of McClellan, the inevitable Democratic candidate, began to seem likely, framed a plan for coming to an understanding with him to save the Union by a combined effort, to be made in the interval between the election and the inauguration.

When the prospect was darkest the forces of the opposition party assembled at Chicago, August 29, quite sure of their power to overthrow the administration.[2] The delegates arrived numerous and exultant, but a want of harmony existed which from the first boded misfortune. While many War Democrats were acting with the Republicans, such as Dickinson, Johnson, Tod, Brough, and a number of the best generals in the field, there were many

---

[1] Nicolay and Hay, *Abraham Lincoln*, IX., 76.
[2] McPherson, *Polit. Hist. of Great Rebellion*, 417.

War Democrats at Chicago, led by the delegation from New York — over against whom stood the peace men, out and out Copperheads, Vallandigham at the front, home from his exile, and in exaggerated vigor. The convention was callèd to order by August Belmont, German born, the agent of the Rothschilds in New York, and noted in finance. His brief address was intended to promote harmony, after which ex - Governor Bigler, of Pennsylvania, as temporary chairman, ascribed the woes under which the country suffered to the Republicans, against whom a united stand must be made "to rescue our country—our whole country—from its present lamentable condition."

Horatio Seymour, of New York, the permanent chairman, made the great address of the occasion, a masterpiece of dignified, eloquent, passionate invective. "This Administration cannot now save the Union, if it would. It has by its proclamations, by vindictive legislation, by display of hate and passion, placed obstacles in its own pathway which it cannot overcome, and has hampered its own freedom by unconstitutional acts. If this Administration cannot save this Union, we can. Mr. Lincoln values many things above the Union: we put it first of all. He thinks a proclamation worth more than peace. We think the blood of our people more precious than the edicts of a president. We demand no conditions for the preservation of our Union. We are shackled with no hates, no prejudices, no passions."

Vallandigham, a member of the committee on resolutions, dominated the committee by his energy. He draughted and put through in spite of opposition the only very significant utterance of the platform. "That the convention does explicitly declare as the sense of the American people, that after four years of failure to restore the Union by the experiment of war, . . . humanity, liberty, and the public welfare demand that immediate efforts be made for a cessation of hostilities, and that a convention or some other unmilitary means be employed, that peace may be restored on the basis of the Federal union of the states."[1]

When submitted to the convention, this practical surrender to the Confederacy passed unchallenged with the other resolutions, the gloom of the military situation disposing the country towards peace as never before. Nominations being in order, McClellan received 202½ votes, with a few scattering. Vallandigham moved that McClellan's nomination be made unanimous, which was done. With the nomination[2] for vice-president of George H. Pendleton, an able Democratic congressman from Cincinnati, the work of the convention was over. Great enthusiasm prevailed, but, September 2, almost at once after the adjournment, news came from Sherman which, as Seward said, "knocked the planks out of the Chicago platform"; and McClellan, while accepting the nomination, did it in terms quite out

[1] McPherson, *Polit. Hist. of Great Rebellion*, 419.   [2] *Ibid.*, 421.

of harmony with Vallandigham's resolution. All interest centred upon the men in the field, and in good time, before election day, their work made the outcome certain.

Before we return to the soldiers, we must consider the disappearance from our stage of certain important figures. Chase has constantly been in the foreground, a pure, stately, columnar, though not flawless, personality, bearing upon Atlantean shoulders a heavy part of the burden of the day. The secretary and the president were really in principle not far apart: to both it was a matter dear as life itself to maintain freedom and the Union; but while the secretary put freedom first as the necessary foundation for the Union, the president put the Union first—its preservation a condition without which freedom could not exist.[1] While not far apart in principles, in temperament and disposition the two men jarred; they had a "different taste in jokes." Lincoln did the fullest justice to the ability and worth of Chase, but could not find him congenial. "Chase is one and a half times bigger than any man I ever knew," said he; but Chase failed to appreciate Lincoln, whom he rated much below himself, and whose homely mother-wit he held to be boorish and unbecoming.

Though always at his onerous post, and faithful as a counsellor, he repeatedly asked to be allowed to resign, usually in order to recall Lincoln's mind

[1] Hart, *Chase*, 292.

to his indispensableness. Up to 1864, Lincoln, with
eye single to the public welfare, had good-naturedly
refused. With the opening of 1864 came the effort
by Chase and his friends to supplant Lincoln, followed by other causes for estrangement. Among
these was a quarrel with the Blairs, whom Chase
thought favored by Lincoln. The Blair family, in
the story of the Civil War, is an interesting group.
Francis P. Blair, Sr., a Virginian born, went while
still a child to Kentucky, becoming a friend of
Henry Clay in early manhood. Estranged from him
in John Quincy Adams's day, he attracted Jackson's
notice by opposing nullification, and was invited by
him to Washington, where he founded the *Globe*,
a newspaper of great influence. In 1864, a man
seventy-three years old, he was no longer an editor,
but very active, as always, for the Union: he was
the medium of the overtures to Robert E. Lee, in
1861, to become commander of the Union army;
in the present year he sought to bring about a
better understanding between Lincoln and McClellan: a little later he was a zealous go-between from
Washington to Richmond in the interests of peace.

Two sons of this political veteran have often
appeared in our narrative, as men of power and
patriotism. F. P. Blair, Jr., after saving Missouri
to the Union, in conjunction with Lyon, followed
a most energetic course: now commanding the
Seventeenth Corps in the Army of the West, now a
leader in Congress, he vibrated between field and

forum, always audacious and dominating. Montgomery Blair did almost as much for Maryland as his brother Frank did for Missouri. Equally able, perhaps, he confined himself to politics. In the cabinet he had not the prominence of Seward, Chase, or Stanton; as postmaster - general his work was less concerned with the war than theirs; but his voice in council was never silent and often heeded. Father and sons stood sympathetically together: forceful and aggressive, they became not only a terror to their adversaries in the South, but caused enmity among the friends of the Union at home.

In 1864 the Blairs had fallen out with the radicals, especially with Frémont, who at their instance had received his commission as major-general and an appointment to a department, but soon forfeited their friendship, all who adhered to him becoming their foes. In Maryland, Montgomery Blair and Henry Winter Davis were soon at odds. The radicals took sides against the trio more and more definitely; the Blairs and all who countenanced them feeling their wrath.

Lincoln was suffering from this feud, which brought about the hostility of Henry Winter Davis, so virulent in the reconstruction business.[1] The president was to suffer still further: Chase conceived a violent enmity to Frank Blair, on account of remarks made in debate—enmity which the aggressive sol-

[1] See p. 139, above.

dier-statesman, riding rough-shod, made more bitter. When Lincoln, according to a promise made some time before, allowed Blair to return to his rank in the army from a seat in Congress, he did so with the hope that he might improve the situation; but Chase at once bracketed Lincoln with Blair, his estrangement from the president growing still wider.

Another cause of offence to Chase was what he unreasonably regarded an interference by the president with his appointments. The upshot of it all was that, June 30, 1864, Chase sent in his fourth or fifth resignation. There is reason to believe that he would have yielded as usual to remonstrance from the president, but this time no remonstrance came; and William Pitt Fessenden, chairman of the Senate committee on finance, was at once appointed as his successor.[1] The resignation of Chase, coming after disasters in the field and contentions in Congress, threw the country into painful excitement, an accurate indication being the rise of gold to its highest point, about 286. Chase accepted the situation, after all, in a manly way. To his successor, who naturally hesitated to assume his colossal burden, his words were kind and reassuring. He said truthfully that all the great work of the department was fairly blocked out and in progress; that the organization was planned and in many ways complete, or in a way towards completion.

[1] Hart, *Chase*, 318.

His achievement, indeed, had been a great path-breaking. He was hampered at every step by the lack of precedents for such an exigency, and the belief shared by every one that the war must soon end. His management of the bond issues was in the main shrewd and far-sighted, his scheme for internal revenue at last most effective; while in laying the foundation of the national bank system, he bestowed on his country a noble and permanent good. Chase may justly be called a great secretary of the treasury, deserving of honor and dignity. In October of this year Lincoln appointed him chief - justice of the supreme court of the United States—a post which the president, with all the magnanimity of his great nature, was delighted to bestow.

The resolution of the Baltimore convention re-lating to a reconstruction of the cabinet was of radical origin, and looked towards the retirement not of Chase, but of Montgomery Blair. That re-sult came in September, the president frankly stat-ing that while Blair had lost nothing in his regard, it was expedient that he should give way, which he did with good grace; nor was the devotion of the Blairs to the administration abated. Montgomery toiled manfully in the canvass for his late chief, while Frank rode at the right hand of Sherman in the progress through Georgia and the Carolinas— the septuagenarian father meantime working as ever for the country. William Dennison, of Ohio, became postmaster-general. James Speed, of Kentucky, was made attorney-general, succeeding Bates, who resigned November 24, a faithful servant of the government, who, ill at ease in the crisis, preferred to withdraw to private life. Caleb B. Smith, Lincoln's first secretary of the interior, resigned earlier, December, 1862, his place being filled by John P. Usher, of Indiana.

CHAPTER X

THE CONFEDERACY ON THE SEA
(1861–1864)

THROUGHOUT all its immense extent of coast and numerous rivers, the Confederacy was compelled in naval warfare, with the single exception of the one day's victory of the *Merrimac*, in March, 1862, to accept defeat. All the other important conflicts—on the Mississippi and its affluents, and in the Atlantic region, were gained by Federal fleets and ships. On the open ocean, too, the Confederacy never gained an important victory; yet her few seagoing cruisers inflicted great material damage, and seriously injured the repute of the Federal navy by their depredations on unarmed merchant-men.

On the other hand, the Federal blockading squadron was also capturing merchant-ships, and thereby giving powerful assistance to the land armies in the effort to throttle the power of the Confederacy.[1] The dozen ships stationed in April, 1861, increased gradually to a fleet of three hundred, which effectually guarded thousands of miles of coast. Not far below the Virginia capes begins the peculiar double

[1] *Naval War Records*, VI.–XIX.

coast which characterizes the southern Atlantic sea-
board — the sounds of North Carolina, behind the
outlying beaches; then after an interval the inlets
among the Sea Islands of South Carolina, and the
sand-barred estuaries of Georgia and Florida. The
North Atlantic squadron patrolled the coast as far
down as Wilmington, whence the South Atlantic
squadron kept watch to Cape Canaveral; the East
Gulf squadron took the stretch from Key West to
Pensacola, and the West Gulf thence to the Rio
Grande. Though the line was so long, the harbors
practicable for ocean commerce were few; and in
1864, Wilmington, Charleston, Mobile, and Galves-
ton, with a few inlets, were the only ports that ships
could enter.[1]

The task of the blockaders was tedious and vex-
atious rather than dangerous. The enemy could
harm them little, and good sailors in stanch and
well-equipped craft soon learned not to dread even
the storms of Cape Hatteras; but there were long
months of monotonous watching, broken only by
occasional excitement; for the sailor must be always
ready on the instant to spring into the fullest activity. Night was the time to be on the alert; small
open boats patrolling close to the surf and on the
bar were stations more fruitful of results than the
comfortable ships.

As experience developed the faculties and resources of the blockaders, the blockaded kept even

[1] Soley, *Blockade and Cruisers*, 26 et seq.

pace, practising ever new methods of evasion.[1]
Privateering, which in 1861 Jefferson Davis sought
to encourage by the issue of letters of marque, did
not prove profitable, as private ships found better
profit in blockade - running. Soon ordinary craft
gave way to vessels built especially for this purpose. Cargoes shipped from Europe were transferred at the Bermudas or Nassau to long, narrow
vessels, in which everything was sacrificed to speed;
gray in color, these veritable ocean greyhounds
could not at the distance of a few hundred yards be
distinguished in the shadows against the sea, the
horizon mist, or the sandy shore. Creeping stealthily landward, they dashed by night at full speed
through the blockading line, the breakers on the
bar making the engines inaudible, the swiftness of
the almost invisible apparitions baffling the keenest
vision. The sharpest competition prevailed between
pursuer and pursued, but the clutch of the pursuer
became ever more inevitable. Early in 1864, about
two out of three blockade-runners escaped; but before the year ended, forty out of sixty-six that fre-
quented one port were captured. The total number
of blockade-runners of every size captured or destroyed during the war was fifteen hundred and
four.[2]

Great as the risks were, adventurers were always
found to run them, for the gains were enormous.

[1] Scharf, *Confed. States Navy*, 428 et seq.
[2] Soley, *Blockade and Cruisers*, 44.

The ingoing cargoes brought huge profits; and the cotton, laden with which the blockade-runners came out, was better than a gold-mine. It was no uncommon thing to clear one hundred and fifty thousand dollars each way. With such gains possible, blockade - running was profitable even though the vessel made only a trip or two before capture. To captains and crews such bounties were paid that they could soon retire with fortunes. The spirit of adventure was reinforced by the love of gain, and owners were never at a loss to man their ships. The *Robert E. Lee*, from Nassau, ran the blockade twenty-one times within six months, bringing out six thousand bales of cotton and carrying in a miscellaneous assortment of merchandise to a voracious market.[1]

Though the South had at the start few ships to defend her coast, and almost no ship yards, machine shops, or skilled labor, the Confederacy showed, as has been explained, most noteworthy ingenuity in supplying this lack.[2] In coping with the results of this skill, the monotonous life of the Federal blockaders was sometimes relieved. Such was the conflict with the *Virginia*, and certain other achievements of the monitors. At last, in the summer of 1864, came one of the few general fleet engagements on a great scale.[3]

At this time the only port of the Gulf available

[1] Soley, *Blockade and Cruisers*, 156, 166.
[2] See above, p. 62 et seq.
[3] *Battles and Leaders*, IV., 379 et seq.

to blockade-runners was Mobile.   New Orleans had
fallen long before; the ports of Texas since the sun-
dering of the Confederacy by the Federal occupation of the Mississippi were of little service; at
Pensacola the Federal garrison at Fort Pickens
prevented entrance. Farragut had long desired to
attack Mobile, which Grant, Sherman, and Banks
had threatened from the land side. But not until
the midsummer of 1864 did Farragut range his
fleet, the West Gulf blockading squadron strongly
reinforced, before the sandy capes between which
opened the strait that he must force.

Mobile itself lies thirty miles from the Gulf, between which and the city extends the bay, a sheet
of water in some parts fifteen miles in breadth, in
many places too shallow for ocean-going ships, but
in its lower part affording the necessary depth and
space.[1]   To defend this bay, on Mobile Point, the
cape to the east, stood Fort Morgan, an old-fashioned fort of brick, supplemented skilfully by earth
works and sand-bag facings, and heavily armed.
To the west, guarding shallow inlets, lay smaller
works, Fort Gaines and Fort Powell, too distant to
be effective. The main reliance for defence was
Fort Morgan, aided by four vessels, of which by
far the most formidable was the *Tennessee*, the most
powerful of the several rams constructed by the
Confederates during the war, craft always inspiring terror and often inflicting disaster. Upon a low-

---

[1] Mahan, *Gulf and Inland Waters*, 218 et seq.

lying hull was mounted an iron-plated casemate two hundred feet long, its sides sloping at an angle of forty-five degrees, built of solid oak and pine two feet thick, and covered with six inches of iron. Noticeable was the projecting rim or "knuckle" of iron which surrounded the hull, projecting well beyond, and which at the bow was prolonged into the beak which was her principal means of offence. She carried six large Brooke rifled guns, and was commanded by Franklin Buchanan, who commanded the *Virginia* at Hampton Roads. Fatal defects in what otherwise was a most menacing instrument of war, were a weak engine, and steering-gear exposed without protection to shot and shell. More dreaded perhaps than even fort or iron-clad were the torpedoes, then instruments unfamiliar and almost untested. It was known that these were thickly scattered about the harbor, and that a line of them crossed the channel where the ships must pass.

To encounter these obstacles, Farragut had a fleet of eighteen ships; four of these were monitors, and seven wooden ships of over a thousand tons, one, the *Brooklyn*, over two thousand. The *Hartford*, as at New Orleans, was the flag-ship, and several of her consorts with their crews had also taken part in that action. In the early morning of August 5, 1864, the fleet was ranged for battle, the monitors, led by the *Tecumseh*, forming a line by themselves nearer the fort than the wooden ships. As at Port Hud-

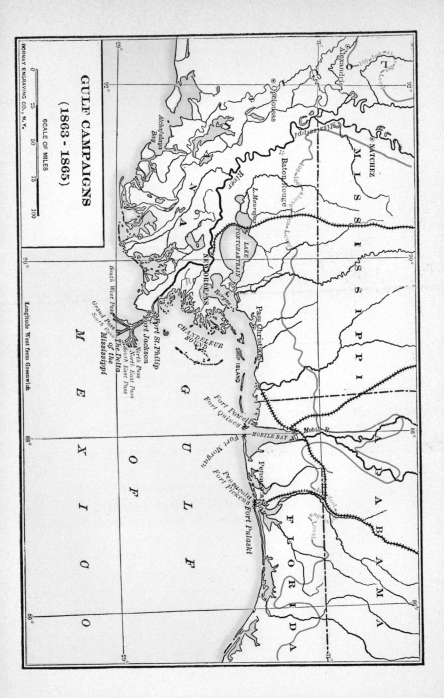

GULF CAMPAIGNS
(1863 - 1865)

DORNAY ENGRAVING CO., N.Y.

SCALE OF MILES

0   25   50   75   100

Longitude West from Greenwich

son, lashed to the port side of each large ship was a smaller vessel, to carry her out of action should she be disabled. Some vessels had been strengthened at the bow, to serve as rams; the *Brooklyn* carried a device for grappling torpedoes; all were stripped of superfluous spars and tackle. Very unwillingly Farragut, yielding to the pressure of his captains, allowed the *Brooklyn* to lead the line of wooden ships, which was formed just west of the monitors. The flood-tide set strongly, a mild west wind was dissipating the haze as the squadron started.[1]

Immediately upon reaching the perilous point in the channel, where the guns of Fort Morgan, now in full activity, told with most effect, the startling drama began. The *Tecumseh*, whose guns opened the battle for the fleet, suddenly sank out of sight before the eyes of friend and foe, her screw still whirling in the air as she plunged head-foremost. Her captain, T. Augustus M. Craven, in the pilot-house, gave the one chance for life that offered, to the pilot, perishing himself heroically. It was the work of a torpedo, so deadly that but twenty-one out of her crew of a hundred or so escaped. At once the *Brooklyn* halted, signalling that a line of buoys was immediately in front, a sign of danger. The ships behind, urged by their engines and also the powerful current, were fast drifting together in a disordered huddle, while the hostile cannon overwhelmed them with its deadly fire, and the passage

---

[1] L. Farragut, *David G. Farragut*, 407.

was blocked ahead. The audacity and quick decision of the admiral saved the day. He ordered the *Hartford* ahead; to get a view above the battle-smoke, he climbed high into the rigging, where he was lashed to the shrouds by a watchful sailor lest wounded he should fall to the deck. Rushing at full speed past the halting *Brooklyn*, the *Hartford's* company soon heard beneath the hull the knocking of torpedoes and even the discharge of the primers; but by good fortune not one exploded.

Presently the *Hartford* passed into the bay, and now had new adversaries to confront in the hostile fleet, which, though few in number, showed no lack of spirit. While smaller gun-boats raked her from the front, the *Tennessee* approached, slow but terrible. Buchanan, seeing that his unwieldy vessel could cope but poorly with the more active *Hartford*, changed his course, running amuck down the line of Federal ships, which were pushing fast after the admiral through the channel into the bay. The crew of the *Tennessee* were intrepid, not shrinking from the broadsides which rained at close quarters upon her armor. Her guns were not idle, but through some defect in the ammunition they often missed fire; her beak, too, through the weakness of her engine, could not well be brought to bear in the swift flood-tide. Nevertheless, the spectacle and uproar were frightful; the fleet in general suffered, and the *Oneida*, completely crippled, was towed along by her consort.

When at length the ships had gathered near the *Hartford* within the bay, the fort batteries now wholly passed, the *Tennessee* approached again, throwing herself into the fray alone. A wilder mêlée than now ensued has rarely been seen upon the waters. Following the admiral's signal, every ship sought to run down the *Tennessee*, which, selecting the flagship, thrust her beak steadily forward. The *Hartford*, nothing loath, rushed head on towards her adversary, swerving just before the impact so that the ram failed to strike fairly. The "bluff of the bows" on each side came together, the ships grating past each other, the broadsides thundering into the opposing muzzles. The other ships were quite too near at hand. First the *Monongahela* struck her blow, her prow crumbling against the "knuckle" of the *Tennessee*, which received no harm. A blow from the *Lackawanna* was equally fruitless, and as that vessel swept round to repeat her dash, in the confusion where each ship was eager for a chance, missing her foe she crashed into the starboard side of the *Hartford*, cutting through to within two feet of the water-line. The end was now near. As the *Ossipee* drove forward in her turn, the monitors at the same moment closing up, a white flag tied to a boat-hook was thrust up from the *Tennessee*. Her exposed steering-gear had been shot away, her smoke-stack was demolished, she lay unmanageable. While inflicting little harm, she had received really little; but two of her crew

were killed and ten wounded within the almost in-
vulnerable casemate; and all the broadsides hurled
upon her were far from having made her a wreck.

The sum of the damage to the Federals was
heavy, though the victory was great. Besides the
drowned crew of the *Tecumseh*, fifty-two were killed
and one hundred and seventy wounded, by far the
longest list of casualties being on the *Hartford*,
which also had the narrowest escape from sinking.
Several other Federal vessels were destroyed by
torpedoes before Mobile Bay was fully possessed.
Fort Gaines and Fort Powell soon surrendered; after
which a land force of five thousand men co-operat-
ing with the fleet, the resistance of Fort Morgan was
beaten down, and it was captured on August 23.
The port was thus closed to blockade-runners, though
the city held out till the following spring.

One ram still remained to the Confederacy, the
Albemarle, which in North Carolina waters threatened the blockade as the *Virginia*, *Arkansas*, and
Tennessee had done elsewhere. On the Roanoke
River, in April, 1864, she destroyed a man-of-war,
and played an important part in the recapture of
Plymouth by the Confederates, and now lay moored
at Plymouth preparing for another onslaught. No
bolder or more brilliant achievement was performed
by the navy during the war than the sinking of this
dangerous ship, October 28, 1864, by Lieutenant
W. B. Cushing. Stealthily making his way up the
river by night with a small crew of picked men, his

launch lay beside his victim before it was discovered. Forcing his craft at full speed over the boom of logs which surrounded the ship, at the moment when a heavy gun, discharged within a few feet, almost shattered the assailant by concussion, he coolly applied to the ram's side a torpedo, then pulling the cord, was submerged with his men in the destruction that followed the explosion. The shattered vessel was sent to the bottom; of Cushing's crew, some were drowned, some made prisoners in the water, while two or three, among them the lieutenant himself, were saved by swimming. The destruction of the *Albemarle* was perhaps the last noteworthy achievement of the blockaders, crowning well their long service of watching and exposure.[1]

The Confederate navy accomplished little on the western rivers; such craft as could be brought to bear were no match for the northern gun-boats, which after the fall of Vicksburg nearly had the field to themselves. Against the blockade, too, while the Confederacy maintained the struggle longer, it had, as we have seen, only small success. On the open ocean, however, the southern commerce-destroyers performed remarkable feats, bringing to the Union great disaster.[2]

The Geneva arbitration tribunal in 1872 awarded to the United States fifteen and a half millions of

[1] *Naval War Records*, X., 620; *Battles and Leaders*, IV., 635 et seq.; Soley, *Blockade and Cruisers*, 104.
[2] *Naval War Records*, I.–III.

dollars for ships destroyed by Confederate cruisers
constructed in British ports, at the same time dis-
allowing all claims for indirect or consequential
losses.[1] Scharf gives a list of two hundred and
fifty-eight prizes captured by nineteen cruisers.[2]

While the money awarded at Geneva was an
offset to this loss, for the large indirect loss there
was no compensation. The case of the United
States at Geneva states that in 1860 two-thirds of
the foreign commerce of New York was carried on in
American bottoms; that the transfers to the British
flag, to avoid capture of ships, were, in 1861, 126;
in 1862, 135; in 1863, 348; in 1864, 106. In 1865
the number of foreign ships frequenting the harbor
of New York was three and one-half times greater
than in 1858.[3] The merchant-marine of the United
States was near extinction. The vessels, large and
small, by which this remarkable result was accomplished—258 captures and 715 transfers, most of
them because of fear of capture—appear to have
numbered nineteen.

The actual damage done was but a part of the
effect of the Confederate cruisers' action; they
involved the United States and Great Britain in a
passionate controversy. Under the usual practice
in time of war, no war-vessel or privateer of either
belligerent enters the waters or ports of neutrals

[1] For the award, see *Am. Annual Cyclop*, 1872, p. 261.
[2] Scharf, *Confed. Navy*, 814 et seq.
[3] *Am. Annual Cyclop.*, 1865, p. 183.

except by special leave of the authorities: if such
permission is granted, vessels are expected to go to
sea within twenty-four hours, except in stress of
weather, and take on only supplies necessary for
immediate use. Neutral ports and waters must not
be places of resort for war-purposes or for equipment:
only coal enough should be sold to take ships to the
nearest port of their own country; if supplied once
they ought not to be supplied again within three
months. The British foreign office issued for the
guidance of colonial authorities instructions [1] in this
sense: but in the British colonial ports often little
attention was paid to the obligations of neutrals.
The Confederate cruisers were sometimes allowed
to coal to their full capacity, and even to refit, and
in violation of the British foreign enlistment act to
replenish their crews; while at the same time the
cold shoulder was turned to the vessels of the United
States. [2] In the rest of the foreign world also there
was much carelessness as to the obligations of
neutrals, the neglect of international rules becoming more marked when the cause of the Union was
depressed.

Such were the conditions which made possible
the extended careers of the Confederate cruisers;
let us now turn our attention to particular vessels.
The agency of one man here was so noteworthy
that he must be put in the foreground. Raphael

[1] Moore, *International Arbitration*, I., chap. xiv., 495.
[2] Porter, *Naval Hist. of Civil War*, 817.

Semmes was an officer of the old navy, a man of enterprise and capacity, who, forsaking his allegiance, presently became captain of the *Sumter*,[1] the pioneer of the commerce-destroyers. She was a Havana trader of five hundred tons, converted into a man-of-war, and in the summer of 1861 Semmes succeeded in eluding the Federal fleet at the Mississippi passes and getting to sea. He could give and take hard blows, but to cripple the commerce of the Union was the task set for his ship; and with an eye single to that end he avoided the men-of-war that swarmed after him, as he swooped down upon the defenceless merchant-ships in his path. From the first he displayed great astuteness, escaping from the powerful *Brooklyn*, which was overhauling him off Pass à l'Outre, by a manœuvre which made her sails useless in the pursuit. He began his work at once, finding his weapon in the torch rather than the cannon, and terror soon prevailed. It was an ignoble warfare directed against the civilian ship master, unarmed and unsuspecting: it was, however, very effective, a blow at the Union resources which told forcibly.

It is only fair to say that, except for burning his prizes, Semmes did nothing for which there was not precedent in the usages of war.[2] Forgetting their own history of intrepid service on privateers and cruisers from early colonial days, throughout the War of 1812, the United States set up an angry

[1] Semmes, *Service Afloat*, chap. ix.
[2] Soley, *Blockade and Cruisers*, 229.

outcry against the operations of the *Sumter* as
barbarous. The conscience of the world was beginning at that time to be sensitive. In 1856 the
United States, through Marcy, then secretary of
state, suggested an amendment to the Declaration
of Paris, with a view to prohibiting in war the
seizure of private property on the sea.[1] This was
not adopted, and though the more active spirit
of humanity among civilized men plainly favored
such a prohibition, the practice both on land and
sea, during the American Civil War, fell away on
either side into methods transmitted from the rude
past. Such were the methods of Semmes: such, before
the war ended, were the methods of many honored
Federal leaders at which we shall later have to glance.

The *Sumter* was active throughout the rest of
1861, destroying many ships and eluding all pursuit.
By a clever ruse at Martinique, Semmes sent the
swift *Iroquois*, which had overtaken him, on a wild-
goose chase southward while the *Sumter* sped north.
In the West Indies neutral obligations hung light-
ly on officials, and the cruiser was little troubled.
Crossing at last to Spain, the authorities at Cadiz
were colder, and in January, 1862, the *Sumter* found
herself at Gibraltar with Federal men-of-war close
by. She could not escape, and was at last sold,
ending her career later as a blockade-runner.[2]

[1] Cf. Smith, *Parties and Slavery* (*Am. Nation*, XVIII.), chap.
xviii.; *Exec. Docs.*, 34 Cong., 3 Sess., 35.

[2] Soley, *Blockade and Cruisers*, 173 et seq.

Following the course of Semmes, we pass now to
the *Alabama*, which, having been constructed in
and having escaped from England amid circumstances already described,[1] was now awaiting her
captain. The cruises upon which she was about
to enter and the results following from them make
her one of the famous ships of history. Taking
command of the *Alabama* in the Azores, August 20,
1862,[2] Semmes utilized his previous experience in
the *Sumter*, establishing accurately in the main
ocean highways the strategic points where his
depredations would tell best. He estimated how
long it would take the news of his operations to
reach the United States; and before the eager Federal ships could find him, the commerce-destroyer,
which could render more important service than to
wait for a fight, was off to new fields.

Semmes began the cruise of the *Alabama* in the
North Atlantic, in two months seeking the West
Indies, whence after a second two months he dropped
southward into the track of the South American
traders; thence, after many successes, to Brazilian
waters, to the Cape of Good Hope, to the Straits
of Sunda, and still more distant spots—in each case
choosing a station where main arteries of traffic
interlace. Wherever the *Alabama* turned, the ocean
was enlivened with the conflagration she kindled,
the cargoes, after being rifled, perishing with the

[1] See Hosmer, *Appeal to Arms* (*Am. Nation*, XX.), 315 et seq.
[2] Semmes, *Service Afloat*, 404.

ships; the captured crews were disposed of with little reference to their well-being or convenience. She was in constant motion, getting supplies from her prizes or obsequious neutrals; and when repairs must be made, some obscure port was found where there was no danger of disturbance. Sometimes Semmes, arming his prizes, commissioned them to act as ships-of-war.

Such was the *Alabama's* course for nearly two years, during which time, though swift ships and able commanders were ever hot upon the scent, the enemy was baffled and the purpose of the long cruise thoroughly carried out. Rarely has a great end been accomplished with means so small. The commerce-destroyer justified her name, her list of captures amounting to sixty-eight.[1] In merchant-shipping the United States, at the appeal to arms, stood second among the nations: this position she lost, to a great extent through the *Alabama* and her consorts, though partly through the coming in of iron ships.

The *Alabama* met with a dramatic fate. Fatigued perhaps with his success, Semmes in the summer of 1864 brought his ship back to the English Channel, and while sheltering in Cherbourg, was challenged by the *Kearsarge*, only slightly superior in size and armament. A fierce passage-at-arms took place off Cherbourg, June 19, 1864. Like fighting eagles the two ships circled at speed through mile after mile.

[1] Scharf, *Confed. Navy*, 815.

The practice of the *Kearsarge* was more certain, though a shell lodged in her stern-post by the *Alabama*, had it exploded, would have been fatal. But it was the *Alabama* which sank at last beneath the waves.[1]

The career of the *Alabama* far surpasses in interest that of any other of the Confederate cruisers. Semmes was both skilful and lucky; but while his prizes surpassed in number and value those of any other craft, much has been attributed to his ship which belongs to others. Of the nineteen vessels which Scharf enumerates, several were small, and others never got fairly to sea. Glancing at those whose activity was important, the next to note is the *Florida*, which, as has been mentioned, escaped from England in the spring of 1862 as the *Oreto*.[2]

She reached Nassau, in the Bahamas, April 28, and not far away from there was suffered by the near sighted officials to arm and equip herself as a man-of-war. Entering upon a cruise, her crew, including her captain, Maffitt, were attacked by yellow fever: on this account, and also because she found her armament imperfect, she sought Mobile, getting safely under shelter of Fort Morgan in September.[3]

In January, 1863, the *Florida* emerged, and, eluding the blockaders, appeared once more at Nassau,

---

[1] *Battles and Leaders*, IV., 615; *Naval War Records*, III., 71 et seq.   [2] Hosmer, *Appeal to Arms* (*Am. Nation*, XX.), 315.
[3] Soley, *Blockade and Cruisers*, 183 et seq.

with a fresh crew and with her defects remedied.
It was just after Fredericksburg, and the British
officials were very indulgent; while the people of
the little town, who were prospering greatly because
the blockade-runners made it their rendezvous, gave
the *Florida* an ovation.   She was allowed to stay
thirty-six hours instead of twenty-four, to obtain
coal for three months, and shortly after to obtain
still more at Barbados—all of which was contrary
to the instructions laid down in London by the
foreign office.   Well supplied now in every way,
her depredations became important: she ranged
from the latitude of New York to Bahia, in Brazil,
capturing and burning many prizes in much fre-
quented seas.   One prize, the *Clarence*, was preserved
and set out independently, having a history worth
remarking.   Receiving a small armament and a
crew under Lieutenant Read, the *Clarence*, in June,
1863, after Chancellorsville and when Vallandigham
was stirring up Ohio, appeared close off the coast,
and between capes of Virginia and Portland, Maine,
made several captures.   Making a transfer to the
Tacony, one of his prizes, a better ship, Read soon
had ten more prizes.   By still another transfer, the
bold sailors found themselves on the *Archer*, from
which craft, in a daring boat-expedition into Portland harbor, they cut out the United States reve-
nue-cutter *Cushing*.   The activity of this handful of
men much aggravated the depression of the North,
now at its lowest point.   But Read was presently

captured by an expedition sent out from Portland, and consigned to Fort Warren.

In the summer of 1863 the *Florida* crossed the ocean to Brest, in France, whence six months later she appeared again refitted. Allowed to coal at various places, through negligence or favor, she patrolled the Atlantic until October, 1864, when her work came to a sudden end at Bahia, in Brazil. Here, in port, she encountered the Federal ship *Wachuset*, whose commander, Collins, paying no attention to neutral rights, captured her, October 7. This seizure, a gross violation of international law, Collins sought to justify as proper retaliation for breaches of the law of which Brazil had been guilty. It was, however, disowned by the government as an assumption of authority quite unwarranted.[1] The *Florida* was ordered to be returned, but by an accident, the nature of which was never a mystery, she sank in Hampton Roads.

Several vessels from which the Confederacy had hoped much either failed entirely to get to sea or found their efforts frustrated. The "Laird rams" served no good purpose;[2] the *Alexandra*, crossing to Nassau in 1863, was there held, and accomplished nothing; the *Rappahannock*, which had once been a despatch-boat of the British navy, frightened off early in 1864, while unprepared, and taking refuge at

[1] Porter, *Naval Hist. of the Civil War*, 813; Scharf, *Confed. Navy*, chap. xxvi.

[2] Hosmer, *Appeal to Arms (Am. Nation*, XX,), 317.

Calais, was kept inactive there under the guns of a
French man-of-war; the *Nashville*, a beautiful ship,
was destroyed by the monitor *Montauk* near Savannah, February, 28, 1863. The *Georgia* had only a
brief career: built in the Clyde, and escaping in
April, 1863, her construction and equipment managed by a British firm which was afterwards prose-
cuted, she cruised for some months in the middle
and south Atlantic. Seized at last by the *Niagara*,
she was taken into Boston and condemned. An
especially formidable craft was the *Stonewall*, a
French-built partially armored ram, which had belonged to Denmark. Coming late into Confederate
ownership, in March, 1865, she defied, off Ferrol, in
Spain, two Federal ships, the *Niagara* and *Sacra-
mento*, which, safe in harbor, pursued the discreet
course of remaining there. In the end she was sold
to Japan.[1]

With the exception of the *Alabama*, the most
famous and the most fortunate commerce-destroyer
was the *Shenandoah*, a ship of seven hundred and
fifty tons, with auxiliary steam-power, very fast,
which had been in the East India trade. She cleared
for Bombay from London, October 8, 1864; but
having been bought beforehand by Captain Bulloch, met near Madeira a vessel containing Captain
I. T. Waddell of the Confederacy, together with a
crew, and also an armament; and was presently
equipped for her work. Since now American mer-

[1] Scharf, *Confed. Navy*, 805.

chant-ships were becoming rare in the ocean highways, the *Shenandoah* followed a new course, planned
by Commander J. M. Brooke, at Richmond, who
in 1855, as a member of the North Pacific ex-
ploring expedition, had learned the habits and
haunts of the great American whaling-fleet. Forsaking the Atlantic, the *Shenandoah* sailed far south
to Tristan d'Acunha, landing there the crews of
prizes she had taken: afterwards she appeared in
Melbourne, Australia, where, with small respect for
the neutrality laws, the authorities allowed her to
remain a month, meantime undergoing repairs, coal-
ing abundantly, and finally, in spite of the foreign
enlistment act, recruiting forty-three men.[1] Thence
she started in February, 1865, upon the track of the
whalers—ships often manned by their owners, poor
men winning a livelihood in the most exposed and
dangerous of callings. Following her prey from
point to point, she was heard of among the Caroline
Islands, in the neighborhood of Honolulu, and later
in the sea of Ochotsk and at Bering's Straits. It
was an inglorious warfare, but carried on with skill,
and telling heavily. The whaling industry was almost extinguished. So remote were her operations
that she long failed to hear of the close of the war,
her commander not being convinced until June 28,
1865, that his cause was lost. He then set sail for
Liverpool to deliver up his ship to the British gov-

[1] See text of award of the Geneva Tribunal, *Am. Annual
Cyclop.*, 1872, p. 262.

ernment. These operations, continued two months after Lee's surrender, were the final throes of the expiring Confederacy.

The Federal navy, at the end of 1864, when its work in the Civil War had been substantially accomplished, comprised 671 vessels (a few of the number being under construction), carrying 4610 guns, measuring 410,396 tons, and manned by 51,000 officers and sailors. The captures by the navy during the war amounted to 1379 vessels, of which 267 were steamers.[1] But, aside from its prizes, what the navy achieved in its various fields of effort, on the rivers, the blockaded coast, and the high seas, cannot be put down in figures. If it be admitted that the army was "the right arm of the government" in maintaining the Union, then the government had two right arms, for the work on the waters can be postponed to no second place.

[1] Lincoln, *Works* (ed. of 1894), II., 609 (Message of December 5, 1864).

CHAPTER XI

SHERIDAN IN THE VALLEY
(JULY, 1864–FEBRUARY, 1865)

WHILE the navy, in July and August of 1864, by the victory of the *Kearsarge* in the English Channel and the triumph in Mobile Bay, did much to lighten discouragement at the North, nothing happened on land to relieve the situation either in the eastern or western theatre. About Petersburg and Richmond, Grant was constantly beaten back. His strategy, so successful at Vicksburg, now came to naught; and his hard blows accomplished no more. No doubt the trouble was partly due to inefficient subordinates men retained in high command for other than military reasons, who lacked the soldierly quality. The chief cause, however, of Union disaster, was the ability of Lee, who applied his armies and resources with consummate generalship, to the confusion of his foes. Grant could not press him so hard as to prevent his sending a corps of his best troops to the suburbs of Washington. Though Early just failed to capture the capital, it was more than three months before he ceased to cause anxiety. As he withdrew, July 12, 1864, to the

valley of Virginia before the Sixth Corps, opportunely arriving, Wright followed him hard; while Hunter,
having made a toilsome circuit by the Kanawha
and Ohio, after his attempt upon Lynchburg, could
bring the Eighth Corps to bear near Harper's Ferry:
could Hunter and Wright but unite, Early would
be in danger. Grant, anxious to strike a blow near
Richmond before Early could return to Lee, wished
to divert the Sixth and Nineteenth Corps (the latter
just arriving from Louisiana) to strengthen the force
before Petersburg. While Wright drew back towards Washington in preparation for embarking,
Crook with the Eighth Corps alone confronted
Early, and July 24 was struck heavily on the old
battle-ground at Kernstown. Plainly it was no
time for withdrawing troops from the valley.[1]

The Sixth and Nineteenth Corps marched back
through the dust and heat—for forty-six days no
rain fell—to find Crook in Maryland guarding the
South Mountain passes, with Averell at the Potomac
fords; while Early, more alert than ever, broke up
the Baltimore & Ohio Railroad and despatched a
raiding-party under McCausland into Pennsylvania.
The latter failing to receive from Chambersburg a
requisition of one hundred thousand dollars in gold,
burned the town to the ground, July 30, and departed
on similar errands. Though panic reigned, the situation presently improved. Wright joining Crook,

[1] Pond, *Shenandoah Valley*, 94 et seq.; *Battles and Leaders*,
IV., 500 et seq.

the Federals again became formidable; Averell, pur-
suing McCausland into Virginia, defeated him at
Moorefield, August 7, 1864. Grant, much harassed,
now arrived upon the scene.

C. A. Dana, at this time in Washington, makes
very vivid the need of a head;[1] things were at sixes
and sevens, and a radical change was demanded.
Four military departments, not long before constituted—West Virginia, Pennsylvania, Washington,
and the Middle Department—were consolidated into
the Middle Military Division, to command which the
best man must be found. Grant suggested W. B.
Franklin, whom he highly esteemed; but a shadow
from Fredericksburg and the Red River campaign
hung over Franklin. The lieutenant - general then
spoke of Meade, whom Hancock might replace
at the head of the Army of the Potomac, while
Gibbon took the Second Corps.[2] That, too, seemed
inadmissible; whereupon Grant fixed upon Sheridan, a selection straightway approved. He was
thirty - three years old, so young, Lincoln frankly
told him, as to cause apprehension in view of the
vast responsibility he was to assume. His principal subordinates, and even officers less prominent,
outranked and in some cases had commanded him.
Wright, when at the head of a department, had
recommended Sheridan for a brigadier's commission;
W. H. Emory, the excellent veteran at the head of

[1] Dana, *Recollections*, 230.
[2] Pond, *Shenandoah Valley*. 112.

the Nineteenth Corps, graduated from West Point
the year Sheridan was born;[1] D. A. Russell, a di-
vision-general of the Sixth Corps, when a captain,
long had Sheridan under him as a subaltern. These
worthy seniors, however, took up their work without a murmur, doing their best; while a noble band
of younger men pressed on towards high places.
Crook was Sheridan's classmate; Merritt and Custer,
in their portraits of that time, look like boys; while
Charles Russell Lowell, first scholar of the Harvard
class of 1854, was brilliantly leading a cavalry brigade.

Though the force in the Middle Military Division
was large, Sheridan's army in the field numbered
only about twenty - six thousand men, to whom
Early opposed about twenty thousand.[2] Early was
backed, however, by a friendly population, among
whom the young men were eager for partisan service. Ashby was gone, but Gilmor, McNeil, above
all Mosby, remained, and at the head of guerilla
bands hung always upon the skirts of the Federals,
cutting off detachments, stragglers, and all trains not
strongly guarded. It is not pleasant to record that
the war was now assuming a more ruthless aspect
than heretofore.[3] "In pushing up the Shenandoah
Valley," wrote Grant, August 5, "it is desirable that
nothing should be left to invite the enemy to return. Take everything necessary for the troops—
horses, mules, cattle, food, and forage, and such as

[1] Cullum, *Register of U. S. Military Acad.*, art. Emory.
[2] Sheridan, *Personal Memoirs*, I., 471–475   [3] *Ibid.*, 486.

cannot be consumed, destroy. The people should
be informed that so long as an army can subsist
among them, recurrences of these raids must be
expected, and we are determined to stop them at
all hazards." [1] While dwellings were to be preserved, the devastation was to be so complete that
"a crow flying over the country would need to carry
his rations." The garden of Virginia was to be
made a desert. The valley population, among
whom were a considerable element of non-resistant
Dunkards and Quakers, had been allowed to a large
extent to commute for service in the field by furnishing subsistence, which had been rendered plenti-
fully.[2] By laying waste the farms this was made
impossible. If the Confederates never systemati-
cally practised like measures, it was due to the lack
of opportunity and not of disposition. McCausland's raid on Chambersburg showed them to be
without scruple.

As Sheridan, in the first days of August, with his
strong army resting on a secure base near Harper's
Ferry, faced the Confederates, Early retired southward along the valley pike, so much tramped in
these years, to Strasburg, whither Sheridan cau-
tiously followed, the mountain Massanutten, as two
years before, looking down on the manœuvres.[3]
Here Early was formidably reinforced, and Sheridan

---

[1] Pond, *Shenandoah Valley*, 118; Cf. Sheridan, *Personal Memoirs*, I., 464.   [2] Pond, *Shenandoah, Valley*, 2.
[3] *War Records*, Serial No. 90, pp. 8–613 (Shenandoah Valley).

prudently countermarched before the refluent enemy,
once more to Harper's Ferry, which, said the wits,
ought rather to be called, from its periodical occu-
pations, *Harper's Weekly*. Once more Early wrecked the Baltimore & Ohio road, and set Pennsylvania into panic; while Sheridan, whose reputation
with many was merely that of a hare-brained and
foolhardy fighter, kept to his lines, with what the
impatient country deemed sluggishness.

Towards the end of August, Grant demonstrated
heavily before Petersburg; Lee, it was believed,
must withdraw troops from his valley army to make
good his hold at Richmond, and at last the withdrawal was announced. Through Crook, Sheridan
communicated with a young Quakeress, a school-
mistress of Winchester, who loved the old flag.
When one day tidings came from her that Anderson had marched southward, Sheridan sprang impetuously upon his weakened adversary.[1] On the
morning of September 19, 1864, to Sheridan's 37,711
effectives, Early could oppose scarcely half as many;
yet, thinking light of his opponent, he marched
away from his post at Winchester, with a heavy detachment, leaving in fact but the one isolated division of Ramseur to hold the place. Sheridan
crossed the Opequon Creek, and the infantry was
soon driving Ramseur to the rear. An unfortunate
delay on the part of the infantry gave Early time
to return, when Rodes and Gordon hurried at once

[1] Sheridan, *Personal Memoirs*, II., 5.

to Ramseur's help. A brilliant flank attack, in
which Russell, of the Sixth Corps, lost his life,
checked the Confederate advance. Just here fell,
on the other side, Robert E. Rodes, a splendid soldier, who led Stonewall Jackson's charge at Chancellorsville, and had never failed in action. Early
now was forced back, fleeing south to Strasburg
without pause. The losses in killed, wounded, and
missing were, Federal, about five thousand; Confederate, about four thousand.[1]

The victory of Opequon Creek, though decided,
was not crushing, Early declaring that Sheridan
showed great incapacity in not destroying him.[2] It
was, however, the first good news that had come to
the North from Virginia for many a day, and it
was made the most of. Closely related to this fight
was that of Fisher's Hill, where Early in his flight
paused in a strong position west of Massanutten.
Sheridan, whose natural impetuosity, long pent up,
now had full course, stormed after him, his numerous and excellent cavalry vexing the Confederate
rear and flank by every art known to troopers.

Early made the most of his resources, posting two
brigades of cavalry in the narrow Luray Valley, east
of Massanutten, besides his main front in the western
valley. September 22, 1864, while Sheridan directed
his main army against Fisher's Hill, he sent Torbert,
with a strong cavalry force, up the Luray Valley

[1] Livermore, *Numbers and Losses*, 127.
[2] Early, *Last Year of the War*, 75.

with the idea of crossing the mountain to assail Early's rear from Newmarket. Through the slack conduct of Torbert the Confederates escaped complete surrounding and capture, though they suffered a great disaster. While Crook charged from the west at Fisher's Hill, Wright and Emory attacked in front. A large number of prisoners and many guns were taken, and the remnant of the army driven south in a disorganized mass.[1] The pursuit continued to Harrisonburg, to Port Republic, and thence to the gaps of the Blue Ridge, through which the fugitives hurried; for the moment the dispossession of the Confederates from their beloved valley was complete.

While the troops of Sheridan now ranged at will from Staunton to Harper's Ferry, and his triumphant corps occupied every point of vantage, neither the spirit nor the resources of the foe were exhausted, so that swiftness and vigilance were as necessary as ever. The policy of devastation drove the population to fury, and guerillas led by Mosby and his colleagues swarmed like hornets wherever there was a chance for reprisal. Nor could Grant so threaten Lee as to prevent the detachment from Richmond of a new army. Kershaw's infantry and Rosser's cavalry were immediately put in motion to succor the valley, and Early, undiscouraged, rallied the fugitives and stragglers till he was strong again. Meantime, on

[1] *War Records*, Serial No. 90, p. 170 et seq. (Fisher's Hill).

13

the Federal side the scheme of devastation was in
full course. Two thousand barns and seventy mills,
filled with the products of the recent harvest, went
up in flames; while all horses, mules, beeves, and
sheep that could be found went to the victors: to
break their power to produce food, even the imple-
ments of the farmers were destroyed. As a rule,
dwellings were carefully spared; but near Harrisonburg, Lieutenant Meigs, a young engineer officer,
was killed by guerillas; whereupon every house
within a circuit of five miles, by Sheridan's orders,
was burned.[1] It was through smoke and ashes at
last that the Federals marched from the upper
valley back to Strasburg, and close in their rear
followed Early, strengthened and confident.

October was now advancing, and Grant pressed
more urgently than ever for aid from Sheridan in
his ill-starred campaign east of the Blue Ridge.
Why did the situation in the valley need a great
army? Surely, after what had been done, the Eighth
Corps, with cavalry, ought to suffice for a guard,
while Wright and perhaps Emory might come back
to the James. The Sixth Corps was indeed put in
motion, but at the moment occurred a thing ominous. At a point on Three Top, the triple summit
of Massanutten, twenty-five hundred feet high, was
a hostile signal-station, from which one day the
Federals made out from the waving flags the following message: "Be ready to move as soon as my

[1] Sheridan, *Personal Memoirs*, I., 484 et seq.

troops join you and we will crush Sheridan.—Longstreet." It was true that Longstreet, after his
wounds in the Wilderness, was in the field again.
Was he coming to the valley, or was it only a Confederate ruse? Sheridan was in doubt, but to be
safe he kept together his three corps and his cavalry.
As to himself, however, he thought he might be
spared for a few days, since Halleck was urgent for
a consultation with him at Washington. Leaving
his camp October 16, he took a train east of the
Blue Ridge and was in the capital on the 17th.
His errand accomplished, he was back at Winchester,
twenty miles from his army, on the evening of the
18th. Hearing from the front that all was quiet,
the general slept soundly till morning.

The message caught from the flags on Three Top
was probably the hoax of some irresponsible joker:
it could not have been sent with Early's connivance,
for its natural result was to strengthen the force in
front of him: Sheridan, on departing from Washington, left his army alert and concentrated, with the
trustworthy Wright in command. But the Confederates were not idle. General J. B. Gordon and
Captain Jed Hotchkiss, the latter an accomplished
engineer officer, climbed Massanutten and surveyed
from Three Top the Federal camps in the valley
below. Through the autumnal woods could be seen
on the Federal left, where Cedar Creek enters the
north fork of the Shenandoah, the tents of the
Eighth Corps, the division of Thoburn on the Fed-

eral left: farther back, *en echelon* towards the west,
lay the Nineteenth Corps; and last the Sixth Corps,
the latter well towards Middletown, the hamlet north
of Strasburg along the line of the valley pike.[1]

What happened to Wright on October 19, 1864,
Sheridan generously declares might easily have
happened to himself.[2] Long before light, Kershaw,
fording the creek, assailed the Eighth Corps in front;
while Gordon, having closely marked the pathway, threw himself upon the left flank.   In the darkness, thickened by a fog from the streams, the
Confederates, who had left even their canteens
behind lest a rattling might betray their approach,
effected a complete surprise.   No Federal commander was warier than Crook, but no warning
came even to him.   Thoburn was killed at once,
and his division thrown into confusion.   Gallantly
active in the wreck was Colonel Rutherford B.
Hayes, commanding the other division, but the
charge could not be stemmed, and soon the Nineteenth Corps was scarcely less demoralized, capable
and well-disciplined though its divisions were, under
William Dwight and Cuvier Grover.   At length the
Sixth Corps became involved, as the lava-flood of
Confederate valor poured northward, Early himself,
now at the head of the troops of Wharton, stimulating the fervor.   The Union lines had time to form.
Ricketts replaced Wright in command of the corps

[1] Gordon, *Reminiscences of the Civil War*, 333.
[2] Sheridan, *Personal Memoirs*, II., 96.

when the latter took the army; but both generals were struck down with wounds, whereupon Getty took the corps, Lewis A. Grant, "Vermont Grant," heading Getty's division. Though the losses and confusion were appalling, the Sixth Corps stood, Grant's Vermonters being conspicuous in their steadfastness. It was now between eight and nine o'clock; the fog was lifting so that the peril could be seen; the Confederates, as often before, too confident of victory, were leaving their colors to plunder the captured camps.[1] Wright, in spite of a wound in the jaw, was still on the field, and though driven from his position some miles northward, was not conquered.

Sheridan at Winchester, on the morning of the 19th, took a comfortable breakfast, undisturbed by reports from the southern outskirts that cannonading could be heard. The night before all was quiet: Wright had announced a reconnoissance, and the volleys might easily come from that. As he set out up the valley at a leisurely pace, the low, continuous rumble became alarming, and he soon encountered signs of a great disaster—frightened fugitives and trains on a run to the rear. Ordering the brigade at Winchester to form a cordon across the turnpike and arrest all flight, he sped forward upon the road, the evidences of rout becoming more plain with every mile. To the unvarying tales of terror he opposed appeals, commands, imprecations, incite-

---

[1] This is denied by J. B. Gordon, *Reminiscences*, 355 et seq.

ments to action; and behind him as he passed, the
fugitives, with courage restored, turned about and
hurried back to duty. Probably during the war
no other such exhibition occurred of the power contained in the magnetic spell of a born leader. He
halted at the position of "Vermont Grant's" men
before the forenoon ended; and Custer, galloping
across the fields from the cavalry, threw his arms
about his neck. The retreat had gone far enough:
there was still time to repossess the old camps, perhaps to do more.

The afternoon brought a Federal triumph. Against
the wall of Massanutten the thunders of the battle
were redoubled: in the disordered mob were extem-
porized formations that proved effective: right and
left the cavalry swept forward pitiless; the unbroken
Sixth Corps was in the heart of the conflict; the hold
of Early upon the field was beaten off; by nightfall
no enemy remained north of the stream save as a
captive. Fifteen hundred and ninety-one Federals,
most of whom Early had taken in the first onset,
were carried off to Richmond: besides these there
was a Federal loss of 4074, among them several of
the best officers of the army. Said Sheridan of
Lowell, who received his death wound in the moment of victory: "I do not think there was a quality I could have added to him: he was the perfec-
tion of a man and a soldier." [1] A Confederate loss of
nearly three thousand was inflicted, young General

[1] Pond, *Shenandoah Valley*, 240.

Ramseur being especially lamented; the cannon which Early had captured were all retaken, with twenty-four of his own. While the infantry paused, the horsemen pursued, until Early's army, stripped of its trains, its flags, to a large extent of its weapons, seemed to melt away into the friendly country that surrounded it.[1]

It was a great defeat, but there was no sign of yielding. Sheridan retired to Winchester, pressed by Grant to operate east of the Blue Ridge and detach troops to Richmond. But even now it was not safe. Rosser was boldly active in the lower valley; and Early, though with only two brigades, stood threatening at Staunton; the irregulars were by no means disposed of. It was not until winter that a part of Sheridan's army reached City Point; with the remainder he undertook winter expeditions of great hardship against the Virginia Central Railroad; and finally, in February, against Early about Staunton. March 2, Custer swept up at Waynesboro all that remained in the way of a regular force, a few war-worn men and trophies, more pathetic than glorious, of battered arms and tattered banners, leaving Sheridan free to appear in a new theatre.

The Federal armies in Georgia and in the Shenandoah Valley had, after difficult struggles, won great triumphs: the Army of the Potomac met harder fort-

[1] Early, *Last Year of the War*, 82; Gordon, *Reminiscences*, chaps. xxiv., xxv.

une. Its labors and sacrifices were colossal, but the spring of 1865 arrived before the series of humiliations which began nearly a year before fairly ended. We have traced these to the midsummer of 1864. Then follow Deep Bottom, the Weldon Road, Reams' Station, Fort Harrison, the Boydton Plank Road, Hatcher's Run—a line of names with most melancholy associations, stretching on to the end of the winter. With dreadful loss, Grant tried now on this side, now on that, to pierce Lee's impregnable defence—a dismal monotony of failure.[1] Yet Lee's communications were partially broken; the strait at Richmond became acute; and the constant impact of the Federal hammer, though often as disastrous to the smiter as to the smitten, slowly told on the scanty resources of the South; the North could stand attrition. In the Federal grip, Lee could send no help to Johnston and Hood, and only a meagre measure to Early in the valley. The iron will of Grant, hard and constant, day in and day out, bore down upon the Confederate resistance. The breaking-point was near.

[1] *War Records*, Serial No. 87, pp. 1–956 (Richmond Campaign); *Battles and Leaders*, IV., 533 et seq.

CHAPTER XII

SHERMAN'S MARCH TO THE SEA
(September, 1864–December, 1864)

ON the night of September 1, 1864, Sherman, then well south of Atlanta, heard explosions which gave evidence that Hood was abandoning the city. Next day he learned that he had not been deceived. Slocum, who had been summoned from Vicksburg to command the Twentieth Corps in place of Hooker (who now resigned in displeasure at the promotion over his head of juniors, and disappeared from history), left his camp on the Chattahoochee and took possession of the city; the four months' campaign had succeeded.[1]

For a week or two a reaction set in from the intense exertion of the summer.[2] After the fatigue and strain, rest was necessary; the terms of regiments were expiring; new troops were arriving, and must be placed and drilled. The portion of the Sixteenth Corps present in Georgia, having lost through wounds its commander, G. M. Dodge, was distributed, one division going to the Twentieth Corps, and

[1] W. T. Sherman, *Memoirs*, II., 108.
[2] Cox, *Military Reminiscences*, II., 292 et seq.

another to the Seventeenth; the name Sixteenth
Corps henceforth belongs to the two divisions now
in Missouri, commanded by A. J. Smith, twelve
thousand serviceable men, as was often proved.
But neither the situation nor the commander made
a long-continued languor possible. Not far off, at
Lovejoy's Station, Hood by the middle of the
month became active again; and Sherman was
ready for new movements.

We have seen that at this time in the Shenandoah
Valley the war was assuming a severer aspect than
before; Grant prescribed and Sheridan carried out
a policy of devastation that was new. The spirit
in the West was no milder, a foretaste of what was
to come appearing in an order for the destruction of
Atlanta and the deportation of its people. Whatever the city contained that could be made useful
to the Confederacy—factories, storehouses, machine-
shops, mills—whether distinctly public property or
the possessions of individuals which might be used
for public purposes, was to be sacrificed; since
Atlanta had become a great centre for supplies, and
had now little importance otherwise, the order
meant a wiping out of the city; its population must
go elsewhere, the Federal general undertaking no
more than to conduct the exodus humanely.[1] Hood
made an earnest protest against the "barbarity"
of the measure, to which Sherman replied with
equal vigor, a controversy of some length taking

[1] W. T. Sherman, *Memoirs*, II . III.

place. But there was no mitigation of the order on the part of Sherman.

It was, however, a time for weapons rather than words. Jefferson Davis appeared in September in the camp of Hood, to concert plans and apply incitements. Beauregard, too, who had done excellent service about Petersburg, after his successful defence of Charleston, came once more to the West as commander-in-chief,[1] soon making his headquarters in the familiar camp at Corinth; while leaving Hood free in the field, he was near at hand for counsel, his jurisdiction including also the region farther west and south throughout Alabama and Mississippi, over which Dick Taylor had been placed.[2]

Passing around Atlanta, Hood was presently on Sherman's communications, breaking up the railroad to Chattanooga and compelling an advance by the Federal army northward to the neighborhood of Marietta. October 5, the important position at Allatoona was in great danger; but Sherman, giving and receiving signals over the heads of the enemy, from Kenesaw Mountain to a station eighteen miles distant, was at last assured of the arrival of the division of John M. Corse, and that Allatoona would be held.[3] Hood made another attempt at Resaca; but the duplicates were close at hand for every part of the railroad that might be destroyed,

[1] Roman, *Beauregard*, II., 283.
[2] Taylor, *Destruction and Reconstruction*, 206 et seq.
[3] W. T. Sherman, *Memoirs*, II., 147.

and Colonel Wright quickly made good every loss. Hood soon marched farther west into northern Alabama, fixing himself at last near Florence, on the bank of the Tennessee River. Sherman followed, being at the end of October at Gaylesville, near the Georgia line, a point beyond which he did not pursue.

In these days, in fact, Sherman was maturing a memorable plan — namely, to cut loose from his base of the summer and march with a great army to the coast, depending upon the country traversed for his support; exactly where he should emerge he was in doubt—whether at Charleston, Savannah, Pensacola, or Mobile. He was convinced that such a march might be made, and that in his absence, Thomas, with troops that were available, could cope with Hood. His sanguine spirit was sure that, could his idea prevail, the heart of the South might be penetrated while the force of Hood was overcome. It was not easy to persuade others. Thomas, to whom a most essential part was assigned, doubted the feasibility of the plan; Lincoln and Grant were full of hesitation, the latter being disposed to insist that Hood should be destroyed before the march to the sea was attempted.[1]

This reluctance was well grounded, for the idea was far from prudent, and critics still urge that the risks should not have been encountered.[2]   This great

[1] W. T. Sherman, *Memoirs*, 153 et seq.
[2] Ropes, in *Atlantic Monthly*, LXVIII., 200.

army would throw itself, without provisions, into the midst of a numerous, brave, and desperately hostile population, to make its way as it could through hundreds of miles to its new base, leaving behind, unvanquished, an army of more than fifty thousand excellent soldiers under very capable direction. "Nothing venture nothing have" is a maxim more applicable in warfare perhaps than in any other sphere; the brilliant successes of Lee came through discarding prudence and taking great risks. Sherman's superiors considered his idea too audacious; but finally, on November 2, Grant yielded, telegraphing, "Go on as you propose." The plan was pushed at once with all possible energy.

Sherman picked for his expedition sixty-two thousand men, divided into four corps,[1] the Fourteenth, under Jefferson C. Davis, the Fifteenth, Peter J. Osterhaus (Logan, the proper commander, being absent), the Seventeenth, Frank P. Blair, and the Twentieth, A. S. Williams: the Fourteenth and Twentieth Corps constituted the left wing, under Henry W. Slocum; the Fifteenth and Seventeenth the right wing, under Oliver O. Howard. Included in the number were five thousand cavalry under Judson Kilpatrick, and there were sixty-five guns. In the rigid selection, poor or doubtful material was sent to the rear. Every man was a seasoned veteran in the best strength and morale; and as perfect as

[1] *War Records*, Serial No. 92, pp. 1–418 (Savannah Campaign); Cox, *March to the Sea, Franklin and Nashville.*

the force was the equipment, though there was nothing superfluous. There were six hundred ambulances and twenty-five hundred wagons, the latter separated into four trains, one for each corps, each train on the march stretching out five miles. While the arms were of the best and ammunition plentiful, the store of food was small: the country was to supply that. Nor were there tents: Sherman himself had only a "fly"—an outer cover; the army in general had nothing but the blue canopy. Stripped thus for work, well shod, clothed, weaponed, in good heart, used to victory, trusting their leaders, full of American intelligence, it is hard to conceive of a more perfect military instrument than Sherman's army.

Communication with Chattanooga was broken November 12, 1864, Atlanta was left behind on the 16th, the conflagration of everything in the city that could be made of service to the Confederacy concluding the occupation. To the reluctantness of the spirit in which Sherman set forth for Savannah— for he determined upon the eastward march—he gave the fullest and frankest expression: "If the people raise a howl against my barbarity and cruelty, I will answer that war is war and not popularity-seeking. If they want peace, they and their relatives must stop the war." To Governor Brown, of Georgia, whom he hoped to detach from the Confederacy, he sent a message that, "If you remain inert, I will be compelled to go ahead and devastate

the State in its whole length and breadth." He
telegraphed Grant, October 9: "Until we can re-
populate Georgia, it is useless for us to occupy it;
but the utter destruction of its roads, horses, and
people will cripple their military resources. I can
make this march and make Georgia howl." On
October 19 he telegraphed to his commissary,
Beckwith: "I propose to sally forth to ruin Georgia and bring up on the sea-shore. Make all dispositions accordingly."[1]

The formal field orders, issued November 9, were
less truculent in tone. While the army was "to
forage liberally on the country," order was to prevail. Each brigade was to have its foraging party,
properly organized and commanded by "discreet
officers." Soldiers were forbidden "to enter dwellings or commit any trespass," while taking what
they might find in gardens. Corps commanders
alone had power to destroy mills, houses, cotton-
gins, etc. Where the army was unmolested, no
destruction of such property was to be permitted;
but if roads were obstructed or bushwhacking occurred, "army commanders should order and enforce
a devastation more or less unsparing, according to
the measure of such hostility."[2]

"I remember well," says Sherman, describing an
occurrence such as must often have happened, "the
appeal of a very respectable farmer against our

[1] W. T. Sherman, *Memoirs*, II., 111, 138, 152, 159.
[2] *Ibid.*, 175.

men driving away his fine flock of sheep. I explained to him that we were a strong, hungry crowd and needed plenty of food; that Uncle Sam was deeply interested in our continued health. We preferred Illinois beef, but mutton would have to answer. Poor fellow! I don't believe he was convinced of the wisdom or wit of my explanation." [1]

The nature of the general was indeed kindly and wholesome, and that, too, was the character of the men whom he commanded: they were really averse to cruelty, and though in the stern warfare a sad overturn of ordinary ethics came about, yet in some ways there was a remarkable abstention from violence: there was almost no wanton slaying of men or maltreatment of women from first to last. No doubt the disposition of the soldiers would have been far milder but for the fact that thirty-two thousand Federal prisoners at Andersonville, within the state, they believed were dying of starvation, though in a land of apparent plenty.

The army set out in perfect autumnal weather, in the highest spirits, and it soon became apparent that their enterprise was to be in the nature of a cheerful excursion, rather than a course of peril and hardship. The country teemed from an abundant harvest. Howard struck southeast towards Macon: [2] Slocum, whom Sherman accompanied, marched towards Augusta, the diverging directions

[1] W. T. Sherman, *Memoirs*, II., 158.
[2] Howard, in *Battles and Leaders*, IV., 663.

of the wings perplexing the foe as to the destination. Indeed, no effective opposition was possible for the South: a skirmish took place near Macon between Georgia troops and one brigade of the Fifteenth Corps; and the left wing was aware of the neighborhood of Wheeler on its flank with a small body of cavalry. In the main, the progress was quite unimpeded, excepting that the negroes trooped from far and near, young and old, sick and well, in a vague, childlike hope of being led into some promised land of plenty and freedom. Receiving a certain number of able-bodied men as pioneers, Sherman turned the rest back: they must patiently await the good time to come.

Three hundred miles lay between Atlanta and Savannah: after a week the two wings were to rendezvous at Milledgeville. Marching from twelve to fifteen miles a day, this was easily accomplished by November 23.[1] Leaving Sherman well on his way, let us turn to Thomas, whose task proved to be more difficult than that of his chief.

Grant sent west from the Army of the Potomac James H. Wilson, to lead the cavalry, with the work of which arm in the Atlanta campaign Sherman had not been satisfied. Grant thought Wilson would increase the value of the cavalry fifty per cent., and at first desired that Wilson should attempt the march to the sea, while Sherman and the infantry should remain behind to dispose of Hood. Different

---

[1] Nichols, *Story of the Great March*, 56.

14

counsel prevailing, Wilson—a young soldier of the
West Point class of 1860—now set against the redoubtable Forrest—remained with Thomas. November was well advanced before Hood was able
to move.[1] He had been slowly accumulating troops
and supplies for a campaign, as the railroads were
everywhere broken up and the region impoverished
and bare of men.   But a formidable army of 53,958
men was at last ready, massed in three corps, under
A. P. Stewart, S. D. Lee, and B. F. Cheatham,
besides the cavalry of Forrest, nearly ten thousand
strong.   The latter was at his best, exciting Sherman's "admiration" by capturing, October 29, with
his troopers and small field-guns, two Tennessee River
gun-boats and five transports.[2]

To oppose Hood, Thomas throughout the fall was
only scantily provided.   Sherman proposed at first
to leave with Thomas only the Fourth Corps, under
D. S. Stanley; but finally spared also the Twenty-
third Corps, under Schofield, the two making up
about twenty-five thousand men. A. J. Smith,
also, with his two divisions of the Sixteenth Corps,
of about twelve thousand men, was to arrive when
he could from western Missouri.   Besides these,
Thomas had Wilson's cavalry, in great part un-
mounted and not organized, and could draw a few
thousand troops from garrisons at fortified posts

---

[1] *War Records*, Serial No. 93, pp. 21–776 (North Alabama and
Middle Tennessee).
[2] Cox, *March to the Sea, Franklin and Nashville*, 15.

and established as railroad guards; and in a strait
he might arm the quartermaster's clerks and em-
ployés at Nashville and elsewhere — untrained men
from whom little could be expected. Thomas,
though not inferior in numbers to Hood, was in
fact ill-prepared, his force being to a considerable
extent raw and widely scattered. Ropes, who
doubts the wisdom of this whole undertaking of
Sherman, urges that he should have at least spared
his lieutenant twelve thousand more men, and made
his march with fifty thousand.[1] Sherman admits
at the time of his departure "things looked squally."
It was with meagre resources that Thomas confronted,
in November, his desperate and skilful adversaries.

The Civil War offers few better examples of military work, from the general-in-chief down, than the
Nashville campaign. Hood's advance began November 20, and was pressed impetuously towards
Nashville, the Confederate leader well knowing his
advantage.[2] Thomas posted Schofield with the
Fourth and Twenty-third Corps, at the moment his
only trustworthy and properly prepared troops,
near the Tennessee line, with instructions to delay
the march of Hood to the uttermost, retiring upon
Nashville only as he was forced.[3] Schofield performed his task with great coolness and ability.
With numbers less than half the Confederate force,

[1] Ropes, in *Atlantic Monthly*, LXVIII., 198 et seq.
[2] Hood, in *Battles and Leaders*, IV., 425.
[3] Schofield, *Forty-six Years in the Army*, 425.

he boldly barred the way northward, yielding only
when Hood, flanking him on the left, was on the
point of striking in upon his rear at Spring Hill.
Here apparently the Confederates lost a great opportunity, and whether the commander or a subordinate was to blame is much controverted.[1] At
all events, Schofield with all his trains and men
passed northward safely on the turnpike, while
their foes slept peacefully about their bivouac-fires
not many rods distant.   A few miles farther on, at
the town of Franklin, the Harpeth River crossed
the line of retreat, and the bridges had been partly
destroyed.   To save his trains, Schofield here made
a stand, November 30.

Leaving the Fourth Corps, under Stanley, and the
Twenty-third Corps, under Jacob D. Cox, on the
south bank, while Wilson with the cavalry obstructed
the fords to the east before Forrest, Schofield himself took post on a fortified hill on the north bank,
whence the whole neighborhood could be overlooked,
and also commanded by the cannon which were
hastily placed   The trains rumbled steadily on over
the bridges which had been partially repaired, and
meantime, throughout the forenoon the two corps
prepared for battle as they could.[2]   Hood was right
at hand, himself so crippled with old wounds as to
be obliged to lie prostrate, but he infused into his
army all possible fire.

[1] Hood, *Advance and Retreat,* 292.
[2] Schofield, *Forty-six Years in the Army,* 175.

The attack was made towards four o'clock of the short autumn day;[1] and into the brief twilight and into a few hundred yards space on either side of the turnpike was compressed one of the most dreadful tragedies of the entire war, the deadly battle between Schofield and Hood, classmates and former friends. Hood's troops were not fully up, lacking two divisions of the corps of S. D. Lee. He had therefore about twenty-seven thousand men, to whom Schofield opposed about the same number.[2] The assailants flung themselves upon the slight Federal intrenchments with a reckless bravery extraordinary even for such soldiers as they, and at the outset came near gaining an advantage that would have been decisive. The division commander who covered the Federal rear in the retreat from Spring Hill, contrary to orders left two brigades isolated on the turnpike, a furlong or so out from the line of works. These were struck with the utmost impetuosity by an entire corps, and fleeing, as they were at once forced to do, in a few moments they came down in disorder upon their friends. Right upon their heels, intermingled with them, indeed, charged the enemy; the troops in position could not fire without killing friends as well as foes; immediately the crowd of fugitives was throwing the lines in the earthworks into confusion, and the pursuers climbed with the pursued into the intrench-

---

[1] Hood, *Advance and Retreat*, 294.
[2] Livermore, *Numbers and Losses*, 131.

ments. Cox was fortunately at the point of danger. The brigade of Opdycke by its steadfastness
prevented a disaster, and, in general, troops could
not behave better.

East, south, and west the assaults were pressed
with fury; the inner and outer slopes of the slight
parapets in some cases were held respectively by
Federals and Confederates, who fought hand to
hand across the crests. But the volleys of the defenders were unremitting and deadly; and from
across the river the rifled guns at Schofield's position crushed many who escaped the musketry. The
repulse at last was complete, and rarely has the loss
been so large in proportion to the number engaged.
About six thousand Confederates fell before Hood
would withdraw, among whom were twelve officers
of the rank of general.[1] One cannot stand to-day
at the Carter House, where the conflict focussed,
surveying the field in front, over which the assailants drove the routed outposts, marking the spot
at the distance of a stone's throw where Cleburne
was slain at the front of his fiery column on the
very muzzles of Cox's infantry, without feeling his
heart beat quick with excitement. It was a narrow chance, but the repulse was complete. Before
the night ended, Schofield, whose losses were scarcely a third those of Hood, took up his march, and

---

[1] Cox, *March to the Sea, Franklin and Nashville*, 97; Cox, *Military Reminiscences*, II., chaps. xliii., xliv.; Cox, *Battle of Franklin*, passim.

next day, with trains, guns, and troops in good order, covered the twenty miles to Nashville.

Great anxiety prevailed as to what Thomas could do to stem Hood's northward rush. In truth, the situation was very precarious. Throughout the fall, Thomas had to face the concentrated force of Hood with an inferior and widely scattered army. The country, the administration, Grant himself, appeared to lack an appreciation of his difficulties. He was censured for sluggishness when he really had at hand no proper means with which to strike. At last, in December, John A. Logan was sent to supersede him, while Grant, quite too impatient, set out from City Point for the West. Nevertheless, all worked to a good end. While Schofield delayed and crippled his powerful adversary, the fine divisions of A. J. Smith had time to arrive from Missouri; an important contingent came in from the outside garrisons, the most numerous and effective part being a detachment from Chattanooga, under J. B. Steedman; the clerks and porters at the great depots stood to arms manfully. When all was ready, a winter storm covered the country with a glare of ice on which neither horse nor man could move. But on December 15 operations became possible.

A Federal victory was now really a foregone conclusion. Hood's force was now only half as large as Thomas's, the Confederates having been reduced by the campaign to less than twenty-four thousand.[1] With discouragement sapping the vigor of the men, and many of the best officers fallen, he was, however, still occupying hills close by Nashville, while the Federal army slowly but surely and thoroughly accumulated. In the attack of December 15, Steedman held the left of Thomas, and did well; Schofield had the centre; but the main work of the day was assigned to the fresh troops of A. J. Smith and to Wilson's cavalry, who were on the right. The Confederates, outnumbered and disheartened, were soon driven: nor was a second attempt to stem the Federal victory the following day more successful. Retreat became rout, culminating in an annihilation such as had followed no previous defeat of the war. Wilson swept from the state of Tennessee every trace of Confederate power. The joy of the North was the more keen from the apprehension which up to the moment of victory had been so oppressive.

The peals and calvoes after Nashville were scarcely quieted when on Christmas eve Lincoln received the following telegram: "I beg to present you as a Christmas gift the city of Savannah, with one hundred and fifty heavy guns, plenty of ammunition, also about twenty-five thousand bales of cotton.— W. T. Sherman, major-general."[2] The march to the sea was accomplished. The later stages were no more difficult or dangerous than the beginning.

---

[1] Livermore, *Numbers and Losses*, 132.
[2] W. T. Sherman, *Memoirs*, II., 231.

The steady rate of twelve or fifteen miles a day was adhered to: no force blocked the path: no storms occurred to mar the pleasure of the excursion. Throughout a belt of country some sixty miles in width, sixty-two thousand men had marched, laying waste as they went—a drastic process, which brought the Confederacy to its knees as nothing else could have done.   The defences of Savannah were easily overpowered, though Hardee was in command.   That prudent general, however, escaped capture, and with a small army made ready as he could for still another fight.

CHAPTER XIII

PREPARATIONS FOR READJUSTMENT OF THE STATES

(September, 1864–March, 1865)

THE series of Federal successes beginning with the victory of the *Kearsarge* over the *Alabama*, June 19, 1864, and followed up by the triumph in Mobile Bay, the capture of Atlanta, the overthrow of Early in the valley of Virginia, the repulse of Hood, and the march through Georgia to the sea, established the administration firmly. It was really a piece of great good fortune for Lincoln and his friends that the depression prevailing at the end of August made it possible for Vallandigham to give tone to the Chicago convention. For the war had no sooner been declared a failure in the Democratic resolutions than the declaration was proved absurd. As victory followed victory till the year closed, the absurdity deepened, until the party that had made the declaration became almost a laughing-stock. The mutterings and contrivings of the opposition, though not discontinued, became impotent. October 19, 1864, occurred the St. Albans raid, an incursion into northern Vermont of twenty or thirty southern sympathizers from Canada, during which a village was badly frightened, but only trifling injury inflicted: this was the most important of a number of attempts to kindle a back-fire, which were of no moment as things came out, but which, had the North experienced the depression of military defeats, would have been dangerous.[1]

As the fall elections proceeded, all went well for the Union party. Maine and Vermont in September gave encouraging majorities: the October states were not behind; and in the presidential election in November came such a "land-slide" as the country has seldom seen.[2] McClellan carried but three among the loyal states, New Jersey, Delaware, and Kentucky, with 21 electoral votes; while Lincoln carried twenty-two states with 212 votes. The early withdrawal of Frémont from the canvass gave to Lincoln most of the radical voters. The congressional elections, for the House which would sit from 1865 to 1867, were overwhelmingly Republican; while in his own party dissensions were quieted, the logic of events thoroughly confuted the error of Lincoln's opponents. He bore himself throughout the canvass with great moderation, dignity, and magnanimity. No point of his conduct is better worth noting than that he discouraged attempts to influence the votes of persons in government employ: civil-service reform was then undreamed of: the

[1] Headley, *Confederate Operations in New York and Canada.*
[2] McPherson, *Polit. Hist. of the Great Rebellion,* 623.

spoils system had full sway; but the president maintained as he could the independent franchise of the office-holder.[1]

The thirty-eighth Congress assembled for its second and last session December 5, 1864, and received on the following day the annual message, which gave main attention to matters connected directly with the war. As to Maryland, which had just abolished slavery, the president declared, "the genius of rebellion will no longer claim her. Like another foul spirit being driven out, it may seek to tear her, but it will woo her no more." He earnestly recommended the adoption of the thirteenth amendment by the present Congress, for the large Republican majority in the next Congress would make sure its ultimate passage.[2]

The receipts from taxation for the fiscal year 1863–1864 were: customs, $102,000,000, internal revenue, $110,000,000, while $623,000,000 were derived from loans. Of this immense total, the war department alone absorbed $691,000,000. The public debt, July 1, stood at $1,740,690,489, which another year of war might raise $500,000,000. Lincoln recommended that loans should be made attractive by exemption from taxation and from seizure for debt to a certain extent, so that the debt, as much as possible, might be owed to the people.

Lincoln referred to the elections as showing the

[1] Nicolay and Hay, *Abraham Lincoln*, IX., 363.
[2] Lincoln, *Works* (ed. of 1894), II., 604.

country was not approaching exhaustion "in the
most important branch of national resources—that
of living men." In spite of the losses, the net increase of voters in the North was 145,551 over 1860.
He declared abandonment of armed resistance to
the national authority on the part of the insurgents
to be the only indispensable condition for ending
the war. As regards emancipation, he declared his
purpose to retract nothing he had said. "If the
people should by whatever mode or means make it
an executive duty to re-enslave such persons, another and not I must be the instrument to perform
it. In stating a single condition of peace, I mean
simply to say, that the war will cease on the part
of the government whenever it shall have ceased on
the part of those who began it."

The pending thirteenth amendment, which had
already passed the Senate, and which Lincoln now
urgently pressed upon the House, came up January
6, 1865, on which day Ashley, who, it will be remembered, had arranged for its reconsideration,[1] took
pains to bring it forward, and made a forcible speech
in its favor.[2] As before, his chief service was in the
way of adroit management; to make up the requisite two-thirds vote, a number of Democrats must
be won; and in reaching these, Ashley's industry and
shrewdness were conspicuous.[3] A debate followed

[1] See above, p. 124.
[2] *Cong. Globe*, 38 Cong., 2 Sess., 138.
[3] Riddle, *Recollections*, 324.

in which a third of the House took part, the stand-
ard-bearer of the opposition being George H. Pendleton, of Ohio, the recently defeated candidate for the
vice-presidency.[1] He again argued that "the power
to amend" did not imply "the power to revolutionize." He was answered at length by Garfield,
and more briefly but effectively by Boutwell, while
the speeches of Scofield, of Pennsylvania, Kasson,
of Iowa, and Rollins, of Missouri, were noteworthy.
The vote was taken January 31, 1865, the galleries
of the House being crowded with a multitude favorable to the amendment. Eleven Democrats threw
their weight in favor, thus assuring the necessary
two-thirds majority—119 to 56;[2] the margin was
narrow, but it was enough. An outburst of excitement and congratulation ensued in which statesmen and spectators took part. Ingersoll, of Illinois,
moved that "in honor of this immortal and sublime
event this House do now adjourn." The Senate
having already taken the necessary action, the
amendment went before the states, and on December 18, 1865, came the official announcement of its
ratification by three-fourths of the number, twenty-
seven out of thirty-five.

To recapitulate here the successive steps of the
process of emancipation, four different methods to
bring it about must be noticed.

(1) By act of Congress, April 16, 1862, slavery

[1] Blaine, *Twenty Years*, I., 537.
[2] *Cong. Globe*, 38 Cong., 2 Sess., 531.

was abolished in the District of Columbia, and June 19 in the territories.[1]

(2) By the definite proclamation of the president, January 1, 1863, as a military measure, slavery was abolished throughout the seceded states excepting Tennessee and certain parts of Louisiana and Virginia.[2]

(3) By direct state action, Maryland adopted an anti-slavery constitution October 10, 1864; Tennessee, which the proclamation had not mentioned, followed, February 22, 1865. Similar constitutions were adopted by Arkansas, January 19, 1864; Louisiana, September, 1864; and Missouri, June 6, 1865.[3]

(4) By the thirteenth amendment, officially announced as ratified December 18, 1865, emancipation was extended to Kentucky and Delaware, besides sanctioning what had gone before, and giving freedom a uniform basis.

The treasury was still a heavy burden to Congress and to the new secretary, Fessenden, who, while he had all mental and moral qualifications for his position, lacked health. During the few months that he held office his service was great, though rather in carrying out policies already entered upon than in originating new devices. In his report of 1864 he urged additional taxation, the people having shown their willingness to bear it; some way for making

---

[1] *U. S. Statutes at Large*, XII., 376, 432.
[2] Lincoln, *Works* (ed. of 1894), II., 287.
[3] McPherson, *Polit. Hist. of the Great Rebellion*, 332, 459, 600.

public lands available for revenue; and the establishment of a sinking - fund. He opposed foreign
loans, advocating the disposal of bonds to the American people, and maintaining that our credit abroad
had been strengthened by the fact that we cared for
the public debt at home—that we had "derived a
pecuniary advantage from self - reliance." As the
disposition to continue the war was unbroken, so
the means for continuing it were in no danger of
failing.[1] Fessenden's suggestions all met with a
good response: the internal revenue was made more
stringent, and the tariff was amended; while, March
3, 1865, a new bond issue of six hundred million dollars was authorized.[2]

Though the war was plainly near its end, the conscription act was made more severe and searching;[3]
there was no neglect or relaxation. Now it was that
the national banking system was strengthened by
further enactment already referred to, imposing a
tax of ten per cent. upon the circulation of state
banks, to go into effect July 1, 1866.[4] This tax was
a practical prohibition of state bank-notes, and before the time fixed that form of circulation had entirely disappeared. The labors of the statesmen
who wrought at the capital were scarcely less ex-
hausting than those of the soldiers. John Sherman,
at the head of the Senate finance committee, de-

[1] Blaine, *Twenty Years*, I., 543.
[2] *U. S. Statutes at Large*, XIII., 468, 469.   [3] *Ibid.*, 487.
[4] Dewey, *Financial Hist. of U. S.*, 328.

clares that when the session closed he was quite broken down;[1] and it may well be believed that the burden borne by his famous brother, then marching through the Confederacy, was no more embarrassing than that of the legislator.

The question of the reconstruction of the states, left in confusion by the controversy over the Davis-Wade bill,[2] was revived in the fall of 1864 by the claim of the "Vest-Pocket Government" to be considered Virginia. After the creation of West Virginia, Peirpoint and his friends removed to Alexandria, claiming as within their jurisdiction the part of Virginia occupied by the Federals—namely, the region about Washington, a county or two on the eastern shore, and the cities of Norfolk and Portsmouth.

Peirpoint made the most of his government, but the result was not impressive. Though his senators remained in their places in the Federal Congress, the House doubted the validity of the election of the one representative appearing; and Butler at Norfolk treated Peirpoint cavalierly. Bates, attorney-general, supported Peirpoint against Butler; and the matter coming before Lincoln, he sustained Bates. Thus reconstruction in Virginia received the countenance of the administration; so in the Southwest, where Lincoln, in November, 1864, checked decisively Generals Hurlbut and Canby,

---

[1] John Sherman, *Recollections*, 297.
[2] See above, p. 139 et seq.

15

officers not considerate of the reconstructed civil
government of Louisiana.[1] When Congress assembled, though the people upheld Lincoln with emphasis, yet Henry Winter Davis and his friends
nursed their wrath; and no long time intervened
before their plan for reconstruction came up anew.
December 15, 1864, the active Ashley, from the
special committee on the rebellious states, of which
Davis was head, introduced a new bill; like the
bill of the previous session, in spite of Lincoln's
public objection, it assumed for Congress the power
to regulate reconstruction; at the same time it con-
ceded recognition to the Louisiana government.
But the temper of the House had changed; the bill
did not find favor, and though Ashley modified it,
presenting it four or five times in different shapes,[2]
it was not made more acceptable. The debate was
earnest, Davis displaying his usual power; while
H. W. Dawes, of Massachusetts, chairman of the
committee on elections, was prominent among his
opponents. A majority of the House had come to
think with Lincoln that it was unwise to prescribe
any one plan; and February 21, 1865, the bill was
laid on the table by a vote of 91 to 64.[3]

In the Senate, February 18, 1865, Trumbull
moved for the recognition of the government of
Louisiana, hinting that should it take place, it
practically involved also that of Arkansas, where

[1] Nicolay and Hay, *Abraham Lincoln*, IX., 436 et seq.
[2] *Ibid.*, 449.   [3] *Cong. Globe*, 38 Cong., 2 Sess., 967 et seq.

the situation was similar. Though a majority was unquestionably in favor, five Republican senators led by Charles Sumner, who was sustained by Wade and Chandler, prevented its passage. The decision was postponed "to to-morrow"—a to-morrow which never came.[1] Thus ended the matter for the thirty-eighth Congress: Lincoln was to make on the subject one more declaration, which will be considered later.

Early in 1865 took place the last and most important attempt to bring about peace, before the final collapse. Francis P. Blair, Sr., whose relations with Jefferson Davis had been intimate, always restless and full of schemes, believed himself to be a medium to bring about an accommodation. Without any authority from Lincoln, who, however, gave him a safe-conduct, if he chose to go at his own instance and risk, Blair made his way to the Richmond outposts, and was admitted to an audience with Davis. He conceived a scheme, according to which, by uniting Federal and Confederate strength, during an armistice, and giving a leading part to Davis, the Monroe Doctrine was to be vindicated and the French driven out of Mexico: the united effort against foreign aggression it was hoped might tend to reconcile North and South; and there was a dream of dominion over Mexico and as far as the Isthmus, when the invaders had been expelled. Davis listened with patience, perhaps

[1] *Cong. Globe*, 38 Cong., 2 Sess., 1011.

with a certain sympathy, as Blair detailed his scheme, agreeing to appoint a commission to represent the Confederacy in a conference with representatives from Washington, with the idea of promoting "peace between the two countries." When Blair returned to Washington and laid the scheme before Lincoln, the latter expressed himself as ready on his part to promote as he could "peace between the people of our common country."[1]

February 3, 1865, the "Hampton Conference" took place on board the steamer *River Queen*, anchored in the Roads, off Fortress Monroe. The commissioners appointed by Jefferson Davis were Alexander H. Stephens, vice-president of the Confederacy, R. M. T. Hunter, senator and ex-secretary of state, and John A. Campbell, assistant secretary of war and a former justice of the supreme court of the United States. Lincoln determined to meet the envoys himself, and was accompanied only by Seward. From the accounts of the participants we know that the Richmond envoys were much occupied by the Mexican project, in which Seward, too, was interested; for it will be remembered that, four years before, he had seen in a foreign war a panacea for our dissensions.[2]   Stephens led up to this point gradually, but Lincoln said at once that he had given no sanction to Blair's project: he could consent to no armistice, nor to any proposition not

[1] Nicolay and Hay, *Abraham Lincoln*, X., 107.
[2] Hosmer, *Appeal to Arms* (*Am. Nation*, XX.), 23.

involving a complete restoration of the Federal authority. The conference in this direction not promising well, the talk fell upon the passage by Congress of the thirteenth amendment, of which the Confederates now heard for the first time. Seward suggested, perhaps not seriously, that if the seceded states would resume their places they might defeat the ratification.[1] Both he and Lincoln expressed their readiness to compensate the South for the manumitted slaves. This was quite in accord with what Lincoln had always professed: he believed the North was as much to blame as the South for the establishment of slavery—that an indemnity was only just, and that the money could be better spent in that way than in warfare. He promised for his part to act with liberality in case of submission; but again and again came back to the declaration that no agreement could be entered into until arms had been laid aside. When Hunter suggested, as a precedent for negotiations between parties in a civil war, Charles I. and his parliament, Lincoln turned that over to Seward, he himself not being strong in history. "All that I distinctly remember about the case of Charles I. is that he lost his head." The conference lasted four hours and resulted in nothing.[2]

A few days later the president prepared a re-markable message, in which he recommended the

[1] Bancroft, *Seward*, II., 414.
[2] Nicolay and Hay, *Abraham Lincoln*, X., 118 et seq.

appropriation of four hundred million dollars, to be paid to the South as the price of peace—the indemnity which he thought it was only just to offer in return for manumission, and which the country could well afford to pay if only the war might cease. This message Lincoln withheld with reluctance after it had received the unanimous disapproval of his cabinet.[1]

The second inauguration of Abraham Lincoln took place March 4, 1865. In the concourse which gathered in front of the east portico of the Capitol, a notable element was the civic associations of negro citizens, and the batallion of negro troops who marched in the procession. The address was brief, and marked by a solemn beauty which places it among the great utterances of history. Rarely from human lips has fallen so perfect an expression of the sweetest and highest wisdom. "Fondly do we hope—fervently do we pray that this mighty scourge of war may speedily pass away. Yet if God wills that it continue until all the wealth piled up by the bondman's two hundred and fifty years of unrewarded toil shall be sunk, and until every drop of blood drawn with the lash shall be paid by another drawn with the sword, as was said three thousand years ago so still it must be said, 'The judgments of the Lord are true and righteous altogether.'

"With malice towards none, with charity for all; with firmness in the right as God gives us to see the

[1] Nicolay and Hay, *Abraham Lincoln*, X., 133.

right, let us strive on to finish the work we are in;—
to bind up the nation's wounds, to care for him who
shall have borne the battle, and for his widow and
his orphan, to do all which may achieve and cherish
a just and lasting peace among ourselves and with
all nations." [1]

Then came the oath, administered by Chief-Justice
Chase: "I, Abraham Lincoln, do solemnly swear
that I will faithfully execute the office of President
of the United States, and will, to the best of my
ability, preserve, protect, and defend the Constitution of the United States."

[1] Lincoln, *Works* (ed. of 1894), II., 657.

CHAPTER XIV

MILITARY SEVERITIES

(1864–1865)

WHAT disposition should be made of Sherman
and his army, whom we left resting in Savannah after the agreeable experience of the march to
the sea, was for a time doubtful. Grant suggested
that all should be put on transports and conveyed
speedily to the lines before Petersburg and Richmond.[1] To Sherman's gratification, however, it
was concluded that he should be allowed to finish
as he had begun, and march to Richmond through
the Carolinas.[2] The army was in fine condition;
the troops had been only invigorated during their
unvexed and well-provided excursion. Whatever
they might now lack was made good from the ships;
their spirits were high. The animals, too, were in
the best condition. All this was fortunate, for the
task to be undertaken thenceforth was difficult: the
winter set in, the streams were at flood, the roads
were avenues of mud, the Confederates were gathering. Johnston had been restored to command by
Lee (now commander - in - chief); and Hardee, at

[1] W. T. Sherman, *Memoirs*, II., 206.   [2] *Ibid.*, 238.

Charleston, was formidable.   The Georgia militia, at Honey Hill, had already defeated in a sharp battle, November 30, a division sent out from Port Royal to seize the railroads.[1]   The spirit of the South was not broken.

With what temper the government and the general were now animated, the following correspondence shows.   Halleck wrote Sherman, December 18: "Should you capture Charleston, I hope that by some accident the place may be destroyed; and if a little salt should be sown upon its site, it may prevent the growth of future crops of nullification and secession."

To this Sherman replied, December 24: "I will bear in mind your hint as to Charleston, and do not think 'salt' will be necessary. . . . I attach more importance to these deep incisions into the enemy's country because this war differs from European wars in this particular: we are not only fighting hostile armies but a hostile people, and must make old and young, rich and poor, feel the hard hand of war, as well as their organized armies.   I know that this recent movement of mine through Georgia has had a wonderful effect in this respect. . . . The truth is, the whole army is burning with an insatiable desire to work vengeance upon South Carolina.   I almost tremble for her, but feel she deserves all that seems in store for her." [2]

[1] Cox, *March to the Sea, Franklin and Nashville*, 48.
[2] W. T. Sherman, *Memoirs*, II., 223, 227.

The Federals set forth from Savannah in January, 1865, thus anticipating the Confederates, who had not looked for a movement while the bad weather prevailed. Through South Carolina there was little opposition from man, but the sky and earth were hostile. Rains were incessant, each brook a torrent, the roads only passable when corduroyed. Following as it could the water-sheds, where the streams were small, and the lowland swamps could be avoided, feinting on the one hand against Charleston, on the other against Augusta, the army waded on.[1] The men did not allow themselves to want for food; the foraging, indeed, became more relentless and vindictive than in Georgia. February 17, Columbia, the capital of South Carolina, was occupied, and forthwith burned.

Who burned Columbia is a question much in dispute. The Confederates laid it to Sherman; and there are Federal writers who hold his soldiers to have been mainly responsible, and see in the occurrence the climax of his "vandalism." On the other hand, Sherman himself strongly asserts his innocence; the conflagration, he declares, resulted from the burning in the streets, by the retiring Confederates, of cotton which they desired to destroy; and the soldiers helped the citizens to extinguish the flames.[2] General Slocum, however, believed that fires were lighted by soldiers made drunk by

[1] *War Records*, Serial No. 98, pp. 1–1149 (Campaign in the Carolinas).   [2] W. T. Sherman, *Memoirs*, II., 286.

whiskey furnished by people of the town;[1] White-law Reid pronounces the burning of Columbia the most monstrous barbarity of the barbarous march.[2] Cox, while admitting that exasperation against South Carolina, and some demoralization in the Federal ranks, had much to do with the destruction of Columbia, yet maintains that the general's policy was "one of mildness to the individual citizen and of destruction only to the public resources of the country."[3] But in war-time how shall the line be drawn between private wealth and the public resources? Confederate writers, naturally, strongly condemn Sherman.[4]

During Sherman's march from Savannah, important events were taking place in other fields. In December, 1864, B. F. Butler, with an army and fleet, appeared off the entrance to Cape Fear River. After the explosion of a powder-boat, on the 13th, in the water near Fort Fisher, which was quite harmless, Butler retired, thus closing his career as a soldier;[5] whereupon General Alfred H. Terry, with the Tenth Corps and a fleet, made a new and entirely successful attempt; Fort Fisher was captured January 15, 1865. With the fall of Charleston, which Hardee evacuated, February 18, after Sherman had severed all its connections and rendered it unten-

---

[1] *Battles and Leaders*, IV., 686.
[2] Reid, *Ohio in the War*, I., 475.
[3] Cox, *March to the Sea*, 176.
[4] For example, see B. T. Johnson, *J. E. Johnston*, 151 et seq.
[5] Butler, *Butler's Book*, 774.

able, the last harbor was closed to the Confederacy.

Meantime, the winter put no bar upon operations in the West. Stoneman, with the Fourth Corps and cavalry, penetrated the mountains from east Tennessee, and seized the great Confederate depot at Salisbury in western North Carolina. Wilson swept southward, ravaging the country, and defeating Forrest at Selma, Alabama. Schofield, too, with the Twenty-third Corps, passing rapidly by a long détour to the Chesapeake, thence sailed southward, and, a few days after the fall of Fort Fisher, joined Terry on the Cape Fear River.[1] Taking command, Schofield captured Wilmington, penetrating thence, March 21, after some fighting at Kinston, to Goldsboro, in the interior. Sherman now, after seizing Cheraw and Fayetteville, important arsenals and depots, was well on his way to Raleigh. His army toiling on through incessant rains, was widely separated on account of the necessity of procuring supplies. Slocum and Howard were far apart, and the columns trailed their attenuated length for many miles.

Here Johnston saw his opportunity, and he now showed, if he had never shown it before, that he could be active and enterprising upon occasion as well as conduct a retreat. While Hampton with his cavalry veiled his movements, Johnston suddenly threw himself upon certain isolated divisions of the left

[1] Schofield, *Forty-six Years in the Army*, 345.

wing near Bentonville, March 19. While Cox declares he had a large superiority,[1] Johnston makes the usual Confederate claim that he was heavily outnumbered.[2] The careful Livermore makes the forces engaged to have been nearly equal, on each side about seventeen thousand.[3] It was a resolute and brilliant attack, repulsed only with heavy loss. The battle over, Sherman and Schofield soon struck hands, and Raleigh was occupied, April 13, 1865.

Sherman's magnificent and epoch-making work as a soldier being now accomplished, a little space may well be devoted to considering the criticisms made upon this striking figure in the history of our country. Says John C. Ropes: "If Sherman purposely destroyed or connived at the destruction of property which was not needed for the supply of his army or the enemy's army, he violated one of the fundamental canons of modern warfare. . . . If we are correct in attributing this position to Sherman, the authorities are against him, . . . and just so far as he directed or permitted this he conducted war on obsolete and barbarous principles."[4] And Charles Francis Adams censures the lightness of Rhodes's condemnation of the "pronounced vandalism" of Sherman, who, with his colleague Sheridan, advocated and carried out in warfare "the

[1] Cox, *March to the Sea, Franklin and Nashville*, 197.
[2] Johnston, *Narrative*, 392.
[3] Livermore, *Numbers and Losses*, 134.
[4] Ropes, in *Atlantic Monthly*, LXVIII., 202.

seventeenth century practices of Tilly." [1]   General
Cox, always calm and sane, one of Sherman's best
officers, who, although himself not in the march
through Georgia and the Carolinas, knew the facts
minutely, and is probably the best historian of the
occurrence, may well be quoted here.

"The tendency of war to make men relapse into
barbarism becomes most evident when an army is
living in any degree upon the enemy's country. . . .
Most of the officers honestly tried to enforce the
rules; but in an army of many thousand men, a
small fraction of the whole would be enough to spoil
the best efforts of the rest. . . . Yet I believe that
nowhere in the world is respect for person and property more sincere than among our own people. The
evils described are those which may be said to be
necessarily incident to the waging of war, and are
not indications of ferocity of nature or uncommon
lack of discipline." [2]

Adams believes Sheridan to have been a graver
sinner than Sherman, both as to precept and example; and if these two are to be censured, the same
condemnation must be visited upon Grant, who
ordered the devastation of the valley of Virginia.
The Confederates are as open to criticism in this
respect as the Federals, so far as they had opportunity, and had no scruples over destroying peaceful commerce, the unarmed ships of private men.

---

[1] Adams, *Some Phases of the Civil War*, 27 et seq.
[2] Cox, *Military Reminiscences*, II., 233.

If Lee in his Pennsylvania campaign was scrupulous, Morgan was not so in his Ohio raid, and Early did not hesitate to burn Chambersburg. In 1864, Confederates in Canada were scheming to lay waste the northern border and apply Greek fire to the cities of the Union.[1] Stonewall Jackson, at the beginning, was in favor of showing no quarter to captured men.[2] Nor is a spirit of ruthlessness confined to the time of the Civil War, or to America. While unpleasant declarations by United States officers of the present time can be cited, there are speeches of the German emperor which befit only the cruel old centuries, the temper of which we had believed obsolete.[3]

"War is hell," said Sherman, and so long as mankind can find no other way of settling their differences, a recrudescence of horrors is inevitable whenever it is waged. When war becomes close and desperate, as it was between North and South, each combatant, in the effort to maintain himself, grasps methods likely to be effective, however cruel, rather than lose his cause. The burning of peaceful merchantmen and whalers was undoubtedly most effective; the devastations supervised by Sherman and Sheridan were undoubtedly most effective. No real line can be drawn in war between public resources and private wealth; what its individual citizens are and possess is the strength of a land, and

---

[1] Headley, *Confed. Operations in Canada and New York*, 264.
[2] Dabney, *Jackson*, 224.
[3] Adams, *Some Phases of the Civil War*, 30.

the crushing must constantly become more ruthless, if the conflict be protracted and uncertain. The thorough-going soldier regards the short, sharp, unsparing method as in the end the humane method, even though the woman and the babe become homeless. It all belongs to the dreadful business, and such things the world will continue to behold until the curse of war shall cease.

No more striking example of what pitiless war may on occasion bring a humane man to do, and no more striking example of the adamantine nerve of the greatest of Union soldiers can be named, than the conduct of Grant, in 1864, as regards the exchange of prisoners. What Andersonville was, all the world knows—thirty-two thousand Union soldiers huddled within a stockade enclosing twenty-six and one-half acres, though in the midst of forests, without the shelter even of trees, against the frost or the burning sun, with scanty and irregular food supply, with a scanty and polluted supply of water, in rags and filth, dragging on month after month of hopeless life. The Confederates desired to exchange them for an equivalent number of their own prisoners in Union hands. The North urged, with breaking hearts, that her sons might be set free from such an abyss of suffering. It may well be believed that the great captain's own heart was oppressed, for he was far from being cruel. But on April 17, 1864, he refused to exchange prisoners; and on August 18, at City Point, when things were at a most critical pass, he explained his refusal: "It is hard on our men held in southern prisons not to exchange them, but it is humanity to those left in the ranks to fight our battles. Every man we hold, when released on parole, or otherwise, becomes an active soldier against us at once, either directly or indirectly. If we commence a system of exchange which liberates all prisoners taken, we will have to fight on until the whole South is exterminated. If we hold those caught, they amount to no more than dead men. At this particular time, to release all rebel prisoners in the North would insure Sherman's defeat, and would compromise our safety here."[1]

Rhodes, whose chapter on this topic is especially painstaking and accurate, finds this subject more difficult to deal with than any other connected with the Civil War.[2] All other things, men once opposed can discuss with charity and good-nature; but as to the treatment of prisoners the soreness persists. The northern man is not more convinced that there were needless horrors in southern prisons than is the southern man that there were needless horrors in northern prisons. While the former flushes at the thought of Andersonville, Libby, and Salisbury, the latter still nurses wrath over Fort Delaware, Elmira, Johnson's Island, and Camp Douglas. The accusations of inhumanity from the South are just as earnest and circumstantial as those that come

---

[1] *War Records*, Serial No. 120, p. 607.
[2] Rhodes, *United States*, V., 483.

16

from the North.[1] It is far beyond the scope of this
work to consider this matter at length. The literature is vast; the second series of the *War Records*,
eight stout quartos, contain the official documents,
and much has been written besides.[2]

The best judgment, based on official records, in-
clines to the conclusion that, up to the end of the
year 1863, little happened in the treatment of prisoners, North or South, to arouse the anger or excite
the sharp criticism of reasonable men on the opposing sides.[3] Embarrassments, of course, there were,
such as the determination of the Washington government, at the beginning, not long adhered to, to
treat privateersmen as pirates and beyond the pale
of mercy; and the determination of the Richmond
government to refuse all rights to captured negro
soldiers and their white officers. There were accusations, too, of the abuse of paroles. But in the main,
when combatant recognized that he had little reason
to complain, and had things gone on in the same
way, the historian of the period would be spared
the writing of some sorrowful pages.

As to what happened after 1863, neither the
Washington nor Richmond authorities intended to
be cruel. On both sides it was ordered that the
same rations should be given to the prisoners as to

[1] E. g., Southern Hist. Soc., *Papers*, 113 et seq.
[2] See J. McElroy, *Andersonville, a Story of Rebel Military
Prisons;* J. V. Hadley, *Seven Months in Prison;* A. B. Isham,
Prisoners and Military Prisons.
[3] Rhodes, *United States*, V., 491.

the soldiers in the field; also that the hospitals for
the prisons should be the same as for the camps:
there was no thought of any harshness in treatment
beyond what might be necessary to hold large numbers of men always trying to escape. But in 1864
new elements came into the problem. Grant was at
the head, and was convinced that in the case of
the men captured at Vicksburg and Port Hudson,
there had been a violation of parole, the men being
returned at once into the ranks: exchanges must
cease until this had been explained and atoned for.
Meantime the prison at Andersonville was established, intended for no large number, but before it
was finished occupied by an overwhelming and un-
looked-for crowd, for whom, as regards all necessi-
ties, no provision was made.

The strait of the Confederacy at the moment was
desperate: it was pressed on all sides, while Grant
and Sherman, each with a hundred thousand men
and more, were advancing through their territory,
upon their eastern and western citadels. The attention of all was concentrated on the approaching
danger. Every man upon whom the Confederacy
could lay hands was needed at the front—every
pound of food was needed for the fighters. Means
of transit were at all times limited: then the railroads far into the interior were wrecked by Federal
raiders, and locomotives and machinery destroyed,
while the blockade prevented their replacement.
There was no time to think of the prisons. The

troops that could be spared for prison-guards were in number the very minimum, and in quality the poorest; the officers to command them were those who could be spared from before the enemy, the incapables therefore. These struggled often ineffi-ciently against the difficulties of the situation which always grew worse: money became worthless; for all work only impressed and reluctant labor could be had. New thousands of prisoners poured in as the summer advanced, largely from before Rich-mond—some part of them, it is said, being "bounty-jumpers," who preferred to surrender rather than fight. Meantime the attention of the heads was absorbed in the terrible battles; or if there was a thought of the prisoners, the answer came that "Grant refuses to exchange, and the responsibility for their suffering lies with their own friends, and not with their captors."

This being the situation, horrors accumulated. The Confederacy, though so distracted, was not insensible to the misery; the truth was sounded abroad by many, in particular in a report made to the government by Colonel D. T. Chandler, which kept back nothing.[1] Various schemes to help were advocated: since Grant refused to exchange, many favored a liberation of the more feeble prisoners, and sending them north on parole. Howell Cobb, who now as commander of the state troops of Georgia, had a supervision of Andersonville, favored

[1] *War Records*, Serial No. 120, p. 546 (Chandler's Report).

the liberation of all such as would at the elections cast their votes against Lincoln.[1] The men directly in charge at the stockade, and who at the North were believed to be especially responsible for the enormities, were General John H. Winder and Captain Henry Wirz. The latter was hanged after the war, for his supposed crimes, and Winder, who died in 1865, no doubt would also have been executed. Yet possibly they were more unfortunate than criminal. They were inferior men set to cope with fearful conditions. Winder urged the policy of paroling and sending north; and Dick Taylor relates a rather pathetic story of Wirz. Taylor, in command of the department, passing by train near Andersonville, late in 1864, was visited by Wirz, who pictured vividly his embarrassments, the enormous requirements, the utter lack of resources to meet them, and begged his commander for help. The Confederacy was tottering to its destruction, with Sherman at its heart, and Grant holding its head in a vise.[2] Nothing could be done. There were at least twelve other prisons, but at Andersonville the difficulty culminated. What can be said in the way of explanation or palliation of Andersonville can in general be more strongly urged for the rest.

As to alleged ill-treatment of southern men in northern prisons, the charges cannot be ignored: the frequent statement that the mortality among

---

[1] *War Records*, Serial No. 120, p. 796.
[2] Taylor, *Destruction and Reconstruction*, 216.

southern prisoners at the North was three per cent. greater than among northern prisoners at the South, rests on no good evidence.[1] Well-remembered testimony, however, from army surgeons, goes to prove that southerners in general showed in the war much less power to endure novel conditions of life than did northerners. The available statistics show that while of southern men in northern prisons a little over twelve per cent. died, of northern men in southern prisons the per cent. was 15.5.[2]

Perhaps the mortality of Confederates ought to have been much less, in view of the vast superiority of northern resources, which removed all difficulties as to the supply of food, medicines, shelter, and clothing. The demands from the front, especially in 1864, affected the northern prison-guards, who were sometimes inefficient, with poor officers. Cases of carelessness, drunkenness, and embezzlement can be cited. While the heat of the South wore upon northern men, the cold of the North wore upon southern men: there was sometimes, with a bare temperature, lack of blankets and fuel, so that pneumonia swept off its victims as well as the fevers of the South. In 1864 a spirit of retaliation became rife. Rumors of the Andersonville situation filled the ears of men, and sentiment was powerfully affected. The prison ration, till now the same as that for soldiers, was reduced twenty per cent. by

[1] Southern Hist. Soc., *Papers*, XI., 113.
[2] Rhodes, *United States*, V., 508.

the Federal government, among the proscribed articles being coffee, tea, and sugar; at the same time the supply of comforts flowing in from outside friends was cut off. It does not at all appear that the reduction was so great as to affect seriously the health and strength of the prisoners;[1] much less were any brought near the starvation-point; nevertheless, there was an experience of privation. It is probable that sometimes at prison-posts the local officials took a hand at retaliation, adding a weight beyond what the government inflicted: the public exasperation was great, and an excess of zeal in this direction likely to be approved or leniently judged. In spite of all, the best testimony favors the idea that a good average of vigor was maintained in the northern prisons; and Grant certainly believed that an exchange, while it brought back men emaciated and powerless, would turn loose upon Sherman and upon himself many thousands of strong and well-fed men.

The investigator who perhaps beyond all others has dived nearest to the bottom of this shocking pit sums up as follows: "All things considered, the statistics show no reason why the North should reproach the South. If we add to one side of the account the refusal to exchange the prisoners and the greater resources, and to the other the stress of the Confederacy, the balance struck will not be far from even. Certain it is that no deliberate

[1] Rhodes, *United States*, V., 505.

intention existed either in Richmond or Washington to inflict suffering on captives more than inevitably accompanied the confinement. Rather than to charge either section with inhumanity, it were truer to lay the burden on war."[1] On war, therefore, let the burden rest. It belongs to the horrors inseparable from a close and desperate war; and such things must be expected to recur again and again until war shall be no more.

[1] Rhodes, *United States*, V., 508.

CHAPTER XV

SPIRIT OF THE NORTH
(1864–1865)

A RENOWNED historian of the Civil War, after describing the colossal labors of the men in authority as it progressed, declares that one reading with care the official records finds it hard to understand how Lincoln and Stanton, in particular, were not crushed by the weight of responsibility, which came to its severest between May and September, 1864.[1] The Stanton of the records he finds in marked contrast with the Stanton of tradition—a patient, tactful, forbearing, as well as resolute and indefatigable character, not the violent and harshly arbitrary man whom many have portrayed.[2]   In these months the burden told heavily upon Lincoln: his boisterous laugh, says his private secretary, was less frequent; the eye grew veiled through brooding over momentous subjects; he became reserved, and aged with great rapidity.   There is a solemn contrast between two life-masks, one made in 1860, the other in the spring of 1865; the earlier face is that of a

---

[1] Rhodes, *United States*, V., 237.
[2] Gorham, *Stanton*, II., pt. viii.

strong, healthy man, full of life and energy. The other is "so sad and peaceful in its definite repose that St. Gaudens insisted at first it was a death-mask. The lines are set as if the living face, like the copy, had been in bronze; the nose is thin and lengthened by the emaciation of the cheeks; the mouth is fixed like that of an archaic statue—a look as of one on whom sorrow and care had done their worst without victory is on all the features: the whole expression is of unspeakable sadness and all-suffering strength."[1]

As the year 1864 closed, for the president there was great relief. The victories made final success certain; the election, while continuing his power, assured him that he possessed overwhelmingly the confidence of the country. His immediate environment had also become more congenial: he had sub-jected the vehement Stanton; he had no longer to bear the ill-nature of Chase; in the place of Bates there stood a warm personal friend, Speed. Indeed, but two of the secretaries of 1861, Seward and Welles, remained in the cabinet. In particular, Lin-coln's relations with the secretary of state were close and harmonious. If at first Seward depreciated the president, that disposition passed after a few months of intimacy, and he worked on loyally in his subordinate place. Any chagrin he may have felt

[1] John Hay, in *Century*, XIII., 37 (November, 1890). The two masks lie together in the Lincoln case at the National Museum in Washington.

at not attaining the highest honor, he suppressed; and there is little evidence that he cherished any further ambition. As to foreign affairs, he declared in these days with truth that "things were going finely." Seward might honestly feel that his own courage and force had helped powerfully to the general success. It is pleasant to read his hearty appreciation of his great chief. In a speech after the election he said: "Henceforth all men will come to see him as you and I have seen him—a true, loyal, patient, patriotic, and benevolent man. . . . Detraction will cease and Abraham Lincoln will take his place with Washington, Jefferson, Adams, and Franklin, among the benefactors of the country and of the human race." [1]

In truth, in Europe things were now going well for the Union. As to the great powers, Russia was always friendly: France, in spite of the unfriendliness of Napoleon III., had not broken with us. In Mexico, Maximilian, after May, 1864, was personally engaged in establishing his dynasty, and seemed for the moment successful; but already there were signs, both North and South, that the Monroe Doctrine was not forgotten, and would some day be vindicated.

By the spring of 1865 all danger of European interference in our quarrel ceased. The Confederate agents were in the background, discouraged,[2] while

[1] Seward, *Works*, V., 514.
[2] Callahan, *Diplomatic Relations of the Confed.*, chap. viii.

Charles Francis Adams enjoyed a consideration such
as no previous American minister had reached. A
different tone was heard in the utterances of statesmen and men of letters. The voices of John Bright,
W. E. Forster, and Richard Cobden more and more
prevailed. At an earlier period Grote had been
supercilious, Dickens unsympathetic, Carlyle roughly
denunciatory, E. A. Freeman and Gladstone proph-
ets of our disruption who were not saddened by what
they foretold. But there were now wiser men, none
more so than Sir Charles Lyell, the geologist, always
a friend to the Union, who showed, with candid
recognition of the merit of the vanquished, his
strong sympathy with the victors. The best English opinion is expressed in one of his letters, March
12, 1865, in which he declares that the Confederates
have certainly shown the power of an aristocracy to
command and direct the energies of the millions;
" Englishmen may feel proud of the prowess of the
southern army, in which there was not that large
mixture of Celtic and German blood found on the
Northern side." He expressed confidence in the
rapidity with which the wounds would be healed,
and believed that the discipline would bring about
in the people of the United States habits of subordi-
nation to central authority, which they needed: he
expected the large national debt to strengthen the
Federal power, which formerly could not control the
states; had the Union been dismembered, there
would have been endless wars, more activity than

ever in breeding slaves in America, a renewal of the African slave-trade, and a retarding of the future course of civilization. The result, therefore, Lyell deemed worth all the dreadful loss of blood and treasure. As to the internal condition of the states, he felt sure of their rapid and successful development. "Whatever it may be for the rich, I certainly think that for the millions it is the happiest country in the world." [1]

When the spring of 1865 opened, although a heavy shadow of death darkened almost every household, and a public debt of three billions gave rise to apprehension, the North was cheerful and buoyant. For the North was not only victorious, but prosperous: though her ocean carrying-trade was nearly destroyed through events which have been described, there was a heavy export and import business despite the high tariff. Legitimate trade with the South was resumed, and intercommerce was extraordinarily active. While there was no large increase of railroads during the war period, in 1865 38,078 miles existed in the North, almost all in good order and fully employed.[2] Symptoms of the spirit of enterprise in railroad building were an act of 1862 for the construction of the Union Pacific and Central Pacific railroads; and consolidations were beginning in the eastern lines. As regards appliances, the air-brake, vestibuled trains, dining-cars,

[1] Letter to T. S. Spedding, Mrs. Lyell, *Sir C. Lyell*, II., 397.
[2] *Am. Annual Cyclop.*, 1865, p. 742.

and palatial compartment-cars were undreamed of; high speed could be maintained only at great risk; roads were commonly single-tracked, and the strap-rail had not entirely disappeared. But the railroad stood fully developed as a powerful instrumentality, already superseding the canal, the wonder of the preceding generation, and promoting transit and traffic to an extent never before known. While the land was thus crossed and recrossed, the internal waters, the Great Lakes, and the navigable streams abounded in sailing and steam craft.

The requirements of the time caused these rapidly developing facilities to be taxed to their utmost. The condition of the farmers in the war period from the first was good. In 1861 the crops were heavy, with a strong European demand.[1] Though the exports of food stuffs dropped off, the vast requirements of the war immediately strengthened the market: there was quick and good sale for every crop and animal which the farmer could produce. Manufactures were no less stimulated: had ships been plenty and Europe clamorous, nothing could have been spared for export, for forge and loom were quite absorbed in satisfying the home needs. The laborer fared worse than the farmer and manufacturer. While wages rose during the war, till in 1865 they stood in the ratio of 183 as compared with 100 in 1861: prices rose far more, being 217 at the end as compared with 100 at the beginning, a law working

[1] Schouler, *United States*, VI., 327.

here which economists have noted.[1] House-rents,✳
too, though advancing, kept no pace with the price
of food and clothes.

The natural resources of the country were ex-
ploited as never before. The northwestern forests
fell quite too rapidly; petroleum, made available in
1859, underwent an extraordinary development in
the sixties. The gold discoveries of 1849 in California were followed by finds of the same metal in
Colorado in 1858 and in Montana in 1861. Meantime, in 1859, silver was found in Nevada; in the
same period became known the stores of copper and
iron in the region south of Lake Superior. The
country was not so busy in the camp as to be unable to make prize of this newly revealed wealth.

In the stimulation of the processes of life, a quick
utilizing took place of inventions lately wrought
out, or now for the first time announced. McCor-
mick's reaper of 1834, Elias Howe's sewing-machine
of 1846, Goodyear's vulcanized rubber of 1839, the
daguerreotype of 1839, the Hoe rotary press of 1847,
the electric telegraph of 1835—all these were improved and made widely available, as could hardly
have been the case among quieter conditions; while
in devising and perfecting breech-loaders, repeating-
arms, and rifled bores, ingenious men were very
active. In 1841, at the Massachusetts General
Hospital, ether had first been used as an anæsthetic
by Morton; what beneficent possibilities were in-

[1] Taussig, in *Yale Review*, II., 244 (November, 1895).

volved in this discovery became fully evident in the field-hospitals of both armies.

Religion grew more earnest in these years. The Protestant denominations, large and small, though divided in the political dispute, lost no vigor. The zeal of the ministers and congregations grew fervent. The men recruited the armies and made sacrifices at home; while the women, using such agencies as the Sanitary and Christian Commissions, gave practical expression to their devotedness. The Catholics were not behind, sending out a multitude of our best soldiers and sailors, while patriotically active at home. Religious activity pervaded, too, the camps; each regiment had its chaplain, usually a worthy man, whose ministrations were earnest and met a response sincere and wide-spread.

As to education, in the North the common school was universal, though sometimes lacking appliances and skilled teachers.[1] In the country districts it was often open only for short terms; and the teachers — farmers' sons or daughters with small training—were not the best. But things were improving. Horace Mann died in 1859, a self-sacrificing enthusiast whose writings and labors were having a marked effect. Normal schools, well established in New England, and fast making their way farther west, were fixing new standards of instruction and management, and effort was made

[1] Mayo, *History of Common Schools* (U. S. Bureau of Education, in preparation).

to profit by the experience of other lands. In the cities were high schools, sometimes open to girls, who, however, usually found a chance for nothing but superficial training. For higher education, denominational colleges abounded, rarely largely attended, usually struggling with poverty, and often esteeming orthodoxy of belief to be more important than sound and broad learning. Of universities only Harvard and Yale had the four faculties of divinity, law, medicine, and science, in addition to the academic course; and neither had more than five hundred and fifty students.[1]

Nevertheless, a new spirit was abroad; the elective system was making its way; endowments were becoming more liberal; and a beginning had been made of the system of state universities which at the present time crown so impressively our public educational system. Among these new institutions the University of Michigan had an honorable preeminence. Since their support came from public funds, it was manifestly unfair that the advantages offered, too costly to be duplicated, should be enjoyed by only half the youth. Hence the co-education of the sexes, which had been successfully tried in several places, notably at Oberlin, Ohio, was generally adopted among state universities, that of Iowa leading the way. In 1862 Congress made

---

[1] Schouler, *United States*, VI., 336; for earlier conditions of education, see Hart, *Slavery and Abolition* (*Am. Nation*, XVI.), chap. ii.

possible the establishment in each state of a college
of agriculture and the mechanic arts: these, combined as they usually were with the state universities, imparted strength and made certain for all
who desired it an education thoroughly practical.
In the pressure of the war the higher institutions
were much affected. At the West it sometimes happened that they were closed, the students, led by
their teachers, departing in companies to the front;[1]
where they remained open the attendance fell off,
the spirited young men finding study difficult in
the prevailing martial excitement. J. W. Sill, a brave
young general killed at Murfreesboro, J. J. Reynolds,
a good commander of a division, J. L. Chamberlain,
J. A. Garfield, J. M. Schofield, and many more officers of distinction, were by profession teachers.

At the end of the war the impression was general
that extravagance and corruption prevailed to an
extraordinary extent; but a survey from this distance may give assurance that the evils were not
excessive or inexplicable. Many became suddenly
rich, for the newly opened mines, petroleum fields,
the vast government contracts, gold gambling, the
chances for speculation afforded by fluctuating
prices, gave unusual opportunity to the adroit and
rapacious. The money made easily was often spent
unwisely. Lavishness was manifest in houses, equi-
pages, and apparel, of women no less than men. But
conscience was active, and societies were formed for

[1] Cox, *Military Reminiscences*, I., 33.

the discouragement of luxury, the spirit prevailing
finding expression in Julia Ward Howe's

> "Weave no more silks, ye Lyons looms,
>   To deck our girls for gay delights!
> The crimson flower of battle blooms,
>   The solemn marches fill the nights.

> "Weave but the flag whose bars to-day
>   Drooped heavy o'er our early dead,
> And homely garments, coarse and gray,
>   For orphans that must earn their bread!" [1]

In the transactions of the government involving
enormous amounts some corruption was inevitable,
but it was resisted manfully, the fighters often
imagining a depth and extent of depravity which
did not exist. A congressional committee in 1863,
of which Senator James W. Grimes, of Iowa, was
chairman, made an appalling report as to waste and
peculation in the management of the army and
navy;[2] and Roscoe Conkling, of New York, in a
speech of April 24, 1866, fiercely criticised the provost-marshal-general, J. B. Fry. When the statistics
were prepared and studied, the charges of Grimes
proved overdrawn. In the vast business of the
department of the paymaster-general, B. W. Bryce,
it was found that from July 1, 1861, to October 31,
1865, $1,029,239,000 had been disbursed—the steals
amounting to less than half a million, the expense

[1] Julia Ward Howe, *From Sunset Ridge*, 5.
[2] Salter, *Grimes*, 229 et seq.

of disbursement to $6,429,600, the aggregate being less than seven-tenths of one per cent. of the amount disbursed.[1] In the department of the quartermaster-general, Montgomery C. Meigs, the amount appropriated was about $1,200,000,000, and the showing was equally good, the business being in fact a model of efficient administration.[2] As to the department of the provost - marshal - general, Fry replied convincingly to his accuser. In the country at large the bounty and substitute brokers, who became numerous towards the end of the war, were generally bad men, and Fry had favored their suppression. Fry's vindication may be regarded as conclusive.[3]

It is enough to confute the charge that wholesale corruption prevailed in the management of these tremendous responsibilities to recall the names of the men who stood as heads: Lincoln, Stanton, Chase, Fessenden, Welles, and his assistant, G. V. Fox, Grant, Meigs, Ingalls, Fry— the country has never had in great positions men of higher ability and integrity That some trace of curiousness and unfaithfulness should occur in the conduct of such affairs was inevitable in view of human limitations, but the need for apology is small indeed in presenting the story of these mighty labors.

Side by side with these men in official station may properly be mentioned citizens in private station,

[1] *War Records*, Serial No. 126, p. 204.
[2] *Ibid.*, p. 254.
[3] J. B. Fry, *Conkling and Blaine-Fry Controversy in 1866.*

who without pay rendered indispensable services—
men like J. M. Forbes[1] and Amos A. Lawrence, of
Boston, who from pure patriotism were government
agents, or became bounty-brokers in the hope of
redeeming a work thought necessary but so often
made discreditable, and scattered broadcast patriotic
literature; Henry Whitney Bellows and Frederick
Law Olmstead, of New York, unpaid heads and
organizers of the Sanitary Commission; and James
E. Yeatman, of St. Louis, well portrayed by Winston
Churchill, in *The Crisis*, as "Mr. Brinsmade."

The years of the Civil War fell well within the
golden period of American literature, which reflects
vividly the wrath, the anxieties, the sorrow, and
the exultation of the time.   In American letters the
humorist is never absent, and the newspapers of
the war-time sparkled with witty effusions that,
rough though they sometimes were, demolished evils
more effectively than attacks sober and labored.
"Artemus Ward" (Charles F. Browne), who was
willing to sacrifice on the altar of his country all
his wife's male relatives, would deserve notice if for
no other reason than that he was a source of much
refreshment to Lincoln.   It is a strange bracketing,
but the "High-handed Outrage in Utiky" will go
down the ages with the Emancipation Proclamation.[2]
The president took great delight also in the deliver-
ances of "Petroleum V. Nasby" (D. R. Locke), as

---

[1] Mrs. Hughes, *John Murray Forbes*, chaps. viii.–xviii.
[2] Hosmer, *Appeal to Arms* (*Am. Nation*, XX.), 215.

did also James Russell Lowell, who declared that "Hosea Biglow" might be spared from the field since a satirist of such vigor had entered it. The letters from the "Confedrit X Rodes" told powerfully against the Copperheadism of the West. Not far behind these was Robert H. Newell, "Orpheus C. Kerr" (Office Seeker), who, as the name suggests, found other political abuses than disloyalty, and sometimes hit out in other fields than politics. An effort being made to obtain a new national hymn, "Orpheus C. Kerr" published "The Rejected National Hymns," the alleged contributions to that end of our better-known poets. His parody of transcendental phraseology was thought amusing forty years ago.

FROM R—LPH W—LDO EM—R N

"Source immaterial of material naught,—
   Focus of light infinitesimal,
Sum of all things by sleepless Nature wrought,
   Of which the normal man is decimal,
Refract, with prism immortal, from thy stars
   To the stars blent, incipient, in our flag,
The beam translucent, neutrifying death,—
   And raise to immortality the rag!"

Often brilliant and genuinely poetic, also, were the poems of John G. Saxe, a Democrat.

In a different class were J. G. Holland, Bayard Taylor, and Mrs. Harriet Beecher Stowe, strong and loyal workers for the Union and for freedom, although the latter certainly had rendered her most memorable service in the preliminary years. Of the

great pulpit and platform orators, Henry Ward
Beecher gave much help in England as well as at
home; while Thomas Starr King, according to the
belief of some, saved California to the Union.
Robert Collyer in Chicago, Phillips Brooks in
Philadelphia, E. H. Chapin in New York, were
constant in their zeal. The eloquence of Wendell
Phillips, on the other hand, tended rather to embar-
rass than assist. William Lloyd Garrison felt that
with the issuance of the Emancipation Proclamation
his work was accomplished, and retired from the foreground. The utterance of these days which especially possesses the hearts of men is the address at
Gettysburg, November 19, 1863, of Abraham Lincoln.

A few ballads and lyrics took deep hold of the
people, their lines becoming household words. Such
were the "Fight in Mobile Bay," of H. H. Brownell,
"Sheridan's Ride," by T. Buchanan Read, and
Julia Ward Howe's "Battle Hymn of the Republic."
Of fiction there was nothing more noteworthy than
Edward Everett Hale's *Man Without a Country*,
which appeared in the *Atlantic Monthly* of December, 1863. This weird and touching story, wellnigh
perfect as an example of literary art, written for the
temporary purpose of affecting sentiment at the
time when Vallandigham was a candidate for governor of Ohio, deepened sensibly northern patriotism
in general, and ever since has been an inspiring
object-lesson for Americans.

As to our great writers, scientists, and intellectual

leaders, most of whom were in the fulness of strength
in the war period, some specimens of their declarations
may well close this chapter.   Nathaniel Hawthorne,
perhaps the chief of all, died in 1864, apparently not
much concerned as to the success or failure of the
government.   While consul at Liverpool, some years
before the war, he wrote to his friend, Horatio Bridge:
"At present we have no Country. . . . The States are
too various and too extended to form really one
country.   New England is really quite as large a
lump of earth as my heart can take in.   Don't let
Frank Pierce see the above or he would turn me
out of office, late in the day as it is.   I have no
kindred with or leaning towards the abolitionists." [1]
He was touched by the uprising in 1861, but only
for a moment.   February 14, 1862, he writes:
"Frank Pierce came here and spent a night. . . .
He is bigoted to the Union, and sees nothing but
ruin without it; whereas I (if we can only put tho
boundary far enough south) should not much regret
an ultimate separation." [2]

In this indifference, Hawthorne stood alone among
his compeers.   The poets were all fervently loyal.
The uncombative nature of Longfellow withheld him
from fiery expressions, but he watched anxiously the
alternations of the struggle, now depressed, now rejoicing—with an earnest recognition of the nobility
cf such things as Lincoln's Gettysburg address.[3]

[1] Woodberry, *Hawthorne*, 281.   [2] *Ibid.*, 284.
[3] S. Longfellow, *H. W. Longfellow*, II., 395.

He was a close friend of Charles Sumner, who always sought Longfellow when he could be absent from the Senate; to give comfort to that strenuous champion was good service, had Longfellow done nothing more. Holmes, both in verse and prose was always spirited and outspoken, in his lighter vein hitting the enemy and the backward patriot at home with sharp ridicule, but most impressive perhaps in the hymns which he wrote in times of special stress. Whittier was strong, aggressive, upon occasion denunciatory, emancipation naturally kindling his spirit; "Barbara Frietchie" is a chivalrous acknowledgment of an opponent's virtue. Bryant, with lyre for the most part laid aside, sometimes overimpatient at the slow progress of freedom, nevertheless made the *New York Evening Post* a source of inspiration.

John Lothrop Motley, minister at Vienna, made a good forecast of events when he said, January 27, 1864: "I have settled down into a comfortable faith that this current year is to be the last of military operations on a large scale. The future will be more really prosperous than the past has ever been; for the volcano above which we have been living in a fool's paradise of forty years, dancing and singing and imagining ourselves going ahead, will have done its worst, and spent itself, I trust, forever."[1]

Emerson, just after the second election of Lin-

[1] To his mother, John Lothrop Motley, *Correspondence*, III., 3.

coln, congratulated his countrymen, "that a great portion of mankind dwelling in the United States have given their decision in unmistakable terms, that a nation cannot be trifled with, but involves interests so dear and so vast that its unity shall be held by force against the forcible attempt to break it. What gives commanding weight to this decision is, that it has been made by the people sobered by the calamity of the war. They protest in arms against the levity of any small or any numerous minority of citizens or States, to proceed by stealth or by violence to dispart a country." [1]

Agassiz pushed in the darkest days of the war, in 1863, the foundation of a National Academy of Sciences and his own Museum of Comparative Zoology, alleging "that the moment of political danger may be that in which the firm foundations for the intellectual strength of a country may be laid." In proof he cited the founding, immediately after the prostration of Prussia, in 1806, of the University of Berlin, by the advice of Fichte, the philosopher, "which has made Berlin the intellectual centre of Germany." [2] But while thus devoted to science, Agassiz was not indifferent to the welfare of his adopted country. He wrote to an English friend, August 30, 1862: "I feel so thankful for your words of sympathy. It has been agonizing week after week to receive the English papers and

[1] Cabot, *R. W. Emerson*, II., 610.
[2] Mrs. Agassiz, *Louis Agassiz*, 510.

to see there the noble devotion of the men of the
North to their country and its Government, branded
as the service of mercenaries.   Your warm sympathy
I needed the more, as it is almost the first friendly
word I have received from England, and I began
to question the humanity of your civilization." [1]

Lowell was especially fervent and indefatigable in
his patriotism.   He wrote for the *Atlantic Monthly*
the second series of the *Biglow Papers*, in which his
pathos, humor, and invective were at their best, and
applied marvellously to the support of the cause he
loved.   At the end of 1864 he greatly mourned the
death of three noble nephews killed in battle.

> "Rat-tat-tat-tattle through the street
>   I hear the drummers makin' riot,
> An' I set thinkin' of the feet
>   That follered once and now are quiet. . . .
> 'Tain't right to hev the young go fust
>   All throbbin' full o' gifts and graces,
> Leavin' life's paupers, dry as dust,
>   To try an' make b'lieve fill their places.
>
>   .   .   .   .   .
>
> " My eyes cloud up for rain; my mouth
>   Will take to twitchin' roun' the corners:
> I pity mothers, tu, down South,
>   For all they sot among the scorners.
> I'd sooner take my chance to stan'
>   At Jedgment where your meanest slave is,
> Than at God's bar hol' up a han'
>   Ez drippin' red ez yourn, Jeff Davis!" [2]

[1] Mrs. Agassiz, *Louis Agassiz*, 577.
[2] *Biglow Papers*, second series, No. 10.

With Charles Eliot Norton, Lowell undertook the
editorship of the *North American Review,* infusing
into that long-established and respected publication
a new life and loyalty. "Everything looks well,"
he writes to Motley, December 28, 1864. "I think
our last election fairly legitimizes democracy for the
first time. . . . It was really a nobler thing than you
can readily conceive so far away, for the opposition
had appealed to every base element in human nature,
and cunningly appealed too." [1]

[1] John Lothrop Motley, *Correspondence,* III., 69.

CHAPTER XVI

SPIRIT OF THE SOUTH
(1864–1865)

TAYLOR, one of our best authorities, declares that the generals at the head of the southern armies resigned all hope of success "after the campaign of 1864 had fully opened. . . . The commanders in the field whose work and position enabled them to estimate the situation, fought simply to afford statesmanship an opportunity to mitigate the sorrows of inevitable defeat."[1] A Confederate soldier of lower rank, George Cary Eggleston, asserts, too, "we all knew from the beginning of 1864 that the war was hopeless."[2] Though that may have been the opinion of the army, they did not confess it to themselves, but, as we have seen, faced with great resolution the forces of the Union. The civil officials, too, made no sign of want of confidence in a good issue, and the tone of the Richmond press was bold: it gravely discussed in the fall of 1864 how to treat the discomfited Yankees when the war is over.

[1] Taylor, *Destruction and Reconstruction*, 197.
[2] Eggleston, *A Rebel's Recollections*, 235.

No man in the Confederacy faced the situation with more courage than Jefferson Davis, and when in 1865 many whose hearts till then had been stout gave up hope, he worked on with unabated confidence and zeal.   If the labors of Lincoln were great, those of Davis were no less arduous; but now while Lincoln was on the point of final victory, and the resources and confidence of a great people were poured out to him as the recognized chief agent in bringing about success, the cause which Davis upheld was failing fast, and condemnation more often than praise was visited upon him.

While what the Confederate soldiers did in the field was as a rule well done, the military administration and commissariat were very defective. Since the advent of Moltke, military writers have had much to say about the importance to a fighting nation of a proper general staff;[1] such a body the southern army certainly had not—a want which was offset by a similar lack in the northern army. It must be admitted that Davis was a poor judge of men: he looked with disfavor upon officers of the merit of Beauregard and Joe Johnston, while he esteemed Braxton Bragg, adopting him as his adviser when Bragg stood discredited with all others.   It must also be laid upon him that Colonel L. B. Northrop was retained as commissary-general. It is a Napoleonic maxim that an army moves upon

---

[1] Henderson, *Science of War*, 69, 401; C. F. Adams, Hist. Soc. of Mass., *Proceedings*, series 2, xx., 159.

its belly; that it shall be fed is vital, but according
to much testimony from southern men the management of the commissariat was execrable. The resources, so scanty as compared with those of the
Union, were clumsily and wastefully handled, and
red-tape strangled efficiency to a disastrous extent.
Eggleston portrays in many pages the resulting
hardships to the soldiers. Stationed in South Carolina, the force of which his battery was a part was
in the midst of rice - fields, furnishing excellent
food. It had been determined, however, to feed
the army on bacon and flour, which must be brought
hundreds of miles; the supply failing through bad-
ness of transportation, there was no thought of
having recourse to rice, but the troops were put on
short rations, being thus made to hunger in the
midst of plenty.[1]

In the first Bull Run campaign red-tape and bad
judgment neglected to use the meat and grain of
the valley of Virginia, close at hand, accessible and
likely to fall soon into the hands of the enemy, but
depended rather upon stores brought with cost and
inconvenience from Richmond. So it was at the
beginning; and far towards the end of the war,
January 5, 1864, we find Lee writing to Northrop a
letter in which his dissatisfaction with the commissariat is very apparent: no beef had been issued to
the cavalry corps for eighteen months, and the
suggestions made by the commissary for bettering

[1] Eggleston, *A Rebel's Recollections*, 204.

matters were disapproved.[1] It is, indeed, hard to see why Lee did not interfere to remedy evils which crippled him seriously; but the inefficiency went on. In the department, too, of the provost-marshal-general, the trouble was as great. The system of guards, passports, and permits was in a high degree annoying to soldiers not only on furlough but on duty, giving rise to often-expressed wishes that Lee would take things into his own hands.[2]

The executive departments in general had many critics. That there was unwisdom in the treasury has been made plain:[3] the postmaster-general could not regulate the mails; the secretaries of war and the navy were targets for abuse. Much of the discontent was no doubt unreasonable, but from beginning to end Benjamin seems to have been the only cabinet officer who made his influence powerfully felt.

The ability of the country, in fact, was in the field, and men could not remain in civil positions, even the highest, without loss of reputation. An able-bodied man away from the front, whether a clerk or a congressman, was liable to unpleasant reminders that he might be in a better place; and in this state of public opinion it came about that men inferior in energy and talent made up the mass in the legislatures and departments. Since the debates of the Confederate congress have been only

[1] Long, *R. E. Lee*, 637.
[2] Eggleston, *A Rebel's Recollections*, 210, et seq.
[3] See above, p. 19.

partially preserved, its action has received little attention, but the popular view was that it was unduly
subservient to Davis and played an unimportant
part. "Congress seems to be doing little or nothing," writes J. B. Jones, January 7, 1865; "but
before it adjourns it is supposed it will as usual pass
the measure dictated by the President. How insig-
nificant a legislative body becomes when it is not
independent! The Confederate Congress will not
live in history, for it never really existed at all; but
has always been merely a body of subservient men
registering the decrees of the executive." [1]

As to commerce, external and internal, while in
the war-time the North lost its merchant-marine,
the South never had a merchant-marine to lose:
before the war the ships of the North and of foreign
nations cared for her trade, and during the war the
blockade-runners were usually of foreign construction and ownership. As to internal commerce,
nearly fifteen thousand miles of railroad existed in
the seceding states in 1861; [2] but notwithstanding
the lack of a through line from Mobile to the north-
eastward, almost no railroad building took place
during the war. No forges, mills, and machine-
shops existed adequate to keep the existing tracks
and rolling-stock in order, much less to start new
enterprises: the rigidity of the blockade barred out
importations. Although throughout the war a se-

[1] Jones, *Rebel War Clerk's Diary*, II., 379.
[2] *Am. Annual Cyclop.*, 1865, p. 742.
18

cret and illegitimate trade went on between North and South, connived at by the authorities on both sides, through which first and last much money was made by individuals, yet no supplies came in which at all answered to the requirements of the South. The ordinary wear and tear of a railroad makes necessary constant repairs and replacements, and the southern roads and their equipments were usually light and cheap: the traffic grew heavy with the transport of armies and their belongings, so that the natural use was destructive. As the war progressed, the pressure from the Federal invaders constantly increased, until for hundreds of miles the communications, if not in hostile hands, were wrecked by raiding parties beyond the possibility of reconstruction. Wagon-roads, always poor, went more and more to ruin; the navigable streams became useless through the destruction by the gunboats of the craft that plied upon them.

Hence, transportation, whether by sea or land, became a matter of the greatest difficulty. As early as the spring of 1863, Fremantle, who made a journey throughout the Confederacy, from Brownsville, Texas, to Gettysburg, makes plain the difficulties of travel everywhere.[1] In the fall and winter of 1864, when Sherman had penetrated Georgia and the Carolinas, people who sought to flee by the overtaxed trains often found it impossible. The graphic Mrs. Chesnut makes an amusing reference

[1] Fremantle, *Three Months in the Southern States*, passim.

to the trials of an over-stout lady of dignity and
standing who was pushed and pulled through the
small window of a car the doors to which were
blocked by crowds.[1] General Johnston, on his way
in 1864 to take command against Sherman, was delayed and endangered in his passage; and Dick Taylor, sent to command the Department of the Lower
South, found it scarcely possible, a little later, to
cross the Mississippi: it must be done at night;
his guides carried on their shoulders from its place
of concealment to the river the small skiff, the best
conveyance that could be found for a lieutenant-
general: the horses swam alongside; the party spoke
in whispers, so that the attention of the close at
hand Federal gun-boat might not be attracted.[2]
The soldiers of Sherman remember that in marching through Georgia they found food in abundance,
and were angry because the prisoners at Andersonville were so near starving. The truth at the moment was that the abundance of Georgia could not
be got northward to the Confederate armies; it was
equally difficult to send it southward to the prisoners, who naturally to the Confederates were of
secondary importance. The apparatus for equali-
zation and distribution failed: for transit of every
kind, the highways and the appliances, if not
broken to pieces by violence, were ruined through
wear and neglect.

---

[1] Mrs. Chesnut, *Diary from Dixie*, 351.
[2] Taylor, *Destruction and Reconstruction*, 197.

As to production, throughout the period until the territory was entirely overrun by Union armies, the South remained fruitful. While all the able-bodied white men from sixteen to seventy at last were in the camps, the negroes, under the direction of the old men and the women, tilled the plantations as before the war. The government made efforts, often successful, to promote the raising of a variety of provisions rather than cotton. If what was raised could have been got to market, and if when there transactions could have been assisted by a proper currency, the situation might not have been distressing. As to manufactures, we have seen the heroic efforts made by a people who had heretofore depended upon what they could import, to furnish for themselves clothes, shoes, tools, and machines.[1] On many a plantation, and often in the towns, homespun was woven and dyed butternut, leather was tanned and worked into foot-gear, straw plaited, baskets woven, and wooden-ware contrived, while rough carpentry and blacksmithing were applied to making what was indispensable. Thus life was maintained. The hardships of those forced to live on salaries were greater than those of farmers and planters, living in cities being not by any means as easy as in the country.[2]

Paper money became at last worth scarcely one per cent. of its face value, and in the disorganiza-

---

[1] See above, chap. iv.
[2] Eggleston, *A Rebel's Recollections*, 95.

tion all proper relation of prices was lost. Eggleston bought in the same day coffee at forty dollars
and tea at thirty dollars a pound; while a dinner
cost twenty dollars, and a newspaper one dollar.[1]
The value of money constantly fell, and the temp-
tation to speculate prevailed widely. An article
bought to-day was sure to bring more to-morrow,
and the scrip, though felt to be worthless, somehow
because it pretended to be money was held to be
desirable. Speculators fell under suspicion, a fate
shared at last by all who had to do with merchan-
dising. The Confederate Congress, which enjoyed so
little credit during its existence, perhaps did nothing which helped more towards its disrepute than
the funding act of February 17, 1864, upon the
principle "that the best way to enhance the value
of the currency was to depreciate it still further."
The scheme of repudiation proved quite futile, and
the condition grew worse to the end. The day before Lee's surrender, a cavalry officer, offering a
five-hundred-dollar note for a pair of boots priced
at two hundred dollars, the store-keeper could not
make the change. "Never mind," said the cava-
lier, "I'll keep the boots anyhow. Keep the change.
I never let a little matter of three hundred dollars
stand in the way of a trade."[2] With flour selling
at last at one thousand dollars a barrel, the currency broke down. Foreigners, who sometimes

---

[1] Eggleston, *A Rebel's Recollections*, chap. iv.
[2] *Ibid.*, 92.

came in on blockade-runners, and were able to afford to the people the rare sight of gold or silver coin, found no trouble in buying at prices near those prevailing before the war. United States greenbacks, too, were eagerly taken at rates not far different from those at the North, a practice which, as has been mentioned, the government sought to correct by statute.[1] A general recourse was had at last to barter, everybody, so far as he could, paying "in kind" for what he purchased.

Education at the South before the war, so far as it was cared for by a public system, was in a rudimentary stage.[2] The common school led a languishing life in a very few cities, and in vast regions the people were quite unprovided. Private academies and seminaries for well-to-do boys and girls existed in every southern state; above this was an apparatus of denominational colleges, wide-spread and undoubtedly useful; but it was a usual thing for the sons and daughters of the planters to seek the North or Europe for advantages which they could not find at home. At every centre of southern life were men and women highly accomplished, whose culture, however, was gained in distant schools, or from tutors and governesses brought from thence.

At the appeal to arms, the colleges for men were in great part closed entirely: while the students went into the ranks, the teachers and heads also often

[1] See above, p. 21.
[2] Hart, *Slavery and Abolition* (*Am. Nation*, XVI.), 20 et seq.

entered the public service in various capacities.
John and Joseph Leconte, as we have seen, when
the University of South Carolina was closed, directed
laboratories and powder-factories. D. H. Hill and
Stonewall Jackson, men trained at West Point, and
many more who had been teachers, figured in the
front of battle. For children, schools sometimes
continued, though much inconvenienced and interrupted in the turmoil. A glimpse into the life of
teachers of those days may be had in the following story. The *Richmond Examiner*, "a newspaper
Ishmael," charged Mr. Sydney O. Owens, a teacher,
with extortion; to which Mr. Owens replied that
while his charges were five or six times as high as
in 1860, "your shoemaker, carpenter, butcher,
market-man, demand from twenty to thirty or forty
times as much as in 1860. Will you show me a
civilian who is charging only six times the prices
in 1860, except the teacher only?   As to the amassing of fortunes by teachers, make your calculations,
sir, and you will find it an absurdity." [1]

In religion, the South has always been more faithful to old doctrines than has the North. While
several of her greatest men, like John C. Calhoun,
John Marshall, and Thomas Jefferson professed a
very liberal faith, the people in general have
not followed them. Wherever the Creole French
and Spanish prevail, as in the Southwest and lower
South, the Catholic church is zealously upheld.

[1] Eggleston, *A Rebel's Recollections*, 106.

In other regions Baptists, Methodists, and Presby-
terians absorb the community, clinging fast to
Biblical land-marks and the sternest traditions of
the founders. In the cities and among the great
planter-class the Protestant Episcopal church, coeval
in its establishment with the settlement of the
country, has possessed an authority which though
not formally admitted since colonial times, has remained scarcely less definite than that of the Church
of England. As at the North, so at the South, the
excitement of the war greatly stimulated religion.

At home the churches were aglow, revival followed
revival; no regiment departed for the front without
consecration; and in the camps a fire of devotion
often prevailed not surpassed in history. The leading characters of the period were men full of pious
ardor. Scenes recorded in the life of Bishop Polk
recall the enthusiasm of the crusades, and his environment, when his strong personality had oppor
tunity to make impression, recalls the Templars and
the Knights Hospitalers. Stonewall Jackson made
his life as near as he could a perpetual prayer,[1] and
he so powerfully swayed his troops that a campaign became almost a long-continued camp-meet-
ing, interspersed with marches and battles. The religion of Lee and Jefferson Davis was calmer, but, it
may be believed, not less earnest and profound.
St. Paul's Church, in Richmond, is a stately temple,
and as a spot where the flower of the Confederacy

[1] Hosmer, *Appeal to Arms* (*Am. Nation*, XX.), 139.

especially gathered, and whence many a leader
slain in battle was carried to his grave, it has tragic
and interesting associations. One contemplates to-
day with reverence the places within its walls where
each Sunday the president and chief-general of the
Confederacy bent the knee, men sincere, able, and
hard-striving, if misguided.

In this time, at the South, the refined enjoyments
which ordinarily adorn and afford relief to life, gave
way to sterner things: music was mostly silent,
except as employed for martial and religious incite-
ment:[1] art ceased to appeal: literature found few
votaries, excepting that certain noble lyrics and
ballads, like "Stonewall Jackson's Way," and the
"High Tide at Gettysburg," showed that there were
still poets. Few books were imported; still fewer
written and published.[2] Pamphlets abounded relating to one or another phase of the war: the
religious warmth caused the issue of many tracts
and sermons; each large town had its newspaper,
those of the cities often conducted with ability and
playing a great part in encouraging resistance. The
straits to which printers were at last reduced were
very grave; while ink and presses failed, paper, too,
grew scarce until coarse wrapping and wall paper
were used for want of anything better.

[1] W. R. Whittlesey, *List of Music of the South, 1860 – 1864*
(Library of Congress, in preparation).
[2] H. A. Morrison, *List of Confederate Documents and Books
published in the Confederacy* (Library of Congress, in preparation).

In struggles like the Civil War in America, it is no doubt usual and natural that the passion of the time should seize especially upon the more emotional sex. To say the least, the women of the North felt as keenly as the men the sentiment of loyalty; and at the South the women surpassed the men, if that were possible, in devotedness. The day went against them, and in the humiliations and injuries which came upon the South through the defeat, women especially suffered. It was their part to endure without the power to strike back; and when, at the close, the country was laid waste by invading armies, as witnesses and helpless victims in the inevitable desolation they had really a harder lot than the men, who at the front found a relief in the excitement of battle. Of course, in such a storm, good taste and delicacy were sometimes torn to shreds. The manifestations of the women of New Orleans which provoked the "woman order" of Butler,[1] were in some instances not less rough and exasperating than the means taken to suppress them. When the Federal foragers appeared upon estates whose owners were absent fighting under Lee or Johnston, the wives, mothers, and daughters left behind could have no smiles and soft words for the intruders. The bitterest wrath flashed out as a matter of course, and wrath as bitter in the answer; and there was no weighing of words in accusation or retort.

[1] Hosmer, *Appeal to Arms* (*Am. Nation*, XX.), 119.

A young woman of New Orleans, who was particularly obnoxious through her demonstrations and activity in thwarting the plans of the victors, framed upon her wall, as her "diploma," a note wherein, over the signature B. F. Butler, it was recorded that "the black-eyed Miss B. is an incorrigible little devil whom even prison-fare won't tame." [1] At a plantation a Federal colonel, in the parlor, uninvited but aiming to be polite, asked the gentle-mannered daughter of the house to play. She declined, upon which the colonel seated himself at the instrument; thereupon the girl, seizing a hatchet, severed with rapid blows the piano chords. "It is my piano, and it shall not give you a moment's pleasure." [2] Eggleston declares that he "never knew a reconstructed Southern woman," and it is very plain even now that while the men often look back calmly on this war, the injuries still rankle in the hearts of the women.

Yet after forty years the embers burn low: even their ancient foes may well pay tribute to the spirit, fortitude, and self-sacrifice of the women of the eracy. The suggestion publicly made by one late in the war, that all the southern women ut off their hair and sell it in Europe, where lieved it might bring forty million dollars, [3] ve been promptly and gladly carried out, have been managed. "There is not a

1 Rebel's Recollections, 66.   2 Ibid., 64.
peal to Arms (Am. Nation, XX.), 68.

woman worthy of the name of Southerner who
would not do it, if we could get it out of the country
and bread or meat in return." [1] To furnish the
nitre needed for powder, women dug up the earth
of smoke-houses and tobacco-barns from which it
might be extracted. They denied themselves meat
and coffee that it might be sent to the army. An
invalid suffering for proper food said: "I think it is
a sin to eat anything that can be used for rations."
In besieged towns, while nursing wounded men in
hospitals, the coolness of the women under fire was
always remarkable.[2] In a party of refugees driven
out of Atlanta by the edict of Sherman in September,
1864, a beautiful girl was seen to step from among
her companions, and kneeling to kiss passionately
the soil she was about to forsake.[3] Such tales make
up the record of the southern women of the war
period: self-sacrifice could go no further.

The behavior of the three and a half million
negroes of the South during the Civil War is an
interesting subject, and not altogether easy to
understand. Unmistakably they rejoiced, in th
main, in the freedom which the war brought
yet there were no attempts at insurrection.
Brown's effort at Harper's Ferry was ba
a complete misapprehension,[4] and perhaps
South the misapprehension of the negro

[1] Mrs. McGuire, *Diary of a Southern Refugee*, 341.
[2] Eggleston, *A Rebel's Recollections*, chap. iii.
[3] Miss Gay, *Life in Dixie During the War*, 141.
[4] Chadwick, *Causes of the Civil War* (*Am. Nation*

However it may be explained, it is certain that at the breaking up of the old relations of master and slave there was often mutual respect and affection. "They were our greatest comfort during the war," exclaims Mrs. Smedes. "They seemed to do better when they knew there was trouble in the white family."[1] Miss Gay relates an anecdote of a slave at once naïve and shrewd. She was one day surprised by a request from "King," a valuable slave, that she would sell him to "Mr. Johnson," a man whom King was known to dislike. When pressed to explain, King declared to Miss Gay and her mother a strong attachment, but said that he had been sent by Mr. Johnson to arrange the bargain which he, King, was anxious to conclude, a lot and store in Atlanta being offered in exchange. "I tell you what, Miss Polly, when this war is over none of us is going to belong to you. We'll all be free." By parting with him to Mr. Johnson, who did not see the near ending of slavery, as King explained, Miss Polly might transfer the loss to him, while she possessed comfortably the Atlanta real estate. "He's a mighty mean man, and I want him to lose me." Thus King proposed, in the transaction, to enjoy a triple pleasure: while obtaining his own freedom, to benefit the mistress whom he loved, and to satisfy his grudge against the man whom he disliked.[2]

[1] Mrs. Smedes, *A Southern Planter*, 196.
[2] Miss Gay, *Life in Dixie During the War*, 54 et seq.

Joseph Le Conte, an intelligent and conscientious owner of slaves, "felt distressingly the responsibility of their care; because I felt that those who owned slaves ought personally to manage them, as my father did. I could at any time during the twenty years previous to the war, have sold my land and negroes with great advantage to myself. This I refused to do out of a sense of responsibility for their welfare"; and he found that emancipation took from his shoulders a great burden, though he had fears as to the welfare of his people so suddenly manumitted.[1] Eggleston describes the behavior of his negroes when the white men were all gone. Most of them desired freedom and quite understood the situation: they knew that they had only to assert themselves to make their freedom certain, but they remained faithful and affectionate. At the end of the war they acted with modesty and wisdom, a great, calm patience being their most universal characteristic.[2]

At the beginning of 1865 the seceding states contained a people overwhelmed by bereavements, by material ruin, by the disappointment of every hope. The face of things was very stern: famine was close at hand to many: in the field there was desperate battle, the ultimate result of which none could doubt. With one or two concrete examples let the story end.

[1] Le Conte, *Autobiography*, 231.
[2] Eggleston, *A Rebel's Recollections*, 255 et seq.

The rebel war-clerk's entry for January 27, 1865, is: "Clear and coldest morning of the winter. Only the speculators have a supply of food and fuel. . . . My wood-house was broken into last night and two of the nine sticks of wood taken. Wood is selling at five dollars a stick. The thermometer at zero." [1]

Mrs. Chesnut writes, January 17, 1865: "Hood came yesterday. He is staying at the Prestons' with Jack. They sent for us. What a heartfelt greeting he gave us! He can stand well enough without his crutch, but he does very slow walking. How plainly he spoke out dreadful words about 'my defeat and discomfiture; my army destroyed, my losses.' Isabella said, 'Maybe you attempted the impossible,' and began one of her merriest stories. Jack Preston touched me on the arm and we slipped out. 'He did not hear a word she was saying. He had forgotten us all. Did you notice how he stared in the fire? and the lurid spots which came out in his face, and the drops of perspiration that stood on his forehead?' 'Yes, he is going over some bitter scene. He sees Willie Preston with his heart shot away. He sees the panic at Nashville, and the dead on the battle-field at Franklin.' 'That agony on his face comes again and again,' said tender-hearted Jack. 'I can't keep him out of those absent fits.'" [2]

---

[1] Jones, *Rebel War Clerk's Diary*, II., 400.
[2] Mrs. Chesnut, *Diary from Dixie*, 342 et seq.

19

CHAPTER XVII

DOWNFALL OF THE CONFEDERACY
(APRIL, 1865)

FROM the battle of Chattanooga, in October, 1863, to the spring of 1865, General Grant underwent severe trials. His labors were incessant, his responsibilities enormous, his capacity exercised to its fullest. Nevertheless, he was disappointed where he tried hardest; for after a year's steady campaigning, Richmond and the Army of Northern Virginia were still defiant. Though Meade continued to command the Army of the Potomac, Grant was always at his side, the real leader; and it was he whom the people judged for whatever that army did or failed to do. Meantime, Sherman, Sheridan, and Thomas reached high distinction. Their success, no doubt, was in great part due to Grant, who put those generals in place, had a hand in all their planning if he was not absolutely the director of their movements, and kept Lee from reinforcing their opponents; but to the popular eye this was not quite apparent. Grant's tenacity, indeed, through protracted disaster, excited wonder. Really, his heroic quality was never more manifest than in that long year's endurance of hope deferred; but this is plainer in the retrospect than it was at the moment.

In the other camp, Lee had reached a better recognition; his fame filled the world. January 19, 1865, the Confederate Congress, by making him commander-in-chief, conferred on him practically supreme power: he was the idol of the South, and could do what he chose within his lines. But to the Confederate capable of measuring the situation the end was evidently near.

The state of things at Richmond when the campaign was about to open is well indicated by an entry in the *Rebel War Clerk's Diary*.[1] "At a public meeting, Mr. Benjamin, being a member of the cabinet, made a significant and most extraordinary speech. He said the white fighting men were exhausted, and that black men must recruit the army—and it must be done at once. That General Lee had informed him he must abandon Richmond if not soon reinforced, and that negroes would answer. The states must send them, Congress having no authority. Virginia must lead the way and send twenty thousand to the trenches in twenty days. Let the negroes volunteer, and be emancipated. He also said that all who had cotton, tobacco, corn, meat, etc., must *give* them to the government, not sell them." March 13, the Confederate Congress passed an act authorizing the

[1] Jones, *Rebel War Clerk's Diary*, II., 415 (February 10, 1865).

enlistment of slaves as soldiers.[1] The opposition was great; the vote was carried by the influence of Lee, who declared, February 18, "that it was not only expedient but necessary"; that "the negroes, under proper circumstances, will make efficient soldiers." The end came before the effect of this policy, judged by many desperate, became apparent.[2]

Lee could oppose to the one hundred and twenty-five thousand men of Grant probably not half as many.[3] Warfare, which all winter long had to some extent continued, became in March as active as possible.[4] Lee, resolving to abandon Richmond, planned to unite with Johnston, in North Carolina: after which, Sherman having been crushed, there was a desperate chance that Grant might be overthrown. Lee could accomplish colossal tasks with small resources, and was sanguine enough to see an opportunity here. March 25, he began operations by strongly reinforcing the divisions of J. B. Gordon, and sending him to attack Fort Stedman, a work near the centre of the Federal line south of Petersburg. Confederate deserters had been coming over in considerable numbers to the Union lines, and when the Federal pickets before light saw the approaching crowd, they misjudged them to be fugitives, an error resulting in Confederate success.

[1] War Records, Serial No. 129, p. 1161. ·
[2] For Lee's letter, see Jones, Rebel War Clerk's Diary, II., 432.
[3] War Records, Serial No. 95, p. 62; Humphreys, Virginia Campaign, 1864–1865, p. 323.
[4] War Records, Serial No. 95, passim.

But it was temporary: the Federals rallied, and Gordon was driven out with heavy loss.[1]

March 26, Sheridan arrived,[2] after severe winter operations on the line of the Virginia Central Railroad. Next day also came Sherman, by steamer from North Carolina: and at the same time, from Washington, no other than the president. The heads consulted, but there was no pause in operations. A plan for despatching Sheridan's cavalry south to join Sherman's army was frustrated by floods which made the rivers impassable. The troopers, therefore, crossing to City Point, were sent at once by Grant to Dinwiddie Court-House, on the extreme left, where it was designed to turn Lee's right, the Confederate intrenchments running from Richmond thirty-five miles in that direction. Lee speedily reinforced the threatened point, and the Federal cavalry, supported by the Fifth and Second Corps, struggled at first unsuccessfully; but April 7, Sheridan gained a victory at Five Forks, having attacked with forty-five thousand men not half that number of infantry and cavalry:[3] but the defence was very brave and able, Pickett and Fitzhugh Lee being conspicuous.[4]   A regrettable incident of the day was that Sheridan saw fit to remove from the command of the Fifth Corps the veteran

---

[1] Gordon, *Reminiscences of Civil War*, 395.
[2] Sheridan, *Personal Memoirs*, II., 125.
[3] Livermore, *Numbers and Losses*, 137.
[4] *Battles and Leaders*, IV., 708 et seq.; Long, *Lee*, 409 et seq.

Warren, an officer of the highest distinction: this action was authorized and approved by Grant, who found Warren overcritical and assuming.[1] The case cannot be discussed here: a court of inquiry, many years later, found nothing wanting in Warren's conduct on that day, and his reputation bears no stain.[2]

Henceforth things moved rapidly. April 2, Wright and Parke, with the Sixth and Ninth Corps, feeling sure that Lee had thinned his lines in their front while strengthening his right, expressed confidence in their ability to break them; by this time, indeed, Lee had made up his mind to abandon Petersburg. The Federals attacked at daybreak from advanced positions gained a week before in the battle of Fort Stedman; while Ord, with the Army of the James, assaulted farther to the left: they carried the intrenchments of Petersburg, occupying next day that long-defended stronghold. Among the fallen was the brave Confederate General A. P. Hill, whom whether as man or soldier it would be hard to overpraise. April 3, Lee evacuated Richmond, the beginning of the end!

The Confederates marched westward for Amelia Court-House, to which point supplies had been ordered. While Weitzel, with the Twenty-fifth Corps, occupied Richmond, most of Grant's army streamed after their retreating foes, now greatly reduced in number. At Amelia Court-House, Lee

[1] Grant, *Personal Memoirs*, II., 306.
[2] Humphreys, *Virginia Campaign, 1864–1865*, p. 357 et seq.

found that by a mistake in orders the supplies were
not there. With no food, therefore, except what
they could gather from the country, losing a precious day in the effort, the doomed and scanty
columns toiled on. The South Side and the Danville railroads were now lost to them, the Federals
having seized the junction at Burkesville. Was
there a possibility of escaping westward? April 6,
Ewell, with eleven general officers and his division
of eight thousand men, was captured at Sailor's
Creek. Longstreet, near by at Rice's Station, with
whom marched Lee himself, evaded the pursuers
a little longer. Barlow's division of the Second
Federal Corps, marching at double-quick, saved,
April 7, a bridge already on fire, at Farmville.
On the evening of April 8, Custer's troopers seized
supply-trains at Appomattox station; and by the
9th Sheridan's cavalry, hurrying forward, barred
the road before Lee's head of column.[1] Already a
deputation of officers headed by General Pendleton
had expressed to Lee the conviction that their cause
was hopeless: he now saw himself that the end had
come.

The capitulation took place in the house of a
man named McLean, at Appomattox Court-House,
on April 9. Between March 2 and April 7, Lee had
lost in killed and wounded 6266, and in prisoners
13,769; thousands more had deserted, so that at

[1] Longstreet, *Manassas to Appomattox*, chaps, xlii., xliii.;
Battles and Leaders, IV., 729.

last but 26,765 laid down their arms.[1] "Men, we
have fought through the war together. I have
done my best for you. My heart is too full to say
more," was Lee's simple and manly farewell.[2]

At the interview between the two leaders, Lee
appeared in a new and handsome uniform, complete to the elegant sword at his side. No finer
type of manly grace and dignity can be imagined
than the Confederate leader as he stepped down
that day from his eminent position. Grant, on the
other hand, not anticipating the meeting, was in
the blouse of a private soldier, dusty from riding.
His face was haggard from illness which he had
suffered during the preceding night. The two men
met courteously, exchanging reminiscences of experiences which they had undergone together in the
old army. At last Grant wrote out his terms—
arms to be surrendered, the Army of Northern Virginia to be paroled until exchanged, the officers
to retain their side-arms and private horses: after
a little talk the "horse clause" was extended to
include each private soldier claiming to own a horse
or a mule, Grant conceiving that as "small farmers,"
which most of them were, the animals would be
needed "to put in the crop." This concession Lee
believed "would have a happy effect."[3] On these

[1] Livermore, *Numbers and Losses*, 135.

[2] Fitzhugh Lee, *R. E. Lee*, 396.

[3] Grant, *Personal Memoirs*, II., 341 et seq.; Sheridan, *Personal
Memoirs*, II., chaps. vii., viii.; *War Records*, Serial No. 95, pp.
557–1305 (Appomattox Campaign).

conditions Lee's army, "fought to a frazzle," [1] at last succumbed. The final campaign cost a Federal loss of ten thousand. The capitulation of Confederate commands far and near followed as the natural sequence. At Mobile a bloody and unnecessary battle was taking place at this very time: the city would have fallen without it.[2] April 26, Johnston surrendered, adding 37,047 to the number of paroled prisoners. The impetuous Sherman here, in arranging the conditions, exceeded his authority; and on the other hand, Stanton was captious and arbitrary, an unpleasant hitch, in which there was no superior guiding hand to bring the two parties together.[3] May 4, Dick Taylor gave up to Canby all troops still in arms in Mississippi and Alabama, a procedure followed, May 26, by Kirby Smith, in the trans - Mississippi. The total number paroled after surrender on the Appomattox terms, throughout the Confederacy, was 174,223.[4] On May 10, Jefferson Davis, who till then had evaded his pursuers, was captured in southern Georgia, and thereafter imprisoned in Fortress Monroe.

"The news is from Heaven," wrote Lowell, after Appomattox. "I felt a strange and tender exaltation. I wanted to laugh and I wanted to cry, and ended by holding my peace and feeling devoutly

---

[1] J. B. Gordon's expression, see Long, *Lee*, 421.
[2] *War Records*, Serial No. 103, pp. 87–322 (Mobile Campaign).
[3] W. T. Sherman, *Memoirs*, II., 347 et seq.; Gorham, *Stanton*, II., 170 et seq., for Stanton's relations with Sherman.
[4] *War Records*, Serial No. 126, p. 532.

thankful. There is something magnificent in having a country to love. It is almost like what one feels for a woman. Not so tender, perhaps, but to the full as self-forgetful." [1]

As we take farewell of Grant and Lee, figures so strongly contrasted as they meet in the interview at Appomattox, a word or two of characterization may be properly spoken. Both are held deep within the hearts of Americans as heroes sincere and manly. Of Lee, perhaps, it may be said that he has been unfortunate in biographers, who have painted him as free not only from all faults but also from all foibles. Not content with traits of greatness, those who describe him dwell often upon petty things—his well-cut beard, the correctness of his dress, the whiteness of his teeth, his proper deportment—until one almost expects to read, as he turns the page, that his hair was never parted awry and that he never ate with his knife. The only trace of shortcoming in him which one diligent reader of the accounts of him has been able to discover, is that he sometimes slept in church, if the sermon was dull. Such abnormal absence of defect becomes depressing: one longs for the discovery of a fault to redeem to humanity a hero so flawless. We can admire but hardly sympathize with a character entire and perfect.

Grant, on the other hand, always homely and unimpressive, discredited by his ante-bellum record,

[1] Lowell, *Letters*, I., 344 (April 13, 1865).

informal to the point of negligence about all details
of dress and manner, yet withal simple, intrepid,
honest, with an eye single to the great purpose which
he had adopted—here is a character that can be
embraced; he has roughness upon which the human
heart can take hold—worth most substantial, but
with a foil of limitation that makes him a man
among men.

Both men rank among the great soldiers of the
world. The best judgment seems to decide that
Lee constantly grew, being never greater than in
his final campaigns, which are faultless examples
of baffling a great power with small resources. In
Grant's record, the masterpiece is undoubtedly the
capture of Vicksburg. And yet where shall we
parallel the relentless force of will with which, in
1864, he, a man of gentle and humane nature,
smote with his flesh and blood hammer, believing
it to be the only way to success, and even hardened
his heart towards Andersonville, determined to secure by whatever sacrifice the salvation of his
country!

Abraham Lincoln was close at hand, at City
Point, when Richmond fell and the troops of the
Union took possession. In company with Admiral
Porter and a few officers, guarded by ten sailors
from the fleet, he landed from a barge near Libby
Prison and went on foot to the centre of the town.
It was by no means a triumphant march. To such
of the population as he encountered, mostly negroes,

his bearing was friendly. He consented to a meeting of the Virginia legislature, hoping they might withdraw their troops from Lee's army, still in the field, and so close the war without further bloodshed. Nothing came of it, but the incident is interesting as showing Lincoln's continued determination to allow the seceding states, after once submitting under proper guarantees, to have a voice in the settlement. This action of the president displeased many earnest men, Stanton remonstrating in the cabinet, and the committee on the conduct of the war, through its chairman, Wade, protesting with indignation.[1]

Lincoln returned to Washington, where, during the forenoon of April 9, was received the news of Lee's surrender. On the evening of Tuesday, April 11, he made to a company gathered at the White House his last public address. Aside from the interest arising from this fact, the address is in itself noteworthy as a clear description of the course he proposed to follow in reconstruction, and as a particularly good illustration of his calm, lucid wisdom.

The seceding states, being now fixed within the Union by the success of the Federal arms, the president thought it idle to dispute as to whether they had been brought back from without into the Union, or had never been out of it. As to Louisiana, he said: "The amount of constituency, so to speak, on which the new Louisiana government rests,

[1] Julian, *Political Recollections*, 254.

would be more satisfactory to all if it contained
fifty thousand, or thirty thousand, or even twenty
thousand, instead of only about twelve thousand,
as it does. It is also unsatisfactory to some that
the elective franchise is not given to the colored
man. I would myself now prefer that it were
conferred on the very intelligent, and on those who
serve our cause as soldiers."

Admitting that what had been done was not
quite satisfactory, the president contended that
the expedient way was not to reject, but to accept,
with the hope of bettering what was imperfect.
Summing up what had been done — the orderly
organization of a state government, the adoption
of a free constitution giving the benefit of public
schools equally to blacks and whites, the ratification of the thirteenth amendment, the state being
thus committed "to the many things and nearly
all the things the nation wants," Lincoln proceeded:
"Now if we reject and spurn them we do our utmost
to disorganize and disperse them. We, in effect,
say to the white man: You are worthless, or worse;
we will neither help you nor be helped by you. To
the blacks we say: This cup of liberty which these,
your masters, hold to your lips, we will dash from
you, and leave you to the chances of gathering the
spilled and scattered contents in some vague and
undefined when, where, and how. If this course,
discouraging and paralyzing both white and black,
has any tendency to bring Louisiana into proper

practical relations with the Union, I have so far been unable to perceive it. . . . Concede that the new government of Louisiana is only to what it should be, as the egg is to the fowl, we shall sooner have the fowl by hatching the egg than by smashing it."

What had been said of Louisiana, Lincoln urged in concluding the topic, would apply generally to other states. And yet since the situation in each state must be in some ways peculiar, no conclusive and inflexible plan could safely be prescribed as to details and collaterals. Such an exclusive and inflexible plan would surely become a new entanglement, although important principles may and must be inflexible.

The 14th of April was Good-Friday, but was a day of happiness rather than sadness. It was the fourth anniversary of the surrender of Fort Sumter, in 1861, and there was particular fitness in rejoicing on that day over the changed condition of affairs. The country universally was in a thanksgiving mood: even at the South, peace, accompanied though it was by defeat, seemed the greatest blessing. At Fort Sumter, in particular, the ceremonies were elaborate. A great company proceeded thither from the North: an oration was delivered within the fortress by Henry Ward Beecher, and after a prayer by the very chaplain who four years before had prayed upon the same spot, General Robert Anderson hoisted upon the flag-staff the very national flag which had been hauled down at the surrender.

At Washington a cabinet meeting took place in which, among other things, a measure was proposed somewhat careless in its terms as regards the rights of states: the president made known his wish that the just rights of states should be carefully upheld.[1]

General Grant, being in the city, was invited to accompany Mr. and Mrs. Lincoln that night to Ford's Theatre, to a performance of "Our American Cousin." Grant, having planned to visit his children at school, declined, in that way perhaps saving his life.[2] Mr. and Mrs. Lincoln drove in the evening to the theatre on Tenth Street, between E and F streets, accompanied only by two young friends. About ten o'clock John Wilkes Booth, an actor of some popularity, son and brother of much more famous men, a fanatical secessionist, forced his way into the box and shot the president from a point close at hand, making his escape across the stage. About the same time a confederate attacked Mr. Seward in his bed, to which the secretary was confined from the effects of a serious accident a few days before. Seward, though dangerously wounded, recovered. Lincoln, however, having been carried across the street to a bed, sank rapidly. The ball had traversed his brain: on the morning of April 15 he died.

---

[1] Nicolay and Hay, *Abraham Lincoln*, X., 282.
[2] Grant, *Personal Memoirs*, II., 357.

The expression of grief and horror throughout the civilized world was almost universal. Many who had ridiculed and denounced were among the sincerest mourners. Said Stanton, weeping at his bedside: "Now he belongs to the ages!" Nor was the South backward in evidence of sorrow. Some of her wiser men felt from the first, that however sore the calamity might be for others, the South was especially smitten.

It is the conviction of the people of the United States of America, based upon facts which the present record attempts to set forth, that the Union could not have been preserved without the patience, resolution, judgment, and devotedness of Abraham Lincoln. If so much as this can be justly said, perhaps no one among the sons of men has better served his kind.

The victims of the Civil War, among whom Abraham Lincoln was the most illustrious, numbered on the Union side fully three hundred and sixty thousand, counting only those who died in the field through casualties and disease; the war brought death to as many more perhaps, through causes less direct. As to the South, the account cannot be definitely rendered, but probably would not be much less. The death-list therefore runs beyond the million mark,[1] while of men surviving but disabled by wounds or disease, no definite estimate can be made. Rhodes judges $4,750,000,000

[1] Livermore, *Numbers and Losses*, 1-63.

to be a fair estimate of what the war cost the North, whereas $3,000,000,000 would have been generous purchase money for the four million slaves before the war began.   The United States won a position "in the first rank among military nations";[1] and to support the proposition that it is a good thing for a nation to be capable of fighting hard upon occasion, Rhodes quotes Francis Parkman:

"Since the world began, no nation has ever risen to a commanding eminence which has not, at some period of its history, been redoubtable in war. And in every well-balanced development of nations, as of individuals, the warlike instinct and the military point of honor are not repressed and extinguished, but refined and civilized.   It belongs to the pedagogue, not the philosopher, to declaim against them as relics of barbarism."[2]   This opinion we may accept though recognizing the hatefulness of war; and, though sorrowing, also that of Sir Charles Lyell, that the result of the Civil War is worth all it cost in blood and treasure.[3]   The rescued Union at the present moment holds within its forty-six states a population close upon a hundred millions. To form that population, into a strong Anglo-Saxon stock blood has been infused from many of the better breeds of men.   The life of this great people is regulated according to the best polity which has

---

[1] Livermore, *Numbers and Losses*, 77.
[2] Rhodes, *United States*, V., 188.
[3] Mrs. Lyell, *Sir C. Lyell*, II., 399.

been developed in the long evolution of the human race;[1] the appliances of the highest civilization are scattered abroad in it; a patriotism which has become a passion characterizes its citizens.   Through the lives and the resources poured out in the war, it was secured that there should be one nation, not a jarring neighborhood of rival powers, with mutual jealousies, with conflicting interests, with delicate questions as to the balance of power, occuring and again recurring, and only to be settled in the midst of confusion and slaughter.   The war settled not only that the Union should persist, but that its corner-stone should be freedom.   Among the nations of the earth, there is not one whose foundations seem more stable, a stability which North and South are equally anxious to maintain.

[1] Hosmer, *Short History of Anglo-Saxon Freedom.*

CHAPTER XVIII

CRITICAL ESSAY ON AUTHORITIES

THIS chapter continues and supplements the similar chapter at the end of the preceding volume of this series, James K. Hosmer, *The Appeal to Arms*. Many of the works here noticed will be cited also in the succeeding volume, W. A. Dunning, *Reconstruction, Political and Economic*. Selecting from many thousands of works, we mention first the most useful secondary publications.

GENERAL HISTORIES

Of books heretofore listed but not evalued: W. C. Bryant and S. H. Gay, *Popular History of the United States* (2d ed., 5 vols., 1896), IV., 435–600, a work of good character, though Bryant had no hand in the authorship; Rossiter Johnson, *Short History of the War* (1888); J. N. Larned, *History for Ready Reference* (6 vols., 1901), III., 529–675, a body of excellent material made easily accessible; James Ford Rhodes, *History of the United States from the Compromise of 1850* (7 vols., 1893–1906), III.–V., of the highest authority; for strictures on some portions, see C. F. Adams, *Some Phases of the Civil War* (1905); James Schouler, *History of the United States under the Constitution* (6 vols., rev. ed., 1899), VI., comprehensive and well studied; Goldwin Smith, *History of United States* (1893), from the point of view of an extremely able and fair-minded Englishman; Woodrow Wilson, *History of the American People* (5 vols., 1902), IV., 145–312, a well-proportioned and scholarly summary.

AMERICAN HISTORIES OF THE PERIOD

Adam Badeau, *Military History of Grant* (3 vols., 1868–1881), an elaborate technical work by an officer closely attached to Grant; John M. Botts, *Great Rebellion* (1866), the work of a Virginian who remained loyal to the Union; John W. Burgess, *The Civil War and the Constitution* (2 vols., 1901), by a student of political science; J. M. Callahan, *Diplomatic History of the Southern Confederacy* (1901), the subject well studied though clumsily presented; S. S. Cox, *Three Decades* (1865), by an able Democratic politician; Theodore A. Dodge, *Bird's-Eye View of the Civil War* (1897), the straightforward account of a scientific soldier helped out by simple but sufficient maps; John W. Draper, *History of the Civil War* (3 vols., 1867), useful but written too near the time to have proper perspective; which may be said also of E. A. Duyckinck, *History of the Civil War* (3 vols., no date); C. A. Evans, editor, *Confederate History* (12 vols., 1899), a collection of accounts by southern writers edited by a meritorious soldier; John Fiske, *Mississippi Valley in the Civil War* (1900), well studied and attractively presented; J. Fitch, *Annals of the Army of the Cumberland* (1863); J. R. Giddings, *History of the Rebellion* (1864), treats the subject incompletely from the point of view of a strong abolitionist; Horace Greeley, *The American Conflict* (2 vols., 1864–1866), vol. II. occupied by an account of the Civil War, full of information and marked by the writer's excellences and defects; Harper's *Pictorial History of the Rebellion* (2 vols., 1868), made up both in text and in illustrations from *Harper's Weekly*, which portrays most graphically events and characters throughout the four years; J. T. Headley, *The Great Rebellion* (2 vols., 1866), popular and partisan; Rossiter Johnson, *Story of a Great Conflict* (1894), a useful résumé; *Frank Leslie's Weekly*, the rival of *Harper's Weekly*, as a pictorial record; John A. Logan, *The Great Conspiracy* (1886), from the point of view of a War Democrat who figured both in field and forum; B. J. Lossing, *Pictorial History of the Civil War* (3 vols., 1866–1869), especially valuable for its illustrations; Asa Mahan, *Critical History of the Late War* (1877), not conspicuous; J. G. Nicolay, "The Civil War, 1861–1865" (in *Cambridge Modern History*, VII., 443–548, 1903); J. G. Nicolay, "The North During the War, 1861–1865" (*Ibid.*, 568–602)—careful summaries by one of the best-informed of Civil War authorities; Louis Philippe Albert d'Orléans, Comte de Paris, *History of the Civil War in America* (transl., 4 vols., 1875–1888), an unfinished account in detail of military events by a French nobleman, an accomplished soldier who served in the Army of the Potomac, of high authority; E. A. Pollard, *The Lost Cause* (1867), a Richmond editor, brilliant, very unfriendly to Jefferson Davis, writes a book not to be neglected; J. C. Reed, *The Brothers' War* (1905); J. C. Schwab, "The South During the War, 1861 – 1865" (in *Cambridge Modern History*, VII., 603–621, 1903), a résumé by a writer distinguished in the field of economics; William Swinton, *Campaigns of the Army of the Potomac* (1882), also, *Twelve Decisive Battles of the War* (1867), graphic pictures, but less relied upon than once; T. B. Van Horne, *History of the Army of the Cumberland* (2 vols., 1875), by a chaplain who made the campaigns; O. J. Victor, *History of the Southern Rebellion* (4 vols., 1868), superseded by later and better compilations; Woodrow Wilson, *Division and Reunion* (1879), brief discussion by a philosophical historian.

FOREIGN HISTORIES OF THE PERIOD

ENGLISH.—H. C. Fletcher, *History of the Civil War in America* (3 vols., 1865), detailed and intelligent; Percy Greg, *History of the United States from the Foundation of Virginia to the Reconstruction of the Union* (2 vols., 1887), abounds in errors; vol. II. largely taken up with an account of the Civil War, hostile to the North; W. B. Wood and J. E. Edmonds, *History of the Civil War in the United States* (1905), a careful study by British officers designed especially for students of the Staff College.

FRENCH.—E. C. Grasset, *La Guerre de la Sécession* (2 vols.,

1886); E. R. L. Laboulaye, *Pourquoi le Nord ne peut accepter la Séparation* (1863), an able presentation of the northern case; F. Lecomte, *La Guerre de la Sécession* (3 vols., 1866–1867); Louis Philippe d'Orléans, Comte de Paris, *Histoire de la Guerre Civile en Amérique* (7 vols., with atlas, 1874–1890), the translation is elsewhere mentioned and characterized; Philippe Régis, Baron de Trobriand, *Quatre Ans de Campagnes à l'armée du Potomac* (1867), narrates the service of a brave Franco-American.

GERMAN.—H. Blankenburg, *Die innern Kaempfe der Nordamerikanischen Union* (1869); E. R. Luecke, *Der Buergerkrieg der Vereinigten Staaten* (1892); J. A. Scheibert, *Der Amerikanische Buergerkrieg* (1874); E. R. Schmidt, *Der Amerikanische Buergerkrieg* (1867).

CONSTITUTIONAL DISCUSSIONS

The following books may be consulted, table of contents and index in each case affording the necessary guidance.

THE NORTHERN SIDE.—G. S. Boutwell, *Constitution of the United States at the End of the First Century* (1895); A. G. Fisher, *Trial of the Constitution* (1862); John C. Hurd, *The Union-State* (1890), philosophical and erudite; Judson S. Landon, *The Constitutional History and Government of the United States* (3d ed., 1905); John J. Lalor, *Cyclopædia of Political Science* (3 vols., 1881), trustworthy discussions of many topics in large part by Alexander Johnston, these valuable articles have been republished under the editorship of James A. Woodburn under the title of *American Political History, 1763–1876* (2 vols., 1905); E. McClain, *Constitutional Law in the United States* (1905); Joel Parker, *Constitutional Law with Reference to the Present Condition of the United States* (1862), by the eminent head of the Harvard Law School, who had no heart for the struggle; J. N. Pomeroy, *Introduction to the Constitutional Law of the United States* (1868); Joseph Story, *Commentaries on the Constitution of the United States* (4th ed., by Thomas M. Cooley, 1880), of the highest authority; Joel Tiffany

Treatise on Government (1867); H. E. Von Holst, *Constitutional History of the United States* (transl. by Lalor, Mason, and Shorey, 8 vols., 1876–1892), much deferred to; William Whiting, *War Powers of the Government* (1864); Henry Wilson, *Political Measures of the United States Congress* (1866).

THE SOUTHERN SIDE.—P. C. Centz (pseudonym for Bernard J. Sage), *Republic of Republics* (1880), best brief presentation of the southern view; J. L. M. Curry, *Civil History of the Confederate Government* (1901), by a respected statesman and educator; R. L. Dabney, *Defence of Virginia* (1867); Jefferson Davis, *Rise and Fall of the Confederate Government* (2 vols., 1881), detailed, restrained, reticent of animosities felt towards critics at home and enemies outside, but marked by faulty judgment; Alexander H. Stephens, *Constitutional View of the Late War between the States* (2 vols., 1868–1870), a defence of the South by one of the best heads of the Confederacy; James Williams, *The South Vindicated* (1862).

INTERNATIONAL RELATIONS

Montague Bernard, *Historical Account of the Neutrality of Great Britain* (1870); John Bigelow, *France and the Confederate Navy* (1888); Travers Twiss, *Law of Nations Considered as Independent Political Communities* (2 vols., 1875); Francis M. Wharton, *Digest of International Law of United States* (1886); Henry Wheaton, *Elements of International Law* (1892); Theodore Woolsey, *International Law* (1901).

MILITARY GOVERNMENT

Horace Binney, *Privilege of the Writ of Habeas Corpus* (1865); Rollin C. Hurd, *Treatise on Habeas Corpus* (1858); John A. Marshall, *American Bastile* (1869). Very helpful are the biographies of Lincoln, Seward, Chase, and Stanton.

THE NEGROES

T. W. Higginson, *Army Life in a Black Regiment* (1882); M. G. McDougal, *Fugitive Slaves* (Radcliffe Monographs,

1891); Mary Tremaine, *Slavery in the District of Columbia* (1892); G. W. Williams, *History of the Negro Troops in the War of the Rebellion* (1888); Henry Wilson, *Rise and Fall of the Slave Power in America* (3 vols., 1872–1877).

FINANCE

H. C. Adams, *Public Debts* (1893); A. S. Bolles, *Financial History* (3 vols., 1885); Davis R. Dewey, *Financial History of the United States* (1903), an excellent authority; John J. Knox, *American Notes*, a history of the various issues of paper money of the United States (1899); J. C. Schwab, *Confederate States of America, Financial and Industrial* (1901), well studied and presented; C. J. Stillé, *How a Free People Conduct a Long War* (1863); W. G. Sumner, *American Currency* (1874); F. W. Taussig, *History of the Tariff* (1885); Horace White, *Money and Banking, 1860–1894* (1903); Edward Stanwood, *American Tariff Controversies in the Nineteenth Century* (2 vols., 1903).

NAVAL AFFAIRS

C. C. Beaman, *National and Private Alabama Claims* (1871); C. B. Boynton, *History of the Navy during the Rebellion* (1868); James D. Bulloch, *Secret Service of the Confederate States in Europe* (2 vols., 1884), an efficient agent's well-told story; C. E. Hunt, *The Shenandoah* (1867); E. S. Maclay, *History of the United States Navy* (2 vols., 1894); David D. Porter, *Naval History of the Civil War* (1886); A. Roberts, *Never Caught* (1867), blockade running; J. Thomas Scharf, *History of the Confederate States Navy* (1894); Raphael Semmes, *Service Afloat* (1887), a record by the captain of the *Alabama* of the destruction of American commerce; Arthur Sinclair, *Two Years in the "Alabama"* (1895); John Wilkinson, *Narrative of a Blockade Runner* (1877); H. W. Wilson, *Iron-Clads in Action* (1897).

STATISTICAL AND TECHNICAL WORKS

W. F. Fox, *Regimental Losses in the American Civil War* (1889); G. F. R. Henderson, *The Science of War* (1905), chaps. viii.–xii., very important criticism by a scientific soldier; Thomas L. Livermore, *Numbers and Losses of the Civil War in America* (1901), the best authority on that subject; Frederick Phisterer, *Statistical Record of the Army of the United States* (1883); Robert C. Wood, *The Confederate Hand-Book* (1900). Semi-official in character are, G. W. Cullum, *Biographical Register of the U. S. Military Academy at West Point* (rev. ed., 4 vols., 1891–1901), and J. H. S. Hamersly, *Complete Regular Army Register* (1880), and *General Register of the U. S. Navy and Marine Corps* (1882) combined in *Complete Army and Navy Register, 1776 to 1887* (1888). General Cullum's work has particular value as giving a minute and accurate record of the stations held by each West Point graduate; but in using it it must be remembered that in the case of Confederates the record ceases at the date when they gave up their allegiance to the Union.

SONGS AND BALLADS

NORTHERN.—W. F. Allen, C. E. Ware, Lucy M. Garrison, compilers, *Slave Songs of the United States* (1867), with scholarly introduction by Professor Allen; Ledyard Bell, compiler, *Pen Pictures of the Civil War, Lyrics, etc.* (1866); George H. Boker, *Poems of the War* (1864), productions of merit; H. H. Brownell, *War Lyrics and Other Poems* (1866); by a man of genius who saw service in the navy; Frances T. Child, *War Lyrics for Freemen* (1862), interesting work ⁄ the patriotic Harvard professor of English; *Copperhead instrel, a Choice Collection of Democratic Poems and Songs* 67); *The Drum-Beat*, songs with piano-forte accompanit (1865); A. J. H. Duganne, *Ballads of the War* (1862); Henry Hayward, editor, *Poetical Pen Pictures of the War, ected from our Union Poets* (1864); Frank Moore, editor, rics of Loyalty (1864); *Selection of War Lyrics*, with illustrations on wood by F. O. C. Darley (1864); *Soldiers' and Sailors' Patriotic Songs and Hymns* (1864); *Trumpet of Freedom* (1864), martial part songs; *War Ballads published during the United States War of the Rebellion*, a collection of two hundred and eighteen broadsides containing songs, lyrics, and hymns, in Boston Public Library.

SOUTHERN.—F. D. Allan, compiler, *A Collection of Southern Patriotic Songs, made during Confederate Times* (1874); W. L. Fagan, *Southern War Songs* (1890, illustrated); *The Jack Morgan Songster, compiled by a Captain in General Lee's Army* (1864); Emily W. Mason, compiler, *The Southern Poems of the War* (1869); Frank Moore, *Rebel Rhymes and Rhapsodies* (1864); W. Gilmore Simms, editor, *War Poetry of the South* (1866); *War Lyrics and Songs of the South* (London, Spottiswoode & Co., 1866); selection of one hundred and eighty-one secession songs and poems, of various dates, broadsides, in Boston Public Library; H. M. Wharton, editor, *War Songs and Poems of the Southern Confederacy* (1904).

For southern music, consult W. R. Whittlesey, *List of Music of the South, 1860–1864* (Library of Congress, in preparation).

NORTH AND SOUTH.—F. F. Browne, editor, *Bugle Echoes, a Collection of Poems of the Civil War, Northern and Southern* (1866); George Cary Eggleston, editor, *American War Ballads* (2 vols., 1889), a collection general in character, but largely made up of Civil War poetry; Richard Grant White, editor, *Poetry Literary, Narrative, and Satirical, of the Civil War* (1866); H. L. Williams, editor, *War Songs of the Blue and Gray, as Sung by the Brave Soldiers of the Union and Confederate Armies* (1905); each volume of Frank Moore's *Rebellion Record* contains a profuse compilation of the w poetry of the year.

OFFICIAL CIVIL WAR RECORD

The War of the Rebellion, A Compilation of the Reco of the Union and Confederate Armies, a work of vast dime sions carried through with great thoroughness and ski was begun before the end of the war, but long hampered through want of means, till a general pressure from all sections of the country caused Congress to provide for it. A War Records Office was created and placed under the direction of Adjutant-General E. D. Townsend, in 1877. Officers of the army, Lieutenant-Colonel R. N. Scott, Lieutenant-Colonel H. M. Lazelle, Major G. W. Davis, Major George B. Davis, judge-advocate of the United States army, and General F. C. Ainsworth, together with two civilian experts, Leslie J. Perry and Joseph W. Kirtly, worked diligently for many years, with the result that an enormous body of interesting documents has been put into a shape permanent and easily accessible. As regards the Federal records, much care for their preservation was taken from the very beginning of the war. Efforts were constantly made also to supplement these by papers collected from individual participants in the struggle.

The Confederate records underwent greater risks. That they were in great part preserved in spite of all is especially due to General Samuel Cooper (adjutant and inspector-general C. S. A.), who, at the fall of Richmond in April, 1865, fleeing southward with Jefferson Davis, had in his charge the documents of the Confederate government. All these he delivered over to the United States for preservation upon his capture by Sherman at Charlotte, North Carolina. The collection thus preserved was greatly increased by the efforts of General Marcus J. Wright, C. S. A., who, now in the service of the United States, spent years in an indefatigable search among the survivors of the "lost cause" for papers that might be of value.

The result of all this labor is summed up substantially as follows, in a document recently issued under authority of the secretary of war:

The official records of the Union and Confederate armies consist of four series, an atlas, and a general index, namely:

[A] Series I.—Embraces the formal reports, both Union and Confederate, of the first seizures of United States property in the southern states, and of all military operations in the field, with the correspondence, orders, and returns relating specially thereto, accompanied by an atlas. It consists of vols. I. to LIII., comprising one hundred and eleven books, many of the volumes being in parts, each part a book. (Serial Nos. 1–111.)

[B] Series II.—Contains the correspondence, orders, reports, and returns, Union and Confederate, relating to prisoners of war and (so far as the military authorities were concerned) to state and political prisoners. It consists of eight books, designated as vols. I. to VIII. (or Serial Nos. 114 to 121).

[C] Series III.—Contains the correspondence, orders, reports, and returns of the Union authorities (embracing their correspondence with the Confederate officials) *not* relating specially to the subjects of the first and second series. It sets forth the annual and special reports of the secretary of war, of the general-in-chief, and of the chiefs of the several staff-corps and departments, the call for troops, and the correspondence between the national and several state authorities. This series consists of five books, numbered as vols. I. to V. (or Serial Nos. 122 to 126)

[D] Series IV.—Exhibits the correspondence, orders, reports, and returns of the Confederate authorities with regard to the same subjects as those embraced in the third series. It consists of three books, designated as vols. I. to III. (or Serial Nos. 127 to 129).

[E] The Atlas.—Contains 178 plates, consisting of several hundred maps of battle-fields of the war, routes of march of the armies, plans of forts, etc., and a number of photographic views of prominent scenes, places, and objects.

[F] In the preparation of the War Records the convenience of the reader has been carefully consulted: each volume is separately indexed, prefaced by a synopsis of events, and by a table giving not only its own contents, but those of all preceding volumes in the series.

A general index to the entire work, together with an

appendix containing additions and corrections of errors discovered in the several volumes after publication, consists of one book, bearing only the serial number 130.

Series I., II., III., IV., the General Index, and the Atlas, have been published, with the exception of vols. LIV. and LV., and comprise 128 books exclusive of the Atlas.

LIV. and LV. (Serial Nos. 112 and 113) are reserved for volumes to contain such additional matter as it may be decided to publish in future, but they will not be issued unless sufficient material to justify their publication shall be secured. Therefore, as the publication now stands, Series I. ends with vol. LIII. (Serial No. 111), and Series II. begins with vol. I. (Serial No. 114).

This great body of documents is well declared by General Cox, probably the best authority, to be by far the most important source concerned with the Civil War, "a wonderful collection of historical material full of personal life, as well as of formal documentary evidence." The material, indeed, must be used with care: honest mistakes are always inevitable; papers, too, occur in which superior officers declare the reports of subordinates to be false and worthless—attempts to gloss over failure in the performance of duty, or to arrogate credit which does not belong to them. As regards the leaders, the value of what they have written is sometimes discounted from the fact that the writers now seek to screen themselves from the consequence of failure, now claim as their own honors which they have not won, now allow their personal prejudices and animosities to warp their statements. "Alas for history when made up from official reports!" exclaims General George H. Gordon in his *From Brook Farm to Cedar Mountain* (249 note), in wrath over a report of his corps commander. The reader must always bear in mind that these agents in the great conflict were very human instruments, whose imperfections inhere in the records they leave. But the careful seeker can usually get at the truth. The statements of rivals and enemies standing on pages near at hand, can be set over against each other. The untruth of the subordinate will be exposed in the relation of the commander; and, on the other hand, the error of the commander will be revealed in the accounts of his brigadiers and colonels. In great part the mistakes and untruths can be detected by striking a balance within the material contained in the war records themselves. But, of course, the scrupulous investigator will check what he here derives by what may be found in the unofficial records, the vast body of memoirs, reminiscences, discussions, memoranda of every kind, with which the press has teemed since the conflict began.

The world will no doubt coincide in the judgment of General Cox, that while all has a value, the more formal documents yield in interest to the terse, hurried despatches and telegrams dictated among the harassments of a campaign or amid the fire of battle—breathless utterances, as it were, that bring one into the very smoke and flashing of the engagement.

In 1894, under authority of the secretary of the navy, was begun the publication of the *Official Records of the Union and Confederate Navies in the War of the Rebellion*, under supervision of Lieutenant-Commander Richard Rush and Mr. Robert H. Woods. The plan followed is the same as that of the army records, nineteen volumes having appeared up to the present time.

The Medical and Surgical History of the War of the Rebellion, undertaken in 1870 under the supervision of Surgeon-General J. K. Barnes, and finished in 1888, is comprised within six quarto volumes profusely illustrated, three of which, with a supplement, are medical, and three are surgical. It is technical in character, and bears the highest reputation as a scientific work.

The important *Joint Committee on the Conduct of the War*, appointed in 1861, made successive reports, those up to 1863 comprised in three parts, each part occupying a volume; the succeeding ones also in three parts, with two supplementary volumes. These records possess great interest, particularly the portions devoted to testimony.

With regard to many important events of the war the principal actors and their subordinates gave evidence, often under rigorous cross-examination. Thus many facts were brought out which otherwise might not have been in evidence.

PUBLIC DOCUMENTS IN GENERAL

NORTHERN.—In a great number of the documents published by the legislative, executive, and judicial branches of the government during the years 1861 to 1865 (the years of the administration of Abraham Lincoln and of the thirty-seventh and thirty-eighth Congresses), the influence of the Civil War is revealed. The nation's struggle for existence, indeed, subordinates all else, and the activity of the civil departments, as well as of the military, is heavily shadowed by the ever-present crisis. For the Federal side the records are complete. The daily debates of both Senate and House in the thirty-seventh and thirty-eighth Congresses are preserved in the *Congressional Globe;* the texts of all statutes and resolutions passed are in the *Statutes at Large;* the work of the various civil divisions of the administration (state department, treasury, war, navy, interior, post-office), in the *Executive Documents* relating respectively to those divisions. The records of the Federal supreme court were kept up from term to term. The decrees of the district and circuit courts have recently been gathered into a private publication known as *Federal Cases.* See A. B. Hart, *Foundations of American Foreign Policy*, 275 et seq. (1901), for an account of the published decisions of the Federal courts, supreme, circuit, and district.

SOUTHERN.—The civil records of the Confederacy have been less perfectly available. The government is publishing at the present moment (1906) the *Journals of the Confederate Congress*, that of the Senate being already complete. The *Confederate Statutes at Large* (excepting perhaps the acts of the closing session of Congress) were printed at the time. James D. Richardson, in *Messages and Papers of the Confederacy* (2 vols., Nashville, 1905), gives a selection of the manifestoes of the Montgomery and Richmond governments, but the number is not large; the only approach to a full collection of such documents is in the war department at Washington. Exactly how much has escaped destruction cannot yet be told. The remnant is fragmentary, nor are adequate lists available of the things preserved. But see H. A. Morrison, *List of Confederate Documents and of Books published in the Confederacy* (in preparation in the Library of Congress), which will go far to supply the lack.

STATE DOCUMENTS

Respecting the individual states both of the North and South, there is for each one, during the years 1861 to 1865, both a military and a civil series of records; and as in the case of the documents of the central governments, so here, the struggle impresses itself on the civil records as well as on those especially devoted to the war. Here too, as regards the South, gaps occur, while the northern states, better situated, show completeness. In this class, of most interest through time to come, will be the reports of the adjutant-generals, containing the regimental rosters.

NON-OFFICIAL COLLECTIONS OF SOURCES

Almost as interesting and important as the official documents is the mass of material not published by the government, coming from participants in, or eye witnesses of, the events described. The posts of the Loyal Legion, Grand Army of the Republic, Confederate Veterans, and various other societies of survivors, have printed, to a large extent, the papers read before them, officers and private soldiers thus putting on record their reminiscences. Histories of corps, divisions, brigades, regiments, batteries, are numerous, but, of course, differ much in value. The publications of the Military Historical Society of Massachusetts, comprising ten volumes and still in progress, have especial value, containing besides the contributions of accomplished officers, papers by such critics as John C. Ropes, founder of the society.   Albert Bushnell Hart, *Amer-*

ican History told by Contemporaries (4 vols., 1897–1901), contains in vol. IV. numerous extracts from sources on military and civil affairs. *The Battles and Leaders of the Civil War* (4 vols., 1888), made up of papers of soldiers of high and low station, North and South, beautifully illustrated by maps and pictures, is pronounced by G. F. R. Henderson to be one of the most important military authorities ever published. Frank Moore (editor), *Rebellion Record* (13 vols., beginning with the year 1861), preserves ephemeral utterances of the war - time, compiled from newspapers, pamphlets, popular manifestoes of all kinds. Each volume contains a compilation of songs and ballads of the period: the collections of official reports are superseded by the fuller and more accurate publications of the government. *Appleton's Annual Cyclopædia* (beginning 1861, edited by W. T. Tenney), is an admirable digest, made at the moment from contemporary accounts of events; *Campaigns of the Civil War* (13 vols., 1881–1890), published by Scribners, are monographs, usually by participating generals, and are of high authority: *Great Commanders* (1892), a series edited by General J. G. Wilson, comprises biographies of soldiers, North and South, by competent hands; *The American Statesmen* series, Houghton, Mifflin & Co., publishers, comprises several biographies of Civil War figures—Lincoln, Chase, Seward, Sumner, C. F. Adams, Thaddeus Stevens—which cannot be passed over; *The American Commonwealth* series, Houghton, Mifflin & Co., publishers, still in progress, offers in each volume chapters concerned with the relations of the state to the war. The following volumes have appeared: California, Connecticut, Indiana, Kansas, Kentucky, Maryland, Michigan, Missouri, New Hampshire, New York, Ohio, Rhode Island, Texas, Vermont, Virginia.

MILITARY BIOGRAPHIES AND REMINISCENCES

By writers in intimate relations with their subjects, or by the subjects themselves, the following have especial value:

21

NORTHERN COMBATANTS. — B. P. Poore, *Ambrose E. Burnside* (1882); Benjamin F. Butler, *Butler's Book* (1892), racy with the peculiarities of its author; J. D. Cox, *Military Reminiscences* (2 vols., 1900), one of the very best records ; M. Dix, *John A. Dix* (2 vols., 1883), a high-minded War Democrat; Loyall Farragut, *David G. Farragut* (1879); also *Farragut*, by A. T. Mahan (1892), a work of especial value; J. M. Hoppin, *Life of Admiral Foote* (1874), a man of brave religious spirit; Ulysses S. Grant, *Personal Memoirs* (2 vols., 1895), of the first importance as a source, and very charming as revealing a simple and honest personality; also *Grant*, by Badeau, Brooks, Church, Dana, and Wilson, Garland, Knox, and Porter; F. A. Walker, *W. S. Hancock* (1894), a great soldier portrayed by a writer unusually accomplished, closely connected with him; also *Hancock*, by his wife (1887); Herman Haupt, *Reminiscences* (1901), the story of an eminent military engineer; W. B. Hazen, *Narrative of Military Service* (1885), a good general of division in the western army; J. Warren Keifer, *Slavery and Four Years of War* (1900), a soldier of long and wide experience who later became speaker of the House; R. M. Bache, *George Gordon Meade* (1897), appreciations of a much-tried and faithful soldier; also *Meade*, by I. R. Pennypacker (1901); M. Cavanagh, *Memoir of T. F. Meagher* (1892), an Irish patriot who took service for the Union; Whitelaw Reid, *Ohio in the War* (1868), by a newspaper correspondent famous later as editor and diplomatist; John M. Palmer, *Personal Reminiscences* (1901), the record of a good citizen and soldier; J. M. Schofield, *Forty-six Years in the Army* (1897), memoirs of a teacher who became a general, recording valiant service, but disputatious; Philip H. Sheridan, *Personal Memoirs* (2 vols., 1902), direct and candid, with unexpected touches of sensibility; William Tecumseh Sherman, *Memoirs* (2 vols., 1886), brusque, straightforward, frankly confident of his own merit, concealing nothing; Henry Coppee, *George H. Thomas* (1893); also *Thomas*, by Donn Piatt and T. B. Van Horne (1882); P. S. Michie, *Life and Letters of Emory Upton* (1885), a young soldier of great bravery and ability; Lew Wallace, *An Autobiography* (2 vols., 1906), a man of literary genius and delicate tastes, who for a time played a soldierly part.

SOUTHERN COMBATANTS. — A. Roman, *Pierre G. T. Beauregard* (2 vols., 1884), a constant and valiant champion of the Confederacy exhaustively considered; J. A. Wyeth, *N. B. Forrest* (1899), paints the career of a soldier uninstructed but of great gifts; John B. Hood, *Advance and Retreat* (1880), the self-told record of a brave but unfortunate leader; Joseph E. Johnston, *Narrative of Military Operations* (1874), the story of one of the ablest Confederate leaders, told by himself; also *Johnston*, by R. N. Hughes (1893), and by B. P. Johnson (1891); A. L. Long, *Robert Edward Lee* (1886), a work of high military value upon the greatest soldier of the South; also, *Lee*, by Cooke, Fitzhugh Lee, R. E. Lee, Jr., Trent, and White; James Longstreet, *From Manassas to Appomattox* (1903), of the highest value and interest; a so Mrs. James Longstreet, *Lee and Longstreet at High Tide* (1904); J. S. Mosby, *War Reminiscences* (1887), the most famous of bush-whackers; Susan P. Lee, *Memoirs of General W. N. Pendleton* (1893), a clergyman who became a soldier; W. M. Polk, *Leonidas Polk* (2 vols., 1893), the memoirs of a sincere and picturesque character; A. H. Noll, *Rev. Dr. E. L. Quintard* (1905), a Confederate chaplain who became Bishop of Tennessee; H. B. McClellan, *J. E. B. Stuart* (1885), the career of the cavalry leader elaborately described; Richard Taylor, *Destruction and Reconstruc ʼ ʼ* (1879), an indefatigable soldier presents a story with touches of sensibility and literary grace; Joseph Wheeler, *Campaigns of Wheeler and His Cavalry* (1899), from materials furnished by General Wheeler.

CIVIL BIOGRAPHIES AND REMINISCENCES

NORTHERN CIVILIANS.—C. F. Adams, *Charles Francis Adams* (1900), an account of our foremost diplomat by his son; James G. Blaine, *Twenty Years in Congress* (2 vols., 1884), I., chaps. xiii.-xxvi., clear, fair to opponents, good-tempered, accurate; G. S. Boutwell, *Reminiscences of Sixty Years* (1902), by a worthy veteran in statesmanship; Albert Bushnell Hart, *Salmon P. Chase* (1899), restrained, discriminating, marked by thorough knowledge; also, *Chase*, by Schuckers, and by Warden; Mrs. C. Coleman, *John J. Crittenden* (1871); Mrs. S. F. Hughes, *John M. Forbes* (2 vols., 1899), a man without official position, either civil or military, but very useful; Horace Greeley, *Recollections of a Busy Life* (1868), reflecting the very vortex of the political cyclone; George W. Julian, *Political Recollections of War Time* (1884), by a statesman of radical anti-slavery views; E. D. Keyes, *Fifty Years' Observations* (1884); John G. Nicolay and John Hay, *Abraham Lincoln, A History* (10 vols., 1890), a monumental work by Lincoln's private secretaries, written from the amplest knowledge by men of great capacity: of the utmost merit, but undiscriminating in its commendation of Lincoln, who is always in the right, whoever else may be wrong, and not judicial in its attitude towards the South; also, *Abraham Lincoln*, by Arnold, Elbridge Brooks, Noah Brooks, Carpenter, Coffin, Dana, Hapgood, Herndon, Lamon, Morse, Raymond, Rice, Rothschild, Carl Schurz, and Ida M. Tarbell; A. G. Riddle, *Recollections of War Time* (1895), good pictures of the life of a congressman; F. W. Seward, *William H. Seward at Washington* (1891); Frederick Bancroft, *Life of William H. Seward* (2 vols., 1900), marked by candor and careful scholarship; also, *Seward*, by T. K. Lothrop; John Sherman, *Recollections of Forty Years* (1895), one of the most experienced and meritorious of the statesmen of the period; George C. Gorham, *Edwin M. Stanton* (2 vols., 1899), an adequate picture of the great war secretary; also, *Stanton*, by F. A. Flower (1905); Samuel M. McCall, *Thaddeus Stevens* (1899), the leader of the House in the thirty-seventh and thirty-eighth Congresses, portrayed by a sympathetic hand; also, *Stevens*, by E. B. Callender (1882); Moorfield Storey, *Charles Sumner* (1902), the leader of the Senate in the thirty-seventh and thirty-eighth Congresses, sympathetically portrayed;

also, *Sumner*, by E. L. Pierce (4 vols., 1877–1893); T. W. Barnes, *Thurlow Weed* (1883), an account of a figure not in the forefront, but exercising great influence.

SOUTHERN CIVILIANS.—Varina Howell Davis, *Jefferson Davis* (1890), the record of an affectionate wife; also, *Jefferson Davis*, by Alfriend and E. A. Pollard; H. D. Capers, *Life and Times of C. G. Memminger* (1893), a well-disposed man set to cope with impossible tasks; H. Cleveland, *Alexander H. Stephens* (1866), a picture of perhaps the ablest of the Confederate statesmen; also, *Stephens* by Browne and Johnston; P. A. Stovall, *Robert Toombs* (1892); L. G. Tyler, *Letters and Times of the Tylers* (1884–1885); J. W. DuBose, *Life of William L. Yancey* (1892), a plausible statesman active in Europe as well as in America.

PERSONAL EXPERIENCE

NORTHERN WAR EXPERIENCE.—H. V. Boynton, *Chattanooga and Chickamauga* (1891); H. V. Boynton, *Sherman's Historical Raid* (1875), severe criticism of Sherman, judged unfavorably by Cox; Junius H. Browne, *Four Years in Secessia* (1865), a war correspondent; as is also C. C. Coffin, *My Days and Nights on the Battle-field* (1887); Warren Lee Goss, *Recollections of a Private* (1890); J. V. Hadley, *Seven Months a Prisoner* (1898); T. W. Higginson, editor, *Harvard Memorial Biographies* (2 vols., 1866), lives of Harvard men who died in the service in various positions, from that of general to the rank and file, written by comrades: pages full of pathos and heroism; J. K. Hosmer, *The Thinking Bayonet* (1865); A. B. Isham, *Prisoners of War and Military Prisons* (1890); C. McCarthy, *Detailed Minutiæ of a Soldier's Life* (1882); A. K. McClure, *Lincoln and Men of War Time* (1892), by an active newspaper man closely associated with leading characters; J. McElroy, *Andersonville, a Story of Rebel Military Prisons* (1879); George Ward Nichols, *The March to the Sea* (1865), vivid description; George F. Noyes, *The Bivouac and the Battlefield* (1863), has to do with campaigns in the East; *Personal Narratives of Events in the*

War of the Rebellion (5 vols., 1880), by private soldiers and sailors, published by Rhode Island Historical Society; George Alfred Townsend, *Campaigns of a Non-Combatant* (1866), by a war correspondent; Frank Wilkeson, *Recollections of a Private Soldier* (1887), makes real the pains and privations.

SOUTHERN WAR EXPERIENCE.—Interesting accounts of experiences undergone by minor characters are: Heros von Borcke, *Memoirs of the Confederate War for Independence* (1866), by a German soldier of fortune in the army of Lee; Mrs. Mary Boykin Chesnut, *Diary from Dixie* (1905), lively, brilliant, pathetic; John Esten Cooke, *Wearing the Gray* (1867); John Esten Cooke, *Hilt to Hilt* (1871), the Shenandoah campaign of 1864; F. E. Daniel, *Recollections of a Rebel Surgeon* (1899); A. S. Dunlop, *Lee's Sharpshooters* (1899); George Cary Eggleston, *A Rebel's Recollections* (1905), a bright and entertaining story of service in a subordinate station; E. S. Ellis, *Camp-Fires of General Lee* (1886); Miss Mary A. H. Gay, *Life in Dixie during the War* (1892), concerned with Atlanta and its neighborhood; Harry Gilmor, *Four Years in the Saddle* (1866); Miss P. A. Hague, *A Blockaded Family* (1888), a good account of plantation life in war-time; J. W. Headley, *Confederate Operations in Canada and New York* (1906), describes the secret machinations and attempts of Confederates in the North; J. B. Jones, *A Rebel War Clerk's Diary* (2 vols., 1866), experiences of a Richmond official; Sarah L. Jones, *Life in the South* (1863), by a blockaded British subject; General Dabney H. Maury, *Recollections of a Virginian* (1894); Mrs. Judith B. McGuire, *Diary of a Southern Refugee* (1865), good pictures, especially of Richmond life in war-time; J. Scott, *Partisan Life with Colonel J. S. Mosby* (1867); Mrs. Susan Dabney Smedes, *A Southern Planter* (1899), paints plantation life near Vicksburg; *My Cave Life in Vicksburg by a Lady* (1864), a woman's experience during the siege; G. M. Sorrel, *Recollections of a Confederate Staff-Officer* (1905), went through the war by the side of Longstreet; R. Stiles, *Four Years Under Marse*

Robert (1903), record of a Yale graduate who served in a subordinate station; W. H. Taylor, *Four Years with Lee* (1878), a record of intimate association; E. L. Wells, *Hampton and His Cavalry in 1864* (1899); W. Wilson, *Life in the Confederacy* (1887), by an alien; J. S. Wise, *The End of an Era* (1899), a bright youth's experience.

NEWSPAPERS

Files of especial interest among the northern papers are those of the *New York Tribune*, *New York Times*, *New York Herald*, and *New York Evening Post*; *Boston Advertiser* and *Boston Journal*; *Springfield Republican*; *Chicago Tribune* and *Chicago Times*; the *La Crosse Democrat* ("Brick" Pomeroy, editor); the *Louisville Journal*; the *Cincinnati Times*. among southern papers, the *Richmond Whig*, *Richmond Examiner*, and *Richmond Despatch*; the *Charleston Mercury*; the *New Orleans Picayune*.

APPENDIX

Of books published since the preceding list was prepared, there may be mentioned on the Federal side *Life and Memoirs of Comte Regis de Trobriand* (N. Y., 1910); *Autobiography of Oliver Otis Howard* (N. Y., 1909); *Under the Old Flag*, James H. Wilson (N. Y., 1912); and on the Confederate side, *Military Memoirs of a Confederate*, E. Porter Alexander (N. Y., 1907); *A Soldier's Recollections*, Rev. Randolph H. McKim (N. Y., 1910); *Gen. Joseph Wheeler and the Army of the Tennessee*, John Witherspoon Du Bose (N. Y., 1912). *The Crises of the Confederacy*, Cecil Battine; *Lee the American*, Gamaliel Bradford.

Particular episodes are well treated in *Battles of Gettysburg*, Franklin A. Haskell (Madison, Wis., 1908); *Campaign of Chancellorsville*, John Bigelow, Jr. (Yale University Press, 1910); *Battle of the Wilderness*, Morris Schaff (Houghton, Mifflin & Co., 1910); and *The Battle of Gettysburg*, Jesse Bowman Young (Harper & Brothers, 1913).

INDEX